An Anthropology of *Ba*

An Anthropology of *Ba*

Place and Performance Co-emerging

Edited by

Gaku Kajimaru
Caitlin Coker
Kazuhiro Kazama

Kyoto University Press

TRANS
PACIFIC
PRESS

First published in 2021 jointly by:

Kyoto University Press
69 Yoshida Konoe-cho
Sakyo-ku, Kyoto 606-8315, Japan
Telephone: +81-75-761-6182
Fax: +81-75-761-6190
Email: sales@kyoto-up.or.jp
Web: http://www.kyoto-up.or.jp

Trans Pacific Press Co., Ltd.
2nd Floor, Hamamatsu-cho Daiya Building
2-2-15 Hamamatsu-cho, Minato-ku, Tokyo
105-0013, Japan
Telephone: +81-50-5371-9475
Email: info@transpacificpress.com
Web: http://www.transpacificpress.com

© Kajimaru, G.; Coker, C.; Kazama, K. et al., 2021
Edited by Dr Karl Smith, Melbourne, Australia
Designed and set by Ryo Kuroda, New York, USA
Printed by Dai Nippon Printing Co., Ltd., Tokyo, Japan

Distributors

USA and Canada
Independent Publishers Group (IPG)
814 N. Franklin Street
Chicago, IL 60610, USA
Telephone inquiries: +1-312-337-0747
Order placement: 800-888-4741 (domestic only)
Fax: +1-312-337-5985
Email: frontdesk@ipgbook.com
Web: http://www.ipgbook.com

Europe, Oceania, Middle East and Africa
EUROSPAN
Gray's Inn House,
127 Clerkenwell Road
London, EC1R 5DB
United Kingdom
Telephone: +44-(0)20-7240-0856
Email: info@eurospan.co.uk
Web: https://www.eurospangroup.com/

Japan
For purchase orders in Japan, please contact
any distributor in Japan.

China
China Publishers Services Ltd.
718, 7/F., Fortune Commercial Building,
362 Sha Tsui Road, Tsuen Wan, N.T.
Hong Kong
Telephone: +852-2491-1436
Email: edwin@cps-hk.com

Korea, Taiwan
MHM Ltd.
1-1-13-4F, Kanda-Jinbocho,
Chiyoda-ku, Tokyo 101-0051 JAPAN
Telephone: +81-(0)3-3518-9449
Email: sales@mhmlimited.co.jp

Southeast Asia
Alkem Company Pte Ltd.
1, Sunview Road #01-27, Eco-Tech@Sunview
Singapore 627615
Telephone: +65 6265 6666
Email: enquiry@alkem.com.sg

ISBN 978-4-8140-0351-8 (paperback)
ISBN 978-4-8140-0352-5 (ebook)

Table of Contents

Figures

Tables

Photographs

Contributors

Caitlin Coker
Associate Professor at Hokkaido University's School of Humanities and Human Science. Coker completed a PhD in Cultural Anthropology at Kyoto University in 2017. Her research focuses on physical experience and performance, specifically butoh and pole dancing, as topics and practice-based methods to develop anthropological theory and thought.

Gaku Kajimaru
Assistant Professor of Kyoto University. Kajimaru completed a PhD in Anthropology. His research interest is reciprocal singing of Buyi (China), Lao (Laos) and Japan, and the social aspect of Japanese folk song. He was awarded the 13th Tokugawa Munemasa Award and the 31st Tanabe Hisao Prize.

Shuji Kamimoto
Associate Professor of Kurume University. Kamimoto's research interest is in spirituality and locality in Jamaica and Japan. He also produces songs for regional promotion.

Eriko Kawanishi
Lecturer at Professional Institute of International Fashion. Kawanishi was awarded a PhD at the Graduate School of Human and Environmental Studies at Kyoto University. She is an anthropologist of the Goddess movement, contemporary Paganism, alternative spirituality, sacred landscapes and spiritual tourism, who conducted fieldwork mainly in Glastonbury, UK.

Masaharu Kawano
Associate Professor of Tokyo Metropolitan University. Kawano specializes in Cultural Anthropology and completed a PhD in International Political Economy. His research interest is in traditional authority and ritual practice in Pohnpei, Micronesia. He was awarded the 19th Japanese Society for Oceanic Studies Prize in 2020.

Kazuhiro Kazama
Professor of Kyoto University. Kazama is an anthropologist who conducted long-term fieldwork on Tabiteuea Atoll in Kiribati and shorter research among the Gilbertese speakers in Fiji. His research interests include cross-cultural encounters, and an ethnographic approach to the study of historical memory and emotions in Oceania.

Ulara Tamura
Associate Professor at Kanazawa University. Tamura is an anthropologist who has conducted fieldwork mainly in Turkey from 2002. Her research interest includes how local people deal with the transformation of traditions under globalization. She received her PhD at Kyoto University in 2011, with a dissertation titled "The Life-world of Local Craft Articulated with the Global Market Economy: The Preservation and Transformation of Carpet Production in Southwest Turkey" which was published in Japan in 2013.

Fumi Watanabe
Assistant Professor of Doshisha University. She completed a PhD in Anthropology at Kyoto University. Her research interest is in art(s) and material cultures in Oceania. She was awarded the 14th Japanese Society for Oceanic Studies Prize in 2014 for research published on Red Wave art in Fiji.

Tatsuya Yamamoto
Associate Professor of Shizuoka University. His research interest is in consumption and production of popular music by Tibetan refugees in India and Nepal. He was awarded the 3ʳᵈ Japan Consortium for Area Studies (JCAS) Award (Toryu-sho (Budding Scholar) Category) in 2013 for research related to the essay in the present volume.

Preface

Just as the sub-title of this collection is "place and performance co-emerging," the articles in this book co-emerged from a research discussion group at Kyoto University which gathered sporadically from April 2019 and into March 2020. Members of the group were younger researchers employed at different universities across Japan who shared a common background of studying in Kyoto University's Cultural Anthropology program. Our stated intent for meeting was to explore and develop themes of place and performance, which were motifs in all of our fieldwork. A tacit intent was to explore the open-ended questions of what would happen when we all met, and what would happen if we transmitted that happening through an English-language format, such as this book.

As we shared our research results, we encountered two problems. The first was that the English-language word place, a keyword in anthropological theory, did not fully correspond to the Japanese idea for place, specifically *ba*, that we use in our everyday lives and, by extension, think with in the field. The second problem was that due to this mismatch, we had to experiment with the ontological concept of place, reexamining how it comes into being and how we exist in it. We have reached the consensus that *ba* is generated by the co-emergence of performance, place, and peoples. This book offers our insights into *how* thinking with *ba* can unveil further dimensions of the *where* which invariably accompanies the never ending anthropological inquiry into *how* we live.

We would like to thank the Unit of Kyoto Initiatives for the Humanities and Social Sciences as well as the Kyoto Humanities Series for their financial support. The Kyoto Humanities Series offers the achievements of humanities research at Kyoto University to a readership with wide academic interests in order to provide a basis for transnational and transdisciplinary academic exchange.

Introduction: An Anthropology of *Ba*

Gaku Kajimaru, Caitlin Coker, and Kazuhiro Kazama

"What is happening here now?"

All anthropologists must have asked or thought this question in their fieldwork – when they are first invited to an unfamiliar room, when they sit with local people chatting in the local language, and when they attend esoteric rituals. Our lives are filled with events small and large, new and ordinary, rare and common, and anthropologists bear witness to events from which emerge changes in the local milieu. We are directly involved in the events as participants, but we must also step back to ruminate over that experience, analyze it, and write ethnographies. First and foremost, we cannot escape the fact that we become inseparable from local events when we participate in and observe them. It is only later that we rationalize an event, as if we were separate from it and are able to write objectively about it – but we all know this has limitations. Why? What is the power of the event that pulls us in and never quite lets us go?

This book answers that question by focusing on the phenomena of the event[1] itself; that is, a momentary, yet historical and material, socio-cultural place. Often theories about place assume it to be a container for separated individual agents and what they can do; from such perspectives, the focus regresses to the individual and their agential actions in context, and therefore cannot adequately explain what is happening in that place. Place becomes a mute background for the performances of actors who are present in it, yet separate from it, and the focus is limited to those separated actors. However, we contend that actors are not separate or separable from place, especially in the moment in which we question the here and now. In this book we question previous research's underlying assumption of the distinction between place and individual agents, arguing that places and the people in them co-emerge through the performances that occur there.

First and foremost, we base this argument on empirical data collected in our various fields. As anthropologists we deal with real-time occurrences of performances and places through a variety of social practices, regions, and interdisciplinary approaches. Despite the diversity in subject-matter and research methods, we share a grounded perspective. This perspective does not gaze upon the people we research but instead researches with them, getting involved in the thick of local events and recording data with our bodies and

1

---

[1] "A place is more an event than a thing to be assimilated to known categories" (Casey 1996: 26).

feelings as a barometer for measuring what is happening in the moment. This qualitative approach gives us an advantage in investigating performance and place, but it is not only our training as anthropologists that effects how we research. There is the added dimension of our lived-experience in the Japanese context and our connections in the cultural anthropology department at Kyoto University, and how that socio-linguistic context makes us privy to an embedded perspective that may not be available or as apparent from a solely English- language perspective.[2]

Specifically, we base our way of thinking in the concept of *ba* from Japanese philosophy as well as its usage in contemporary Japanese language in our formulation of the co-emergence of performance and place. Coming from the background of Japanese anthropology, the authors of this book live in an academic world that straddles theories and lexicons in English and Japanese and expects them to perform academically in both realms. From this linguistically based academic duality, we can identify conflict between the English and the Japanese perspectives on place. Specifically, in the English context agents are seen as individualized creators of place, while in Japanese the place, called *ba*, is often what moves people, allowing or hindering their actions, and thus guiding the formation of an actor as an individual in the first place. This idea of a moving together as a unified whole of people with places may seem somewhat mystical and thus not practical from a social science perspective; however, the authors of this volume contend that *ba* is an ordinary and concrete perspective, which, when applied, contributes a fresh re-consideration of place and place-situated performance.

Performance

In our view of *ba*, which will be articulated later, actors and their performances do not arise without a place to do so, and that place likewise does not emerge without the performance. The definition of performance is quite broad, and differs across the branches of social science; but it is possible to trace a connecting thread across them.

Erving Goffman (1959) defines performance broadly, encompassing every aspect of human interactional behavior. According to Goffman, "a 'performance'

---

[2] We note that this volume is produced in an academic (semi)periphery in the world system of anthropology (Kuwayama 2004) under a neoliberal urge to publish in English (Kuwayama 2017); we believe that our Japanese-derived term *ba* will be valuable to "dominant anthropological discourse" (Kuwayama 2004: 39) and world anthropologies (Ribeiro 2006: 2014).

may be defined as all the activity of a given participant on a given occasion which serves to influence in any way any of the other participants" (Goffman 1959: 15). By this definition, every behavior in front of other people can be performance as long as it is socially meaningful. Meaning comes from culture-specific characteristics and from socio-cultural contexts; Goffman borrowed anthropologist Gregory Bateson's term "frame" to describe how the actor's society imbues their performance with meaning, and how their performances in turn reproduce, maintain, transform, and create their culture and society (Bateson 1972, Goffman 1986). For Goffman, a "frame" refers to how actors perceive and make sense of an event according to socially decided principles. That perception and meaning-making influences their behavior, which in turn leads to the formation of the event (Goffman 1986: 10–11). Thus, "frame" is a cognitive concept through which actors understand, or rather imbue what they and others do with meaning, and is thus how performance comes about.

In performance studies, performance is not a concept by which to forcibly categorize human behavior but is instead a malleable concept to be adapted to the actual phenomena of human and nonhuman behavior[3] (Kirshenblatt-Gimblett 2016: 29). Richard Schechner proposed two categories for studying performance: "is" performance and "as" performance. Something "is" performance when its historical and social context, convention, usage, and tradition say it is. One cannot determine what "is" performance without referring to specific cultural circumstances (Schechner 2013: 38), while any behavior, event, action, or thing can be studied "as" performance (Schechner 2013: 41). Therefore, almost all behavior (human and nonhuman) can be seen "as" performance.

For Schechner, as well as other performance studies researchers, all kinds of performances, from long dramas to short gestures are composed of "restored behavior," for which past behavior serves as a source.

3

> Restored behavior is living behavior treated as a film director treats a strip of film. These strips of behavior can be rearranged or reconstructed; they are independent of the causal systems (social, psychological, technological) that brought them into existence. They have a life of their own. The original "truth" or "source" of the behavior may be lost, ignored, or contradicted – even while this truth or source is apparently being honored and observed. How the strip of behavior was made, found, or developed may be unknown or concealed;

---

[3] (Communication-oriented) Performance Studies have extended discussion to posthuman relations including plants (Brisini and Simmons 2016, Brisini 2019).

elaborated; distorted by myth and tradition. Originating as a process, used in the process of rehearsal to make a new process, a performance, the strips of behavior are not themselves process but things, items, "material". (Schechner 1985: 35)

Although it originates from past behavior, restored behavior is not repetition; it is a new creation based on raw materials, the ingredients of past behavior. Schechner states that each performance diverges from its source and other similar performances through its embodiment by each individual actor (Schechner 2013: 36–37), thus making it perpetually new, but it is still based in the actors' shared social past and their understanding of it. If we think of Schechner's strips of film as pieces of behavior, the way they are put together into the movie, the narrative of performances is Goffman's concept of framing, the social competence and cultural filters emerging as the actors piece together the strips in the course of the performance.

While folklore and linguistic anthropology have different foci than performance studies, Richard Bauman argued that folklore should be treated as a verbal art, with performance as its key concept. For Bauman, performance is a mode of spoken verbal communication, which "consists in the assumption of responsibility to an audience for a display of communicative competence. This competence rests on the knowledge and ability to speak in socially appropriate ways" (Bauman 1975: 293). So, whereas Schechner's definition of performance relies on a conscious consensus of behavior as performance, this definition opens the possibility of thinking about performances which are not necessarily recognized as such, perhaps transcending Western ethnocentric evaluations of what "is" performance. Basically, for Bauman folklore "is" a verbal form of performance if considered from Schechner's definition of the term.[4]

In the field of ethnopoetics, this does not stop at the verbal form. According to Kuniyoshi Kataoka, poetic structure is not restricted to language but is instead a multimodal activity (Kataoka 2012). Kataoka means that in linguistic research the subject for consideration is not only found in the verbal, but also in the unfolding of the nonverbal; not only in the audio but also the visual generated in its transmission. In this way, a linguistic approach has recognized the necessity to focus not only on the verbal dimension of performance but also how it is seated in the body and environment – in other words, in the physicality of its actors being generated together with their milieu.

4

---

[4] Additionally, in the field of ethnopoetics, Hymes identified the recurrence of behavior as one of the fundamental features of performance (Hymes 1981), which is quite similar to Schechner's idea of "restored behavior".

Furthermore, Bauman claims that by thinking of folklore as performance the researcher can grapple with "a dual sense of artistic *action* – the doing of folklore – and artistic *event* – the performance situation, involving performer, art form, audience, and setting" (Bauman 1975: 290). In other words, the action of performance necessarily comes together with its context (which is also an indispensable background for identifying which frame is at work[5]). This makes the consideration of place a necessity.

In summary, performance is not reducible to the performers' cognition of and involvement in them, because it does not happen in a vacuum. The place in which the performance occurs, including the socio-cultural context in which it is situated, has been the B-side in theories of performance; it tends to be overlooked, but closer inspection reveals that it is an irreducible factor in performance.

Place/space

Place has become a point of discussion across the social sciences. In anthropology specifically, place was relatively invisible before it became a major concern and was then further developed through considerations of place and space.

Human geographer Tim Cresswell (2004) explains the socio-cultural significance of a place by contrasting it with the complementary concept of space. The designation of some place as a place is not universal; a place can only exist as such due to the socio-cultural meaning with which it is imbued. When a certain geographical area is seen as empty, invisible, and not worthy of recognition, it is given the abstract label of space. Thus, where borders or boundaries are drawn and which spaces are named as specific places depends on who inhabits them and how they perceive it (Cresswell 2004: 8–10). However, this view does not account for places that do not correspond to geographical regions but are instead created and reproduced in social practices.

In the collection *The Anthropology of Landscape: Perspectives on Place and Space* (1995), Eric Hirsch states that what distinguishes anthropology from geography is that anthropology sees place and space not as static images or representations but as momentary results of cultural processes. Hirsch explains the significance of landscape as an ethnographic concept for considering how the

---

[5] Again, in ethnopoetics, the poetic function of language (Jakobson 1960) is essential and ubiquitous in this framing by performance (Hymes 1981, Tedlock 1983, Blommaert 2006, Webster 2015).

anthropologist frames her subject of study as well as how local people within that frame endow their surroundings with meaning. In terms of space and place, in the field the anthropologist first sees space before understanding the local, subjective designations of place.

Likewise, the collection *Senses of Place* (1996) sought to give the theme of place a greater prominence in the field of anthropology. This collection purposefully did not attempt to theorize place and space in themselves, but instead presents specific fieldwork cases from a variety of societies to reveal a kaleidoscope of ways that place is perceived and imputed with social meaning and significance. In the introduction, editors Steven Feld and Keith Basso point out how previous research focusing on place could not account for social actors who did not have a place that they could belong to, namely, those who have been uprooted.

After *Senses of Place*, anthropological collections regarding place soon offered visions of how to consider peoples who are uprooted in this postcolonial and de-territorialized world by criticizing conceptions of culture which see it as rooted in specific places. Gupta and Ferguson (1997) argue against assuming that the local is static and bounded, pointing instead to its shifting and blurred boundaries. Rather than assuming geographic boundaries, they call for anthropologists to investigate how places are made through embodied practices and social and political processes, what place-making contributes to the constitution of individuals, and the possibilities for transformative social resistance. Similarly, Kirsten Hastrup and Karen Fog Olwig (1997) claim that while anthropology's idea of culture has traditionally been fixated on the idea of geographically discrete places, the global world in which they write cannot be comprehended in that way. While Gupta and Ferguson call us to look at the practices and processes present that make a place, Hastrup and Olwig highlight how those moving in and out effect a local place. They propose that place be considered not in terms of geographical boundaries but rather through how people site their own culture (hence their title *Siting Culture: The Shifting Anthropological Object*), with that place being considered through social relations. Anthropologist Setha Low and Denise Lawrence-Zúñiga (2003) take up the mantle of anthropological theory of place and space by considering transnational cases in which the idea of place cannot be confined to the lines drawn on a map, as well as cases in which space is embodied, gendered, inscribed, and contested. Low (2017) considers space as being created through bodies moving within it and the historical, political, social, and material forces that they in turn put in motion. At the same time, place is that space which is granted not only individual and social meanings but also the meanings, affects, and perceptions of the individual agents who dwell within it. For example, a house becomes a home through dwelling in it and finding meaning in the cultural practices performed there (2017: 12). The meanings of a place are not unrelated to the forces that create space, but are rooted in them. In other words, space is a field that is shaped through societal organization and regulation as well as the existence of material bodies of people in it; space becomes a place by people living in it, interacting with each other, seeing from one another's perspectives, and finding meaning in themselves and the space (2017: 32). Low demonstrates how place is generated not only in the local sphere but also in a continuum from intimate to global interrelations, including cases of transnationality, in which the demarcations of place may shift with social practice.

In Low's review of ethnographies of place and space, places are generated through cultural practices that emerge from top-down societal productions of space as well as from bottom-up individual and agential constructions of space. Throughout this relationship between human actors and place, there is an inherent tension between the societal forces of established places and the power of individual agency to effect social change. From a phenomenological perspective, the place as well as the individual are both constantly transitioning between emerging states, and thus the individual has potential to change what the place becomes and what it means for its inhabitants (Casey 1996).

We agree that physical experiences and the workings of societies shape spaces, and that the meaning imbued in lived spaces is what makes them places, regardless of whether they can be clearly delineated on a map or not. However, there seems to be a tendency in previous works to consider space and place as merely a backdrop to the tensions between society and the individual and between individuals as they establish their identities and exercise agency. Place and space are basically treated as containers for social actors, whose performances are considered as forces affecting the place, without considering how, conversely, the place itself is not merely a site for human meaning and practice but is also an actor which can affect both human and nonhuman actors. If it is formed through moving social bodies and is permeated with cultural meanings, then place must be a social force in itself. To get at the affect that place has on human and nonhuman actors, we must reconsider the relationship between place and people. This perspective relies on the Japanese linguistic and philosophical concept of *ba*, through which we claim that place co-emerges together with and primarily exists in a state of non-separation from the human and nonhuman actors it envelops.

7

Ba and the co-emergence of social actors

Ba is an ordinary word in the Japanese lexicon, which can be translated as place or space. Its usage differs a little from place or space in English, though; in Japanese the subject can be "moved by *ba*" (*ba ni ugokasareru*) or "influenced by *ba*" (*ba ni eikyō sareru*). This includes the socio-cultural context of what is appropriate in a given situation, but it also denotes the general mood or individual feeling based on that place. It comprises more than the intersubjectivity of social actors; it is instead the whole of which they are a part. That whole is the place, and it affects them to the point that they may perform in ways that are uncustomary to their individual identity or different to what they might do in another place or time.

For example, when a professor delivers a lecture to a classroom of students, that class in itself is the *ba* through which the professor performs and thus is a professor in the first place. Of course, the classroom lecture would not be possible without the materiality of the room in which the students can sit, or equipment like a projector or microphones to make the lecture accessible to them, but there is also the necessity of the students to show up to class and to sit and listen to the lecture itself. However, there is more in how this scene brings about the performance of the professor. By looking at the students' facial expressions and the look in their eyes, the professor is faced with the students' attitudes – i.e., their interest, lack of interest, or general mood that day. The professor has given the same lecture for years, but this mood envelops and changes the course of how he or she delivers it each time. If the students don't seem receptive, the professor may feel like his or her words get stuck, they won't come out, and he or she feels awkward. If, however, the professor can feel the students' interest, he or she can relax, and ideas and additional examples come to mind while speaking.[6] Thus, the professor, the lecture, and the students are different each time, and their emergence, as well as performances, happens together with the emergence of the *ba*.

Another example is the specific *ba* of bars in Kyoto, Japan. Kyoto has a small-town feel (everyone seems to know each other through a degree or two of separation) and is infamous for sometimes being unfriendly to Japanese people from other social circles or prefectures. In bars, the *ba* of the bar itself provides

8

---

[6] When talking about this in Japanese, it is interesting to note that the ideas/words themselves become the implied subject and not the individual professor. In English, where we might say "I get stuck," "I can't think of anything," or conversely "I can come up with more examples than usual" in Japanese there is no "I" in these sentences. Instead "(it) gets stuck," "(it) relaxes," "(the ideas/words) don't come out," or "(the ideas/words) arise." Because there is no need to distinguish "I" in these sentences, it could be said that realizing a non-separated state of the *ba* is a facet of the Japanese language.

a guidebook as to how a customer should act, rather than the collection of individual attitudes at the bar. Depending on the bar, a first-time visitor may feel welcome or not; finding oneself out of place is called *ba-chigai*. In this case, the person is not the subject, but rather the *"ba"* itself is the main actor. Due to the different kinds of *ba*, in some bars it may feel easy to talk to someone new, but in bars that are filled with regular customers, it may even feel like the new customer made a mistake by going there. In other cases, the physical layout of the bar puts the customer face to face with the bartender in such a way that the customer feels obliged to make small talk. In other bars the seats are separated and the lighting dark, generating a *ba* that encourages solo drinking. This sense of the different emerging *ba*'s is something that the new customer gets by sitting there for a few minutes and absorbing the feel of the place, by which time they feel the tacit rule that it is too late to leave without having at least one drink.

William F. Hanks et al. (2019) introduced this idea of *ba* to the field of linguistic pragmatics, elaborating on the relationship between the *ba* and social actors. They explain that *ba* is not an empty container for agents but instead suggests a frame for human interaction through which the force of societal regulations, the circulation of affects, and the contingency of the moment are all implied. Their theorization of *ba* is largely based on *basho* as conceptualized by philosopher Kitaro Nishida and the concept of *ba* by the scientist and independent thinker Hiroshi Shimizu. As *ba* and *basho* both mean *place* and are thus often used interchangeably, they blend the ideas of these two thinkers to propose *ba* theory.

9

Nishida (2012) and his philosophical descendants at the Kyoto School corresponded with German phenomenologists like Husserl and Heidegger in the early 20th century, but their vector towards place and social actors begins from the opposite direction than the conception of place in most phenomenological thought. Hanks points out that while phenomenology starts with the experience of the individual and thus assumes a separation of that perceiving and experiencing individual from the place they inhabit, Nishida's idea of place instead begins with the idea of non-separation, an absence of distinction between anything, in what he called the "primary *ba*." "Secondary *ba*," then, is the place where distinctions between subject, object, and environment are made, and where the space they inhabit is given meaning; basically, the "context" or "situation" of social interaction (2019: 65). Hanks states that Euro-American approaches assume the separation of individuals, thus beginning their consideration of place from the position of the secondary *ba*. Thus, these approaches have to work their way towards conceptualizing states of non-separation, the primary *ba*. However, with *ba* theory, the basis of social life begins in the primary *ba*, and non-separation is assumed; from this perspective, it is separation, distinction and articulation (the secondary *ba*) that must be explained.

Shimizu describes the state of non-separation in the primary *ba* with an allegory of a painter trying to paint a picture of the room in which she is sitting.

> Now, imagine a painter before a blank canvas in a room. His or her task is to depict the room as accurately as possible in its present state. Think photorealism. Of course, the painter and the canvas are part of the room (s)he is portraying with brush strokes, and this interiority poses a challenge (s)he will fail to solve. Starting to paint on a blank canvas, the painter adds details, but because the canvas is part of the room, the room is changing as (s)he adds details to the canvas. The painting of the canvas must include a painting of the canvas, but (s)he will always be a step behind the actual state of the room, which emerges from changes on the canvas. This is the problem of reflexivity. *The painter is in a basho*. (Hanks 2019: 65–66, Shimizu 1995: 70)

10 Because the painter and her actions are in a state of non-separation with the place, the strokes on the painting change the overall image of the room as the image of that room influences the painting. It is the secondary *ba*, the predominant idea of place in linguistics, that takes an egocentric approach and assumes the painter to be an individual agent separate from the painting and the room. From the perspective of the primary *ba*, the artist's actions and expressions happen together with the changes of the room and the paintings; thus we can say that the artist herself emerges together as the place, the *ba*, emerges. This fact is evident in the problem of reflexivity in ethnography; the ethnographer must write about a certain society from an objective perspective and yet the ethnographer's performance in that *ba* influences the ever-shifting forms of the very society they wish to understand. To be able to consider this relationship of non-separation, the focus has to be shifted from the individual agent to the *ba* itself, to the nature of its existence and workings.

For Shimizu, *ba* is a location "within" which life is living. This *ba* is a sort of environment enveloping life itself, like a body and a cell. Living things create *ba* and locate themselves within it. At the same time, *ba* constrains the state and activity of the living. However, living things find creative ways to elude these restrictions and in the process create a new state of *ba*. Shimizu claims that this dynamic may induce harmony between self and environment, if the system works successfully (Shimizu 1993, Shimizu 2003: 66). *Ba* can be seen as physically closed space (Shimizu 1993) but it is a conscious space of self, too (Shimizu 2003: 56). So, in his *ba* theory, self and environment, subject and object are so intertwined that they should be treated primarily as a single system; the starting point of the theory, then, is the interiority of subject to the world, just like the painter sitting in the room she is attempting to portray (Hanks et al. 2019: 67).

Additionally, Shimizu added the allegory of the "improvisational drama model" to explain how social actors emerge together with the *ba* through their social interactions. When an improvisational troupe performs, they share a story line, but the roles they take on and the parts of the narrative they will perform are not decided. Their representative performances aim to align individual actions with the performance choices of their fellow actors while also delivering what they intuitively think the audience expects of them. By taking on the perspectives and feelings of fellow actors and the audience their actions unfold together, and thus the actors themselves emerge. In this process, the actors are not individually organizing themselves and their actions; rather, the *ba* envelops and brings about their performance. They were not individual characters from the beginning; rather, they began as an indeterminate group of actors who became characters through their interactions together with the formation of the *ba* (Shimizu 2003; Hanks et al. 2019: 66).

This volume builds on the *ba* theory proposed by Hanks et al. (2019) to add a new theoretical focus for the analysis of performance and place. Moving beyond linguistic pragmatics, we want to spotlight the social force of *ba* evident in the empirical data from our fieldwork. Whereas Shimizu relied on allegory to illustrate his points, we offer concrete first-hand experience reflexively considered in a *ba*-centered way. For example, in the improvisational drama model, if the *ba* is the whole of that event, it includes the material theater, props, and sets, the actors and the audience, as well as the cultural context of "the theatre" – we cannot know exactly how these aspects of *ba* will influence and shape each other as they emerge until we witness the performance firsthand. Based on *ba* theory and the chapters of this volume, we argue that *ba* is not simply a passive container but instead an active and even creative force in social relations and cultural histories.

Since it wields this social force, *ba* can be defined as a social actor[7] consisting of an aggregation of other social actors, while also including the environments and

11

---

[7] *Ba* may be thought of as an agent being formed together with human and nonhuman agents; even though *ba* theory may reveal agency and the existence of individual agents to be illusory.

contexts which shape their performance.[8] Butler's concept of performativity, which illuminates how "people's social and linguistic practices effectively constitute the identity they are said to express or reveal" (Butler 1990: 141) can also be understood in terms of this emergence of *ba* together with the social actors within it. Within the *ba*, performance is a social dance of pure contingency with the continual emergence of *ba* and what dwells within it. What can be certain is that *ba* is created and re-created[9] through performance, and *ba* likewise maintains or changes the performance of social-actors-in-*ba*; in other words, *ba* and actors co-emerge through performance. Our application of *ba* theory will shift this perspective of performativity from people to place, and especially to its co-emergence with the social actors in it. The chapters outlined below focus on fields around the world but are conjoined by the shared perception of *ba*.

The chapters in the first section "Co-Emergence of Ba and Actor" deal with how place influences participants' behavior, how *ba* and actors co-emerge and affect each other, and how these relationships sustain and remake the social order.

The first chapter by Caitlin Coker attributes agency to the *ba* and considers individual volition as secondary to the formation of the individual with the *ba*. Coker puts forth and analyzes an oral history of how butoh dancers, who are avant-garde performance artists, not only raised money for their stage performances but also became dancers through dancing and stripping in cabarets across urban and rural areas of Japan. Whereas other anthropologies of place (such as Low 2017) seem to assume that the Western cultural value of agency as the individual's ultimate goal is universal, their formation and realization as dancers depended on the place of the cabaret exercising its agency on them.

Next, Gaku Kajimaru develops *ba* by indicating different ways it can arise in singing practices, further developing it in regards to the concepts of space and place. Specifically, Kajimaru examines two contrasting scenes from the Japanese folk song contest "Obonai Bushi National Contest;" one is an official song performance on stage for the contest, while the other involves the singing and dancing at the after-party. In the former, the practice of singing is well organized, and singers may only join it by accommodating their behavior to the frame of

---

[8] This perspective corresponds with Actor-Network Theory (ANT) to some extent but differs in that ANT does not see a network itself as spatial. *Ba* is necessarily spatial or at least imagined as spatial because it emerges through actors' interactions and performances, dissolves into other contingent states, and/or collapses when its dynamics change dramatically.

[9] Though the *ba* emerges through performance and dissolves away, it does not emerge from nothing and dissolve away without any remainder. *Ba* carries a residual aspect of *ba*, a vestige of the past *ba*, which will be used as a resource (Schechner's "restored behavior") for the next performance from which will emerge a new *ba*.

the contest. In this case, the emergence of *ba* seems to be systematically planned, i.e., pre-determined. In the latter, the singing after the contest seems more improvisational, which he argues can be recognized as a spontaneous emergence of *ba*. In regards to theories of space and place, he identifies the former emergence of *ba* as a "*ba* of space setting," and the latter as a "*ba* of place making."

Masaharu Kawano examines the process in which ritual performances and *ba* co-emerge and portrays how performances are influenced by the *ba* through his fieldwork on ceremonial feastings in Pohnpei, Micronesia. From a local perspective, feastings function to express the social hierarchy between participants and reconfirm the rank-order under chiefly authority. However, Kawano argues that, in practice, participants' performances are also influenced by the *ba*, specifically by the emotional bonds among relatives. Kawano concludes that the co-emergence of ritual performance and *ba* enables not only the manifestation of social hierarchy but also emotional relationships through the feasting process.

The second section "Performative Translocality" deals with *ba*, (trans)locality, and identity. The first two chapters by Tamura and Watanabe illustrate how ba collectively create the sense of locally-connected identity and diverse agency, while the latter three chapters by Yamamoto, Kamimoto and Kawanishi illuminate how identity is translocally constructed, maintained, and disrupted in the *ba*.

13

Ulara Tamura applies the concept of *ba* to the largest Yörük cultural festival in Turkey in order to discuss the process of the transformation of Yörük culture from being thought of as "backward vulgarity" to being valued as "our good old origin as Turks." Whereas performance studies on nationalistic events and ceremonies tend to emphasize the strong unifying power of performances which involve the crowd, Tamura describes micro-scale personal experiences and their following reflections within the festival site. While the people participate together in an inclusive *ba*, the ways they reflect and summarize the experience in Söğüt vary. Her work points to diversity in the formulation of culture and the people that can co-emerge in a *ba*.

Fumi Watanabe's chapter focuses on the Festival of Pacific Arts (FOPA), a quadrennial regional festival in Oceania. Watanabe considers FOPA to be a place that foregrounds cultural differences between countries/territories and raises awareness of their uniqueness, while at the same time transcending national/territorial boundaries and confirming, or in some cases constructing, cultural continuity in the Oceania region at large. Focusing on the latter, Watanabe discusses the power of *ba* to involve people through performance. She then examines the pan-Oceanic culture that emerged in FOPA through the lens of Epeli Hau'ofa's concept of 'Oceania'.

Tatsuya Yamamoto's chapter on the performance of Tibetan traditional performing arts in a Tibetan diaspora portrays how the 'co-emergence' of performance and *ba* impacts the undetermined and uncertain processes of lived diasporic ambivalence. In this chapter, ambivalence refers to the attitude of Tibetan performers born and raised in India and Nepal who are expected to embody the oppositional temporalities of pre-1950 Tibetan culture and their contemporary selves in India. This chapter analyzes the discourses and practices of these performers performing the development of Tibetan nationalism and its policies on stage and explores what ambivalence brings to the lives of Tibetan performers.

Shuji Kamimoto describes the processes of the emergence of *ba* through different daily opportunities for confirming EABIC (Ethiopia Africa Black International Congress) Rastafarians' beliefs. He introduces the embodiment of their philosophy in their headquarters and commune called *Bobo Shanti*, the maintenance of their beliefs through their interpretations of daily news and events, and the historical understandings of their collective status at work in their demonstration march on Emancipation day. Through these cases, Kamimoto analyzes the emergence of *ba* as well as the density and agencies within which are based on people's performances.

In the final chapter, Eriko Kawanishi analyzes cases from her fieldwork on the Goddess movement and Sufism in Glastonbury to consider how her agency as a fieldworker co-emerges with her field, and how "vestiges" are left inside and outside the field from performances with her informants. She notes that she is a non-Western anthropologist with Western informants, as opposed to the traditional pattern in anthropology, where a Western anthropologist works with non-Western informants. She asks: "How has my performance, which emerged from the interaction between me and my informants in the field, affected them and changed myself?" She argues that the *ba* of fieldwork is a changing process of the fieldworker's agency.

What follows in this book is an attempt to uproot the anthropology of place from its Western, English-language centered perspective by considering it from the complementary perspective of *ba*, based on Japanese linguistic and philosophical thought. Through this consideration, we aim to shed light on an unseen side of place and agents, revealing the inclusive and reflexive aspect of the agency of *ba*. We hope this book brings readers a fresh understanding of place and place-situated life.

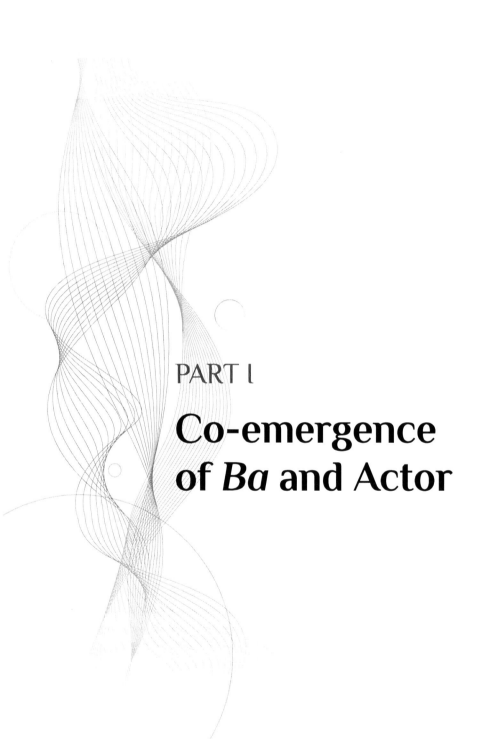

PART I

Co-emergence
of *Ba* and Actor

1. Butoh and the Cabaret
How the place of striptease fueled avant-garde performance in Japan

Caitlin Coker

My first encounter with butoh and the cabaret

Without coming to Japan and actually dancing butoh, I might have never known that many dancers of the avant-garde performance form butoh also danced in semi-nude cabarets[1] in Japan, from the 1950s and well into the 2000s.

Butoh is a concert dance form well known for its grotesque and surreal renderings of the human body; these dancers do not try to dance, but instead commit themselves to becoming a multitude of mostly nonhuman things on stage. For example, when I first came to Japan as a Fulbright Fellow to conduct anthropological research on dance in 2007, I learned how to become a rock, water, a doll, a carp, as well as other things through movement under the tutelage of Butoh dancer Ima Tenko in Kyoto, Japan.

After a year of research, I finally performed with Ima and began to understand her teachings. I desperately wanted to stay and learn more, but I was not sure what direction my research was taking nor how to fund an extended stay. Ima offered to introduce me to her manager who connected her with semi-nude dance jobs. We met at a busy arcade street in southern Osaka, where she took me down some back alleys to a large decadent building. In the basement of this building was Misono Universe, a legendary cabaret.

Cabaret Misono Universe is a grand place. As you enter, the walls are covered in deep red velvet. Overhead are hanging planets and gilded stars, mimicking the universe. The lighting is fantastic and psychedelic, both on stage and in the hall. The hall is spacious – it can hold 1000 people standing or 35 large booths each seating about eight people comfortably. On the left of the entrance are the bar and the audience, and on the right is a large stage from which extends a catwalk toward the audience.

---

[1] They performed at a plethora of places, such as trendy clubs, small bars, hot spring hotels, and even in movies; but I am focusing on the cabaret because it seems to be the place in which they most consistently performed.

Photo 1.1 Butoh dancer Ima Tenko at Kyoto Butoh-kan in 2018. Photo by Kosugi Tomoko.[2]

Ima led me to the dressing room, across the hall from the entrance, and introduced me to the dancer who was performing that night. She was a 28-year-old woman who spoke English fluently, having spent time in the United States. Ima and I went to a table situated between the dressing room and the catwalk and watched her dance. She came out in a thong, chaps, a bikini- style triangle top, and a cowboy hat and gyrated to the song "American Woman" by Guess Who. In this dance I remember her strutting down the catwalk, greeting customers while she danced, and coming to our table, where she stood facing away from us with her legs apart and bent over rolling her bottom at us, so that I could see the thin line of her thong between her legs. She danced to three songs in a row during which she removed her top. At the end of the third song she pulled off her thong at the back of the stage as the lights faded to black, hiding her naked physique. I later learned that this three-song pattern is a staple of semi-nude cabaret shows (as well as all-nude strip shows, which I will not discuss in this paper).

Unfortunately, I could not do this kind of work because of visa issues. However, I did learn that practically all the women and most of the men who joined

17

<hr>

[2] Whereas most butoh dancers perform on select nights at different small theaters, Ima performs each week at the Kyoto Butoh-kan (as of this writing, 2019). Kyoto Butoh-kan is an intimate space that only seats eight people; thus, as Ima performs she and the audience are inseparable in the unfolding of her butoh world. A detailed discussion of butoh is beyond the scope of this chapter; I encourage the reader to look at videos on the internet or see it live at butoh-kan in Kyoto, Japan (see https://www.butohkan.jp/).

18

Photo 1.2–1.4
Butoh dancer Ima Tenko's
show dancer alter-ego
Haruna Kiki in 1988.
Photos by Nogi Torio.

butoh dance companies were automatically recruited to dance in semi-nude shows
such as this. This history stretches back to the butoh company that Ima belonged
to in the 1980s (Byakkosha), as well as the company that her teacher belonged
to in the 1970s (Dairakudakan), the studio where her teacher's teacher learned
butoh in the 1960s (Asbestokan), and to the director of Asbestokan and butoh
founder Hijikata Tatsumi and his wife Motofuji Akiko in the 1950s. Despite this
history, there is no previous research about butoh artists dancing in cabarets, a fact
acknowledged by dance critic Shiga Nobuo (Shiga 2008).

Perhaps this lack of research is because butoh and semi-nude show dancing
are considered to be polar opposites; butoh is avant-garde, high art, whereas semi-
nude dancing is seen as entertainment of lower value. Butoh is highly conceptual
and reveals beauty in the grotesque, while semi-nude dancing can be thought of

Photo 1.5 Cabaret Misono Universe, view of the stage from the entrance, 2015. When I visited in 2007, there was a catwalk instead of the large floor seen in the photo, according to my notes (retrieved from http://universe.osaka/gallery.html on December 29, 2019).

Photo 1.6 Cabaret Misono Universe, view of the audience from the entrance (retrieved from http://universe.osaka/gallery.html on December 29, 2019).

as more straightforward in that it adheres to more conventional ideas of beauty. On the surface, these two forms of performance should have nothing in common, not even a relationship between them. However, a closer look into these butoh dancers' lives reveals that the cabaret was indispensable to butoh's development.

My argument

In this chapter, I will examine interviews and fieldwork conducted with Japanese butoh dancers to consider how the place of the cabaret was an agent in the generation of the butoh dancer and thus the performance form of butoh in Japan.[3] Whereas many considerations of performance and place focus on the agency and identity of the individual dancer, I will portray how in butoh individual agency

---

[3] Many of these interviews and research results have also been published in Japanese as part of a butoh oral history (see Coker 2015b).

and identity are not the ideal; instead, the agency arising from the materiality and milieu of the place, the primary *ba* of nonseparation,[4] are appreciated by the butoh dancers themselves as the source of the chance and contingent experiences which ultimately made them into butoh dancers.

Previous research on performance and place tends to approach the subject from one of two angles: either how the overarching force of society reproduces and maintains the social order or how the micro force of the individual contributes to producing society. Regarding the latter, there is a tendency to focus on the agency of individuals and their moving bodies as the force for creative and positive change (Butler 1990, 1993; Csordas 1993, 2011; Ingold 2011; Sen and Silverman 2014; Simone 2005). Low points out that there has been insufficient consideration of how the material environment affects the moving body (Low 2017: 151). I propose that this affect can be seen in the relationship between the materiality of a place and the materiality of corporeality and affect, especially in the experiences surrounding dance.

In my studies in Japan, rather than focusing solely on individual agency, I have found the idea of agency realized through the collective performativity of the group (Tanaka 2006). Furthermore, in fieldwork I noticed the agency of place, as per Low, but have further seen how place is essential for performance, and not only performance, but for the sedimentation of affect in the physical body and thus the development of the performance and performative ability. To put it simply, without the right place a performer cannot put on a performance, and performance is the ultimate training for the development of not only skill but moreover a certain "X-factor" or charisma and star quality of the performer. Furthermore, the place of performance is not an empty box, but a space with a certain historical and social context, which imbues it with an affect of its own. In this chapter, place, specifically the cabaret, is an indispensable agent in the development of the performer.

In the case of butoh, rather than individual agency, the agency of the place is what shaped the performer and thus allowed this performance genre to evolve. This idea of a material place having a physical affect on social actors is not new in the Japanese-language context: the word *ba*, which means place and space, is recognized as having the power to generate the behavior and social relations of the actors in it. Conversely, the place would not exist without the actors, human and non-human, within it. In this case, butoh dancers were also powerful performers in the last years of the cabaret's golden age in Japan. While

---

[4]   Please refer to this book's Introduction for an explanation of *ba*.

focusing on the agency of the cabaret, this chapter also portrays how the butoh artists performed on these stages and imagines the force of their dances and sheer presence to illustrate the co-emergence of the place and the performers.

While the sometimes radical dancing and underground avant-garde status of butoh dancers might superficially seem to be incompatible with the *ba* of the glittery and glamorous cabaret, it appears to have been necessary for the dancers to surrender their agency to the cabaret in order to fully realize themselves as butoh performers. In this chapter I criticize the tendency of previous research to assume that the development of the individual necessarily includes the realizing of their individual agency in opposition to societal pressures; I argue that, in the case of butoh and the cabaret, a moving together with the *ba* is not a relinquishing of personal power but rather a redirection of it that may lead to the realization of possibilities contingent to the performing individuals and their specific *ba*.

This research, informants, and the history of cabaret performances

21

This research is based on an oral history composed from my interviews[5] with 15 dancers[6] who belonged to one of three butoh dance companies – Asbestokan (based out of Tokyo), Dairakudakan (Tokyo), or Byakkosha (Kyoto) – between 1964 and 1994. These companies are all connected: butoh founder Hijikata Tatsumi was the main figure;[7] Maro Akaji, the leader of Dairakudakan, was close to Hijikata and Hijikata performed as a guest in Dairakudakan's works; and the leader of Byakkosha, Osuga Isamu, was a member of Dairakudakan. In short, these three companies represent three generations of butoh groups. This research spans the period from 1964 to 1994, the year Byakkosha disbanded.[8]

---

[5] Interviews were semi-structured, lasting between two and five hours, with most occurring over several sessions. The author also participated in butoh workshops with almost all of the interviewees.

[6] These dancers are: Tamano Koichi, Tamano Hiroko, Kobayashi Saga, Murobushi Ko, Bishop Yamada, Waguri Yukio, Sakaino Hiromi, Yamamoto Moe, Yuki Yuko, Osuga Isamu, Yurabe Masami, Katsura Kan, Mizuno Ritsuko, Ima Tenko, and Erochica Bamboo. Some dancers go by stage names, while others use their birth names, and the order of the dancers' names is the family name followed by the first name, except for Erochica Bamboo.

[7] I used the term "main figure" because while Hijikata Tatsumi was the teacher and choreographer as well as a dancer, he would probably object to the word "leader." He was a charismatic tornado who drew in young people and organized for them to perform in a variety of places. Asbestokan was also not a company name but rather the name of their studio in Tokyo, out of which many different companies were formed.

[8] Dairakudakan is still performing. However, it has a new generation of dancers, and I am not familiar with how their financial system currently works.

Photo 1.7 Byakkosha. Photo by Abe Jun

22 All the participants in this research were members of at least one of these companies, and almost all share the following characteristics. First, most of the artists joined the company when they were of university age. They were wondering what to do with their lives and their interests in the art and/or literature of their time led to an encounter with butoh, which was largely interdisciplinary in scope, as its main figures collaborated with artists from diverse backgrounds while also publishing intriguing texts and socializing with influential literary figures and academics of their times. Thus, most[9] of them came to butoh companies with an interest in their figureheads or butoh itself, and through this encounter became entangled in the world of the cabaret.

In this chapter, I will discuss how they all came to dance at the cabaret, focusing on how they remembered their cabaret performances and what meaning that held for them, and highlighting the agency the cabaret exercised on their lives.

---

[9] Tamano Koichi, one of the most well-known butoh dancers, became Hijikata's student not after seeing a butoh performance or reading one of his literary pieces but after watching Hijikata and Motofuji's cabaret performance in 1964. Tamano, who was working at the cabaret, packed his things, moved into Asbestokan, and became Hijikata's live-in student soon thereafter.

Photo 1.8 Show Dance Duo "Blue Echoes," Motofuji (Left) and Hijikata (Right). *Courtesy of Keio University Art Center and Butoh Laboratory, Japan*

23

The history of butoh artists performing show dance

According to Hashimoto, strip shows arose in Japan in 1948–49, despite laws against topless dancing. According to news reports, this dancing was tame compared to strip shows in Europe and the United States at the time (Hashimoto 1995: 39–50). In postwar Japan, and into the 1960s and 1970s, strip tease became racier and more diverse, featuring feather fan shows, bathing shows, and topless boxing shows, as well as re-enactments of bunraku puppet plays, Japanese traditional dancing, and folk songs. Overall these shows shared similar stage sets and props with American burlesque dancing, but they also interwove themes from Japanese daily life as well as traditional Japanese forms of performance (Hashimoto 1995). Ozawa classified the women who worked at the cabaret into two categories: the first kind of women needed money, either for their debts or the debts of their lover or their family; while the second danced nude in rebellion against gender norms and to earn money (Ozawa 1969, 1977, Ozawa and Hijikata 1981). Attesting to the diversity of cabaret shows, the butoh dancers interviewed in this research seem to perform different kinds of shows than Hashimoto documents, and for none of the reasons Ozawa reports.[10]

So, why and how did these performers come to dance at the cabaret? According to my interviews, after WW2 it was common in Tokyo for ballet and modern dancers as well as underground theatre troupes to perform at the cabaret to raise money to put on stage performances. Therefore, it was not out of the ordinary for Hijikata and his wife Motofuji to perform as a pair at the cabaret. Motofuji writes that she and Hijikata raised money for their performance in 1959 by forming the dance team "Blue Echoes" and dancing in nightclubs locally and around Japan (Motofuji 1990: 88–89).

Then, from the mid-1960s, when some of my informants began to gather at Asbestokan – living there while learning from and dancing in Hijikata's works – Hijikata quit dancing in clubs and cabarets, sending his students instead.

> One time, Hijikata threw a box with all of his cabaret props from the top of a bridge. He said, "I quit the show. If I go, then I can't do dance, so you all have to work." So, to make a living, Hijikata wasn't working, Motofuji wasn't working. If we were working, the cost of Hijikata's family and of stage performances (would be covered). (Interview with Kobayashi Saga, October 3, 2012)

Money earned from the cabaret went directly to Motofuji who then passed along 500 yen[11] to the performer.[12] Kobayashi said that the performer's fee from the cabaret was "unbelievably good" in the 1960s, and Waguri and Sakaino, who both entered Asbestokan in the 1970s, estimated that pay at about 10,000 yen[13] or more, describing the small portion they received as like a child's allowance. However, neither of them expressed this negatively. Waguri said that because of this system they didn't have to think about money and could focus on butoh, while Sakaino and Murobushi said that other performance groups at the same time had a similar system, so they accepted it as the norm.

---

[10] There are a number of reasons why female cabaret dancers would give Ozawa formulaic answers. First of all, they do not typically tell the truth to customers, but rather tell stories to pique their interest (according to my discussion with a former stripper who was performing in a show pub). Additionally, the style of communication for these kinds of situations often involve telling the listener what they expect or what they would understand, rather than stating the dry reality.

[11] As of December 23, 2019, 500 yen is equivalent to 4.12 Euro or 4.57 US dollars.

[12] This rate of 500 yen seems to have been established in the 1970s.

[13] As of December 23, 2019, 10,000 yen is equivalent to 82.48 Euro or 91.37 US dollars.

Photo 1.9 Hijikata (bottom right) teaching choreography to Ashikawa Yoko (bottom left), Kobayashi Saga (top left) and Tamano Koichi (top right) for the "Avant-garde show" to be performed at Space Capsule, a trendy members-only club (most likely photographed in 1969). *Photo by Nakatani Tadao, Courtesy of Keio University Art Center and Butoh Laboratory, Japan.*

All the students at Asbestokan were sent to dance at the cabaret, regardless of gender. Male student Waguri said that he was sent to dance at a legendary cabaret called France-za in Tokyo one week after he started practicing butoh and living at Asbestokan. Waguri said, "Hijikata choreographed a little for me. But as for the rest, he told me to figure it out" (Interview with Waguri Yukio, December 8, 2012). While all participants in this research spoke positively about dancing at the cabaret, this same obligation led others to quit. Kobayashi Saga expressed this in the following way:

> Most quit because they didn't like the cabaret. Women and men. That's why people kept on quitting. After all, they didn't like getting naked in front of people or gyrating in front of people in the countryside.

While their shows were in high demand in the 1960s, in the 1970s the cabaret drastically lost popularity and began decreasing in number.[14] At this time, there seemed

---

[14] The cabaret's loss of popularity can be attributed to the economic recession triggered by the Oil Shock, the spread of color television, karaoke, and the introduction of VCRs in the 1970s. By the 1980s, people could watch pornographic videos at home, and thus did not need to go to the cabaret to see a naked woman.

to be less demand for male dancers, and thus the obligation to dance at the cabaret seemed to fall mostly on the women, with the men able to quit if they wanted to.

As it became more difficult to draw customers to the cabaret and strip clubs, performances became increasingly erotic. Whereas the cabaret had traditionally featured the art of the striptease, Waguri said that people did not care about that art or dance. As performances became more erotic, some places presented the women naked from the start. At Asbestokan in the early 1980s, Hijikata and his wife opened about six show pubs in Tokyo, where his students danced "in the nude," according to one source. Hijikata's students in the period of 1979–1982 did not perform butoh on stage but instead danced in these bars while pursuing Hijikata's butoh.

Other butoh companies drew inspiration from both Hijikata's butoh, his cabaret performances and performance system. Dairakudakan, which was established by the underground actor Maro Akaji (who also lived at Asbestokan and performed at the cabaret in the 1960s) and Hijikata's student Bishop Yamada in 1972, began their group activities by dancing at the cabaret to raise money to stage butoh performances in a proper theater. Since they were working at the cabaret every day, their first rehearsals were primarily for cabaret performances. Osuga Isamu, a member of the company, left Dairakudakan to begin his own company, Byakkosha, in 1977. Osuga also has said that his first experience as a performer was on the cabaret stage. Through the 1970s, 1980s, and until Byakkosha disbanded in 1994, dancers received 500 yen per night when they danced at the cabaret in these companies.

At Byakkosha as well, if a dancer did not like working the cabaret, they quit. One difference between Byakkosha and the other two groups is that they were based in Kyoto, in the Kansai area, and participants said that more women worked in this area. Byakkosha member Yurabe Masami said that the women danced at the cabaret almost every night, whereas the male members danced four or five nights a month. The dancers who stayed in the company accepted their obligation to perform at the cabaret, and some even reveled in it. Butoh artist Ima Tenko explained that she accepted at first because she was educated in the older style, so she thought this arrangement was fine if she was able to learn and become a butoh artist in the future (interview with Ima Tenko, June 24, 2012). This "older style" is the teacher-student relationship in which the student will do what the teacher asks in order to be around them and have a chance to absorb that dance style.[15]

---

[15] Instead of connecting this to traditional dance, I would rather connect it to dance in the present. In my research of neo-burlesque and pole dance groups in Japan from 2015 to the present, there are also groups in which the teacher can ask the student to work for free in faculties unrelated

A very different example is international neo-burlesque dancer Erochica Bamboo. She began as a member of Byakkosha and was then sent to dance in the cabaret. Initially she did not like dancing there, but she was already booked for shows, so she continued going. Eventually, she fell in love with the glitzy and glamorous world of striptease and the cabaret and in the end chose the international world of neo-burlesque over the grotesque expression of butoh (interview with Erochica Bamboo, May 20, 2015).

Overall, these butoh dancers/ cabaret performers were not moved by social norms of women needing to save money for their husband or family, nor by the discourse of women rebelling against social expectations about dancing in such places; however, they were not moved by their own will or agency, either. It was a given that entering a butoh group meant also dancing at the cabaret, so it became a condition for developing as a butoh artist. The butoh group exercises a collective agency that initiates their movement, but in the following sections I will argue that it was ultimately the material affective force of the cabaret that allows them to follow through with this movement from cabaret to cabaret, and thus from stage to stage.

Co-emergence of the *ba*, the performance, and the artist

27

This section outlines how these butoh dancers remember the cabaret's *ba*, focusing on their co-emergence as cabaret dancers and butoh dancers with that *ba*. While this article focuses on the cabaret as the quintessential place of striptease, there was significant variety in the places these dancers were sent to perform. While they danced at cabarets as large as gymnasiums, holding audiences of 500–600 people, they also danced in small clubs, hot springs resorts, and in strip clubs after the cabaret started to decline in the mid-1970s. They danced on stages within commuting distance of their studios and headquarters, but also went on tour around rural areas of Japan for a few weeks or a month. In the 1980s, Dairakudakan mostly toured the cabarets in the northern half of Japan, from

---

to dancing, perhaps working the entrance, serving as a waitress, or advertising for the teacher's dance shows, and the student will not, or rather, can not object. I was also involved in this kind of relationship as a student. When I tried to quit the seemingly unrelated unpaid jobs due to the difficulty of balancing it with my university work, the pole dance teacher asked me, "do you think you don't have anything you can learn here?" adding seriously "I am giving you a chance others would be envious of." Even now there are dance groups in which the student is expected to be grateful for doing whatever the teacher asks as it is seen as a chance to learn the tricks of the dance-trade. This "old style" of education can also be seen in other hierarchical types of activity, like after-school clubs in Japanese high schools.

Tokyo to Hokkaido, while Byakkosha toured the cabarets in the southern half of Japan, from Nagoya to Kyushu.

Depending on the company and the era, the cabarets were completely different, but there were some similarities to how these material places were remembered. First, there were the well-equipped stages, including enough space to dance and for proper stage lighting. Stage lighting is crucial for the performance, as proper stage lighting can make or break the spectacle. Second, there was a live band, to which the dancers could give their sheet music on the day of the show. And as the live band differed depending on the venue, so too was their music performed a bit differently each time. Perhaps it is an affect of nostalgia, but I never heard of a cabaret, large or small, that did not have an otherworldly, extraordinary, underground, even giddily deviant atmosphere to it. This was in part created by the material characteristics of the place, but was also inseparable from the human actors and the performances.

Thus, the *ba* of the cabaret was generated in part by the human actors surrounding it: the dancers, audience, in-house staff, and production companies, the latter of which were reportedly run by yakuza (gangsters). Kobayashi Saga and Waguri Yukio remembered most vividly the dancers with whom they shared a dressing room, recalling a utopian dance community.

28

> The dancers didn't have fake exteriors or ulterior motives. Everyone was naked when they put on their makeup before a show and naked when they came back from the stage... I learned something really amazing here (the dressing room). What I remembered with my body, or like a warm heart... There were no barriers between us... Dancers are in the lowest status. The lowest social position, having gone that far, there is nothing left to hide from each other. These were relationships stripped of all superfluous things. They were all wonderful people. (Interview with Kobayashi Saga, date as above)

> I fell right into a dance village. We are all segregated from society, right? Apart from riding the train, all day I was either in the dressing room or training in the studio (Asbestokan). Anywhere I am, it was a dance village. Even the studio. Because I suddenly dove in to such a place. In a certain aspect, it was comfortable. Our own thing, with a little distance put up between us and society. (Interview with Waguri Yukio, date as above)

Sakaino Hiromi said that training at Asbestokan was extremely strenuous, and that she could hardly sleep or eat due to their schedule. For her, the dressing room was a place to nap and relax. She said that people would worry about her, give her *onigiri* (riceballs), and wake her up before she was supposed to dance. "It was an interesting era" (interview with Sakaino Hiromi, Sept. 28, 2012).

The dancers regarded their cabaret shows as totally different than their butoh performances. This can especially be said for the strip shows. Sakaino explained that performances had three phases of "Begin, Mambo, and Slow," and Yamamoto Moe talked about how men danced with a female solo dancer in a style called "duo show" or "adagio" in the 1970s.

> "Begin" is where you dance whatever... and you wear a costume. When it cuts to "mambo," you take off some clothes. During "slow," you become nude and strike a pose. When you are told to go on stage you do this, and the band plays some songs. (Interview with Sakaino Hiromi, date as above)

> There were three songs. In the first song the male dancer comes out; in the second song the female dancer comes out, and they dance together. In the third song, the female dancer takes off her clothes. That was the kind of flow to it. Then, when it was my turn to dance, I moved too much, and the female dancer was angry, saying "This is my stage, so don't dance too much." So, I thought that this is a woman's workplace. Actually, with the audience, older men drinking alcohol are watching, and they want to see women. There were times when I heard, "Get off the stage, man" ... So I quit. (Interview with Yamamoto Moe, September 1, 2012)

In addition to this more typical strip show, there were also group shows, of which the *kinpun* is especially well known. *Kinpun* can be translated as the "golden powder" show. *Kinpun* refers to the "golden powder" that dancers mix with vegetable oil and then apply to their entire bodies so that they shine like a golden bodhisattva. The costume is typically only a hand-made golden g-string, so that it looks like they are naked with glistening golden skin. Additionally, they often use eye makeup or hair accessories that add an oriental element and dance with burning torches. Many of the movements are reminiscent of the poses and gestures of Buddhist statues, which may explain why the choreography was called "Oriental" among the dancers who were at Asbestokan.

Although the cabaret show is categorically different than butoh in terms of performance genres, all the participants in this research noted different ways

29

in which cabaret shows contributed to the development of butoh. Waguri and Sakaino[16] directly stated that the cabaret made them the performing artists they had become.

> Actually, I think it is the cabaret that made me who I am today, what I experienced at that time. Ten days after (entering Asbestokan) I was made to stand on the stage of a strip club with no prior experience or career... it's scary. It's scary, or rather, I'm anxious, but I have to go (to dance there) regardless. You gradually go on and learn that sort of thing, though. (Interview with Waguri Yukio, date as above)

> When I think about them letting me go on stage, being able to experience the tough training (at Asbestokan) and the fun shows, I think it's good that I started in that era (when we could dance at the cabaret). I'm here because there were (butoh) performances and shows (at the cabaret). (Interview with Sakaino Hiromi, date as above)

Waguri is a male dancer, while Sakaino is a female dancer, and both were referring to the 1970s. Sakaino also references butoh dancers now, who cannot make a living and pay for performances by dancing at the cabaret, because the number of cabarets has drastically decreased, and those that remain (at the time of writing) are different than they were then. Sakaino said that she feels sorry for the newer generation of butoh dancers who cannot live the lifestyle of a cabaret dancer.

Bishop Yamada and Kobayashi spoke of the affective relationships between the cabaret as a place, their bodies, and the butoh stage. According to Yamada, dancing at cabarets was not just an extremely helpful way to raise funds for butoh stage performances; butoh itself would not have become what it was without the students doing cabaret shows.

> What can I call it, showing oneself in the space of the cabaret? That raw, energetic physical sensation is cultivated there... Because we take that sort of thing and pound it out on stage like "gan!"[17] in the form of butoh. It's not just

---

[16] This is an interesting combination of people to be in agreement, because they seemed to me to be polar opposites personality-wise. Waguri is very warm as a teacher but also has a cool intellectual side; Sakaino has a loveably ditzy side and does not seem to consider herself as very intellectual.

[17] This translation keeps the onomatopoeia for the sound he made for how they take it to the stage while keeping his use of the passive tense, which makes for awkward English.

going along with the plan. This thing, like a weird energy, came out like "gah!"
(Interview with Bishop Yamada, October 13, 2013)

Yamada uses onomatopoeia like "gan!" and "gah!" to express how some unnamable energy was generated in his body and let out when he stepped on stage. This energy did not have to be carefully rehearsed and perfectly executed; in fact, it could not be. As he says, it is simply being in the "space," not doing but simply "showing" himself, from which an energy overcomes and flows through him, a happening that could not be planned. This is one example of how place exercises its agency on these dancers. However, this does not mean that the dancers are passive; rather, it is clear that Yamada was quite active, invigorated in the co-emergent power of that *ba*. Yamada's onomatopoeia and use of the present tense suggests the energy and excitement I saw pouring from his body as he spoke, as if that *ba* remains part of him even now.

As discussed earlier, Kobayashi stated that she learned how to be a social being through her relations at the cabaret, and claimed that dancing in the cabaret was good training as a performer. She also listed another physical sensation gained from this experience:

> Hijikata told me to go to the cabaret... I rode the train for a long time and went to far-away places like Hokkaido and Kyushu. During that time, I would get the sensation that my body was being taken away. (Coker 2018: 413)

In another paper, I discuss how entering the life of butoh was akin to being kidnapped (Coker 2015a, 2018). First, this is based on the idea of traditional dancers being taken as a child and raised completely saturated in their performing art. Hijikata also required a total commitment from the students to immerse themselves in the butoh world. This does not mean being willing to physically go and do the things that Hijikata said, but a deeper attitude, a mode of action that they learned. This physical attitude can be called a willing surrender to being caught up in that world, a ready acceptance of the powers that pull them in, a mode that can also be ascertained from how they move in butoh.

I cannot generalize the movement I was taught in butoh workshops with many of the participants, because each had a different approach. However, I did see the following pattern. They requested that dancers not intentionally plan how we would move and not superficially express what we were told to dance. Instead, we were told to become what we were dancing on the cellular level, and thus to move without planning but rather as a necessary consequence of that becoming.

31

That movement should take over and transform our whole body, as well as our perception of our surroundings (Coker 2019). This sense of our bodies being taken away by the alternative reality of the butoh workshop seems to be quite similar to what Koyabashi and the other participants describe as being physically taken away to the alternative *ba* of the cabaret.

Dairakudakan and Byakkosha also sent their dancers to the same types of cabarets. Dairakudakan's shows were partly inspired by Hijikata's, while Byakkosha's shows were partly inspired by Dairakudakan. This is inevitable, since the choreographer for Dairakudakan (Bishop Yamada) was Hijikata's student, while the leader of Byakkosha (Osuga Isamu) was a member of Dairakudakan. As a result, Dairakudakan developed the kinpun show and the choreography called 'Oriental' in the 1970s, and then Byakkosha made a similar yet different version of the kinpun show, with choreography called "Kafkas" in the 1980s. I performed Dairakudakan's kinpun show with the company at a summer intensive in 2009 and learned Byakkosha's kinpun show from Ima Tenko, a former member.[18] Although the choreography of the two kinpun shows is quite similar, Byakkosha's choreography allows for a wilder and freer interpretation of the movement by each dancer. Although their kinpun show is inspired by their predecessors', they adapted it to suit their own butoh style, as well as the era (1980s) in which they danced.

In these two companies, the kinpun show had an ambiguous position: it was a cabaret dance, entertainment, while at the same time being a form of training for new members of the company. Each of the movements feature different motifs for how to transform the body into different objects, like moving bodhisattva statues, lateral figure-eights, exploding fireworks, and a wine-drinking Nijinsky, among others. However, while butoh is thought to be a slow and improvised, interpretive dance, the kinpun show's choreography has clear physical shapes that resemble jazz dance. When I participated in Dairakudakan's summer intensive, another participant, an American woman, said that she thought that dancing the kinpun show "was not butoh," but regardless she was ready for them to "get me in that thong and paint me gold." Perhaps this attitude of letting go of one's preconceptions of butoh, accepting that one does not know what butoh is anymore, and being willing to let oneself go, get naked and dance in front of an audience is the first step towards doing butoh.

Osuga Isamu put the difference between butoh and their cabaret dancing very clearly: "I guess you can say that when we did a show we did (danced)

---

[18] In Photo 1.7, Ima is the dancer in the front row, second from the right.

very specific images like a flower or an octopus, but in the case of butoh we did extremely abstract images." For example, when I learned the octopus movement (from the kinpun show) from Ima Tenko, I was told that water is shooting from my arms, which are octopus tentacles, and I am an octopus who loves the figure "8," so I am writing the figure eight all over the space, and then I was told to move. This is a fun and easy exercise, we often smiled when we did it, maybe even making water sounds with our mouths or playing with it in other ways. The tasks for getting at butoh movement were typically not as easy. For example, sometimes we were told to crouch down and imagine that we were a person who has been inside a boulder for 1000 years who is endeavoring to stand up and walk out. While it may be equally clear in its imagery, often butoh leaves the performer with a riddle, unclear what they are supposed to do, how they are supposed to move. Perhaps this is the point – butoh is not supposed to be intentional or planned out; the person is just supposed to do it, to become it. In cabaret shows, perhaps there was more leeway to play around and simply do things because they thought they and the audience would get a kick out of it.[19]

Bishop Yamada gave one example of how they developed the kinpun show: a movie director suggested that they have sword fights on stage. They made the swords themselves, cutting them into different sizes, and rehearsing so that sparks flew when they hit their swords together. He said when they performed this version of the show at the top-class cabaret called "Royal Akasaka" the manager rushed to them after the show and said that in his twenty years in this job he had never seen such a fantastic show.

Yuki Yuko gave another, more static image of the kinpun show; she said, "First of all, we paint our whole bodies gold and shiny and surprise the audience" (interview, August 2012). It is like the so-called freak shows that used to be at the circus – they could simply show their bodies, standing still, like a statue, not breathing. The kinpun show had different possibilities, but what connects them is a certain giddy playfulness, a trickster-like characteristic that pulls the audience into a different kind of physical reality.

This performance is not possible without the place, a *ba* that is equally composed of material characteristics as well as the people and things in a space

33

---

[19] This is a very difficult distinction to make – I have also seen cases in which the butoh choreographer came up with a routine in an instant, in the spirit of "because it will be fun and why not." While I want to re-present my participants' perceptions of a big difference between their performance at the cabaret and on the butoh stage, it is impossible to specify what that difference is because of butoh's variety and defiance of being defined.

that co-emerge according to a certain historical timing. Yuki Yuko expressed the *ba* of the cabaret as another world:

> It's a world that you normally wouldn't know. Meeting snake-handlers, magicians, famous singers. Meeting yakuza from Japan's underground, finding out that yakuza have the same view of life. Having the chance to talk to these kinds of people, knowing Japan's unknown underground world. (Interview Yuki Yuko, date as above)

Meeting Yuki Yuko was exciting. I travelled to an art festival in the northern countryside to meet her, and I thought that it would be a typical interview, spending a few hours in a cafe. Instead, the interview was a slumber party, in which we rode bicycles, took off our clothes and swam in the lake, talked late into the night while listening to the cicada chirp and over breakfast as well. While I have a lot of data from what she said, it is the whimsical, joyous character of Yuki that I most want to convey to the reader: the Yuki who while laughing said that she danced at the cabaret while pregnant with her big belly bulging out and the Yuki who accepts all of her experiences as part of some kind of joy engine, propelling her into her dance future. If the reader could find a video of Yuki Yuko dancing, I think this Yuki can be seen in how she moves.

Speaking specifically of what she learned while dancing at the cabaret, Yuki said that the strict expectations of the cabaret made her a top-notch dancer. On top of that, she said that she was also able to bring her own art to the stage.

> In my life, the part of me as a cabaret entertainer and the part of me as a butoh artist were awakened. Then, one thing was born from the refinement of a mutual refining between myself as a cabaret entertainer and myself as a butoh artist. (Interview with Yuki Yuko, date as above)

While she can divide the parts of herself as cabaret dancer and butoh artist, they are one and the same Yuki Yuko. She acknowledged that this Yuki Yuko would not exist without the other people she encountered at the cabaret.

> The hostesses, the cabaret entertainers... it all comes together thanks to them. Right? So, it doesn't matter if it is a big cabaret or a small cabaret, that *ba*, that timing makes the cabaret entertainer, gives birth to them. (Interview with Yuki Yuko, date as above)

In her own words, she confirms the idea of the *ba*: the co-emergence of multiple actors in a state of non-separation makes them what they are. In the interview, she specifically states that in training for cabaret dancing she learned the basics of how to move her body, such as tension and release, but that she also acquired more abstract skills that she described as "dance that surpasses dance, acting that surpasses acting." It is obvious that the process of becoming a dancer cannot be reduced to the cause-effect relationship of training, rehearsal, and performance; supposedly external factors of other actors form the *ba* together. This is because the real actor of becoming is not the individual, but rather the *ba* itself, in which the individual is internalized.

Murobushi Ko deepens the discussion about the relationship between the performer and the place by taking up the *nikutai*, the Japanese word for the corporeal and carnal, material human body.

> It's the realization of the one-night-only festive *nikutai* that dances wildly, the cabaret's "ah!" of holding a woman and drinking alcohol, the deviancy that the entertainer's body inevitably conceives, it's like a festival of darkness... but a festival that is outside of the community's festival. Speaking of the deviancy I mentioned before, there is the afternoon festival, and then there is the night festival. The night festival is a placeless thing that doesn't have a place anywhere; the night festival equals *nikutai*. So it is the place to encounter your own dangerous, precarious *nikutai*.

35

Murobushi's description of the relationship between the corporeal and the place sheds light on the point. The place of the cabaret is outside of productive, hierarchical, and rule-oriented society, and as such, it is placeless. However, if we think of this cabaret as the festival of *nikutai*, or rather as *nikutai* itself, placelessness takes on another meaning. That is, the simple fact that when *nikutai* leaves a place it is not the same as when it arrived; it takes not only the physical memory but also a real physical imprinting from that place with it. The body is forever changed from performing in a certain *ba*. Likewise, *nikutai* is the irrepressible and libidinal aspect of our physical nature as human beings and cannot be completely subjugated to the social norms that operate in a certain *ba*. Therefore, our *nikutai*, our existence as carnal and physical beings can also contingently impact the *ba* and potentially upset our social selves. And the special nature of the cabaret made it one of the few and rare *ba* in which these butoh dancers encountered their own *nikutai*.

Former members of Byakkosha also credited the cabaret with forming them as performers.

> Since we performed at a lot of different places with different atmospheres, with different size stages and different performances of the music by the band, we must've really learned a lot from that. It's like (we had to think of) how to make the best use of that place. (Interview with Yurabe Masami, date as above)

As Yurabe is looking back at his experience, he can't pinpoint which element of the cabaret affected him; obviously this can be the result of remembering something that happened decades ago, but this also supports the idea of non-separation in co-emergence with each element being essential, even irreplaceable, to the emergent whole. Additionally, when he thought of the performer's relationship to the place, he said that the performer had to *ikasu* the place in which they end up. Based on the context, I first assumed this *ikasu* as the most logical meaning of the word in that context, "to make the best use of"; however, it is interesting to note that *ikasu* also means giving life to something. When both of these meanings are employed at the same time, we can say that as the dancer makes the most of the space, music, and atmosphere of the cabaret to create the most impressive show they can, they are bringing life to the place; it emerges as a place through their performance.

Furthermore, this place of the cabaret that emerged from their performance, and the selves as performers who co-emerged, was carried over to the butoh stage, shaping the development of that performing art.

> Being at the cabaret job and standing on the (butoh) stage had a close feeling, and I think they both influenced each other because we could *odoru*. (Interview with Ima Tenko, date as above)

The word *odoru* means "to dance," but these butoh dancers used it differently than other Japanese words for dancing. Other words for dance, like *buyou* or *dansu*, refer to forms of dance that are conventionalized or imported from Western countries. *Odoru* suggests a dance that is more rooted in a local Japanese context. They used it amongst themselves to refer to butoh as neither modern dance nor traditional dance. It was movement that they were reinventing with the development of butoh. They held a clearly different category for this butoh movement than choreographed dance, but with movement and dance, the instrument of the physical dancing body is the same instrument used for everything in a dancer's life. This point could open to the suggestion that every aspect of their lives went in to the development of butoh (see Coker 2015a, 2018), but the generation of affective relationships between place, performer, performance, and audience only occurs where they all co-exist: the theater, the stage. Even if there is a clear difference for the butoh dancer between the dance they did at the cabaret and what they performed on the butoh stage, their body and its formation as an artist is the same material vessel.

Ima and Mizuno Ritsuko, two women from Byakkosha, both noted the effect on gender of performing at the cabaret. It may seem that performing sexy shows at the cabaret would heighten the female dancer's sensitivity to what is expected from women and cause them to adhere more strictly to the gender norms placed upon them. However, they said it was the opposite. By becoming women on the cabaret stage, women were able to erase their female presence on the butoh stage and become something else.

> We were told that the performance will come together if a man stands on stage as-is, but the female body cannot stand on stage unless it is erased of its ego so that it can take on the qualities of anything else. We were told that we can't become something else if we assert ourselves. (Interview with Mizuno Ritsuko, May 23, 2012)

Considering the wild performances of Byakkosha, it is easy to imagine that the performance would not work if the performer showed any shame or hesitation in doing something other people would normally consider as debasing – such as being naked, being covered in dirt, and being connected to a stock like a slave (see Photo 1.7). From my research of pole dancing bars in Japan, I became all too familiar with how ready men in the Kansai area (specifically Osaka) are to get completely naked and make a scene at drinking parties, even if they are not that drunk, if it is to the delight of their co-workers. Conversely, women seem trained to be more demure and careful with how they express themselves and their bodies. Therefore, it may seem paradoxical that being trained to present their bodies as extremely female at the cabaret would help them to erase their femininity on the butoh stage. However, realizing and cultivating the physical practices of emanating the social ideal of the female was their first step to being able to strip it away. This bodily control allowed them to become what they wanted to become in the moment on stage, realizing the diverse differences and possibilities of their body.

Conclusion

In summary, the place of the cabaret changed life courses, dancing bodies, and the performance itself.

This chapter started from the observation of the historical relationship between butoh and cabaret show dancing, and how the butoh dancers perceived their co-emergence as performers with the life of the physical cabaret in their shared *ba*. Whereas much literature on performance and place is based in the tacit idea that the individual is incomplete without exercising agency, to develop as butoh performers they had to surrender their agency; they realized this surrender and convergence with the *ba* while moving from cabaret to cabaret and stage to stage.

These butoh dancers surrendered their place as so-called proper members of society by being branded as cabaret dancers. Performing on the cabaret stage changed lives, changed bodies, and changed the practice of performance itself. The affect of that performance is enabled by the agency of the place, which is enabled by its materiality (the physical stage and space of the cabaret) and contextuality (its socio-historical meanings).

Rather than social change beginning with individual agency, I see a need to consider how collectivity and contingency can set forth creative change. Along with the collective performativity of butoh dancers in this case, the material agency of the place and the individual's contingent relationship to that *ba* is essentially what establishes the meaning and thus the affect[20] of their performance.

---

[20] Why do I use terms like meaning and affect? First, the result of performance is affect – how it makes someone else feel. Unlike sports, in dance whether a performance is good or bad is judged more on how it makes someone feel – thus the affect of the performance. Now, in affect theory it is becoming accepted that affect is not only some shared yet unconscious feeling but also is formed through conscious meaning-making that develops based on experience (Wetherell 2012). This is why I cannot talk about dance performance without also using words like meaning or affect.

2. Space for Competition and Place for Participation

Two Contrasting Sides of a Japanese Folk Song Contest

Gaku Kajimaru

Ba as a musical performance space

Sound is deeply embedded in space and time. Phenomenologist Don Ihde suggested that sound diffuses in every direction from its source and human auditory focus is omnidirectional, but humans generally hear sound as located and directional. People experience sound as a sphere in which they are immersed (Ihde 2007: 75–77). Though Ihde argued that the spatial horizon was obscure and strikingly temporal (Ihde 2007: 107–108), "music and sound can articulate spatial and socio-spatial as well as temporal boundaries" (Born 2013: 14).

Sound and musical practice produce and transform space (Born 2013: 20). Multidisciplinary studies of the relation of sound and space like Soundscape Studies have focused on the aural experiences of people and their cultural, historical, political, and social contexts (Born 2013, Samuels et al. 2010). And since auditory experiences can be embodied and have strongly affective force, sound does not always produce transparent "space" but emerges and connects with intimate "places" where people inscribe meanings (Casey 1996, 1997, Feld 1996, Cresswell 2004, Low and Lawrence-Zúñiga 2003, Low 2017). Furthermore, sound is not material that exists in space, especially if it is performed music. As Christopher Small argued, music should not be understood simply as a noun but should be grasped in its essentially verbal aspect, which he named "musicking" (Small 1998). Behaviors like playing music, speaking, oral performance and just making noise are also essential foci for inquiring about sound, music and space/place.

Playing music is a typical performance medium for creating *ba*. We can find *ba* in a crowd around or in front of musicians on the road, in a room, or in a hall. Ethnomusicologists have recorded and analyzed how musical and dance performances are connected and signified in social-cultural-historical contexts (Blacking 1973), and how participants exert their agency in those contexts (Rice

2014). Musicians play music to enjoy themselves, to earn money, to help people, and/or to make a place in the world. At the same time, musicians and dancers are sometimes inspired to perform by the *ba* in which they find themselves.[1] Musicians create *ba* by playing music, and at the same time they become agents-in-*ba*.

In this chapter, I will explore the variety of *ba* through examining two contrasting scenes of a folk song contest in Japan, "Obonai Bushi National Contest";[2] singing on stage for the contest, and then singing and dancing at the after-party (*naorai*). These two scenes have quite different characteristics, and the emergence of *ba* and agents-in-*ba* is deeply connected with the differences in performance and space. To illustrate the diversity of *ba* in musical performance, two concepts suggested by Thomas Turino will be helpful. Turino (2008) suggested two fields of live music performance: participatory and presentational. He defined the former as a performance "in which there are no artist-audience distinctions, only participants and potential participants performing different roles, and the primary goal is to involve the maximum number of people in some performance role", while the latter is a performance "where one group of people, the artists, prepare and provide music for another group, the audience, who do not participate in making the music or dancing" (Turino 2008: 26). Though these two fields have some continuity, they have contrasting goals, values, musical roles, and styles (Turino 2008: 88–91).

Performance on the contest stage can be classified as presentational while the performance at the *naorai* party provides a good example of participatory performance. Formation of performance is apparently relevant to the type of *ba*. In the next section, I will outline the modernization of *Obonai Bushi*; the historical and social background of the contest. The following sections outline the contest's general setting, process, and on-stage performance, and details the performance in *naorai*. In the last section, then, these two cases will be analyzed and compared, to clarify the relation between the features of music making and co-emergence of *ba* and *agents-in-ba*.

---

[1] The idea that *ba* has its own agency, distinct from participants, was inspired by Akira Okazaki at the meeting of an inter-university research project "In Search of Interacting Musicking Body: An Interdisciplinary Approach" at National Museum of Ethnology (Japan).

[2] This paper is based on my field research of this annual contest in 2017 and 2018.

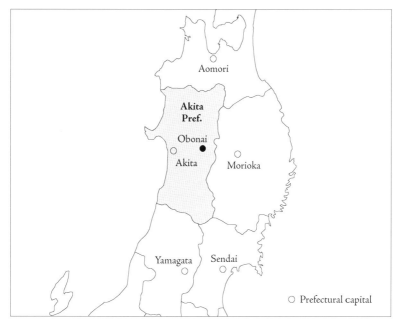

Fig. 2.1 Map of Akita Pref. in Tōhoku region, Japan

41

Modernization of Japanese *Min'yō* and *Obonai Bushi*

As David Hughes points out, Japanese traditional folk songs were dramatically modernized in the latter half of the 20th century, though their central traits (e.g. pentatonic scales, textual content, absence of vocal harmony, vocal style, limited accompaniment, and association of songs with particular regions) have not changed.[3] The changes include standardization, professionalization, and formalized stage performances (Hughes 2008a: 299–301). In premodern Japan, folk songs allowed improvisation to some extent, especially of lyrics. People learned local folk songs by ear in everyday life, and thus there were many variations according to each person's preferences. The repertoire of local villagers was quite limited and all their songs have proper occasions for singing, such as planting rice, drinking parties, marriage, or seasonal rituals (Hughes 2008a: chap. 2).

---

[3] Traditional folk song is called '*min'yō*' in Japanese. As Hughes notes, Japanese folklorists saw *min'yō* as born naturally, locally performed in a community, and transmitted naively and orally (Hughes 2008a: 14-15). Academics have not researched modernized *min'yō* because it is inauthentic, while non-academic people still accept it as 'traditional folk song' (see Hughes 2008a: chap. 1).

Fig. 2.2 Notation of 1st and 2nd verse of an old version of *Obonai Bushi* ("*Obone'a Dashi*") (Nihon Hōsō Kyōkai 1992: 270)

From the mid-20th century preservationism prevailed because of the declining popularity of folk songs, folklorists' vigorously recording for preservation, identity construction of local intellectuals, and the commercialization of folk songs (Hughes 2008a, Takeda 2001).[4] To preserve an 'indigenous' folk song, local aficionados organized preservation societies (*hozonkai*) or similar to fix the standard version of the song, and to transmit and disseminate it. After WW2 *min'yō* experienced two booms in 1947–8 and 1970s–80s, which also greatly increased the standardization of singing styles via TV programs and LPs, and staged folk singing (*sutēji min'yō*, see Hughes 2008b). Japanese folk songs have lost their improvisational qualities, gained accompaniment by Japanese musical instruments such as *shamisen, shakuhachi* and *taiko*, and in some cases folk dances have been invented for stage performances of these songs. Professional singers founded *min'yō* classes (including both songs and musical accompaniment in many cases) and made their own groups like *iemoto* system. Amateur singers began learning to sing folk songs in these classes, and to sing on stage in competitions held by local preservation societies and other organizations. In Turino's terms, Japanese *min'yō* transformed from participatory to presentational performance (Turino 2008) though its musical style has not fundamentally changed, as Hughes found (Hughes 2008a).

Obonai Bushi[5] is one example. This song is recognized as indigenous to the Obonai region,[6] which is now included in Senboku city in Akita prefecture (Fig. 2.1).

---

[4] The earliest example was *Esashi Oiwake*, which started the typical modernization process in the early 20th century, while most Japanese folk songs were modernized much later (Hughes 1992, 2008a).

[5] '*Bushi*' means 'tune' in Japanese. This word is often used for folk songs in Japan.

[6] Most famous (now staged) folk songs in Akita were originally transmitted from other regions by merchants, laborers or itinerants in the Edo era.

Fig. 2.3 Notation of 1st verse of Kodama's version of *Obonai Bushi* with *shamisen*
(Nihon Hōsō Kyōkai 1992: 270)

The contest organizers claim that the song originates in the 16th century[7] and was originally called 'Obone'a Dashi'. It is sung in drinking parties as entertainment (Taguchi 1983: 26). Many local singers sang this tune, improvising lyrics while playing off each other like a conversation at a drinking party. For example; 43

> *sasuzo sakazuki / nakamite agare / nakani tsurukame / mai asobu*
> I will pour sake in your cup. / See inside before you drink. /
> You can see a crane and a turtle inside / dancing and playing.

> *anata sakazuki / hajimete moratta / kin no senryō mo / morata yoda*
> Your treat / I firstly accepted for the first time. / Thousand taels of gold /
> It is like to receive.

> (Yomiuri Shinbun Akita Shikyoku 1979: 31)

This song was praised as "one of the most difficult melodies in Japan" by a professor of music from Tokyo in 1930 who visited this region to transcribe folk songs. In 1931, it was rearranged to make it easier to sing by Gyōson Kodama, who organized a folk troupe in Kakunodate town (near to Obonai) and staged

---

7   This is also written in the program pamphlet of Obonai Bushi National Contest, but it is dubious because the meter of lyrics is typical of the style that emerged in the Edo era (early 17th century). Komine explained that this song consisted of some popular folk songs in the early or middle Edo era (Komine 1970: 42).

performances around Japan and China in the 1930s–40s (Minzoku Geijutsu Kenkyūsho 2013, Taguchi 1983: 23). This version became quite famous in Japan, while the original versions were still sung by the locals (Fig. 2.2, 2.3). One of the original versions was selected and became 'Seichō Obonai Bushi' (Standard Obonai Bushi). This was the style performed by the local amateur Taguchi Kiyono, a member of the local folk troupe 'Kyōdo Geinō Shinkōkai' (Provincial Arts Association)[8] and made famous by professional singer Hasegawa Hisako in the 1950s (Sasaki 2008: 152, Takeuchi 2018: 127). Both versions are now accompanied by *shakuhachi* (end-blown bamboo flute), *shamisen* (three-stringed Japanese plucked lute), *taiko* (stick drum), and *kakegoe* (time-keeping or ornamental calls), and commonly recognized as one of the most popular (modernized) folk songs in Akita. Folk dances for both of these styles were also created, taught in a local elementary school and performed at *Obonai Bushi Bon Odori Taikai* (Obonai Bushi Bon Dance Festival) which is held at Obonai annually and an annual school athletics meeting.

Performative music making on the contest stage

As is common with famous modernized folk songs, the Obonai Bushi National Contest has been held annually since 1986 at the Senboku Civic Hall. This contest was organized by local public organizations for promoting sightseeing[9] and preserving the local folk culture. This local contest was estimated to be one of more than 100 single-song contests held in Japan every year until 1988, in which singers from all over Japan compete to demonstrate their skill in performing one 'local' folk song (Hughes 2008a: 5.5). In the Obonai Bushi National Contest, both *Obonai Bushi* and *Seichō Obonai Bushi* are accepted, but every singer must begin with the following lyrics:

> *fukeya Obone'a Dashi / nanoka mo youka mo / fukeba takara kaze /*
> *no'o ine minoru*
> Blow Obone'a Dashi wind! / seven days and eight days, /
> if it blows it will be a wind of treasure / oh, rice will ripen.

---

[8] This troupe was founded for preservation and promotion of local folk performance including folk songs like Obonai Bushi under circumstances of the declining popularity of folk culture in 1955. See Katsura (2003) for the history and activities of this group.

[9] Though its effect diminished significantly after the folk song's last boom faded away.

Photo 2.1 Obonai Bushi National Contest in 2018

45

Recent Obonai Bushi National Contests have welcomed about 120–160 singers each year. Participants are not all locals (i.e., not from Senboku City), but the majority are from Akita prefecture. Most participants belong to amateur groups or folk singing classes to learn from professional performers. These amateur folk singers join not only their own region's contest but other contests in Akita[10] and sometimes contests in other prefectures, so many of them know each other as fellow amateur singers even if they belong to different folk groups.

This contest is systematically organized and has two age-groups (up to 14 years old, and 15 and above). Participants must apply by submitting an application form on which they declare not only general information such as name, address, age and phone number, but also information about their plan such as, which version they will sing, which age-group they will join, their preferred length of *shakuhachi*,[11] and what musical accompaniment they require from the organizing committee. Singers can change the length of *shakuhachi* and

---

[10] In Akita prefecture there were 13 'national' local single-song contests (though one of them closed in 2019) and some other local single-song contests.

[11] Modern Japanese *min'yō* generally do not have a predetermined pitch for singing. Accompanists normally adapt the pitch to the singer's voice, so a *shakuhachi* player needs to select the length of his instrument to match the singer's pitch beforehand.

their musical accompaniment on the day at the reception. Though the contest schedule and the order of performance is decided in advance, the organizing staff finalize their preparations with this information.

As mentioned, the contest is held at the main hall of Senboku Civic Hall. The performance setting is typical concert hall style. With one large stage at the front (Photo 2.1), the hall has 1,024 seats, but the balcony is closed throughout the contest and many of the seats on the ground floor remain empty.[12] More than half the audience appear to be competitors and their families or members of their *min'yō* groups. The rest are mostly local *min'yō* fans.

After checking in at reception, participants are free until their performance is scheduled. Most participants go to the municipal gymnasium next door, which is arranged as a locker room in which the singers change from their street clothes into *kimono*.[13] While waiting for their turn, or for the announcement of results, many listen to other performances from a seat in the audience, or watching the TV in the lobby which broadcasts the live performance, or chatting with their *min'yō* friends. When their turn is approaching, they go to the stage wing to wait. As the singer before them finishes, they proceed to the center of the stage and sing *Obonai Bushi* to the audience and judges (Photo 2.1). The judges, however, are not in the hall; they listen to the performances in a room at the municipal library next door, where they can see the live performance on screen with high-quality audio.[14]

There are seven judges, including professional *min'yō* singers, the president of a local folk performance society and local media executives in Akita. They must score each singer quickly and accurately before the next singer starts. According to the chief judge at the opening ceremony in 2018, basic rating criteria are "the way to open mouth, the way to vocalize and breath, (accuracy or beauty of) melodic ornamentation (*fushi mawashi*), and accurate lyrics" as well as "not spoiling the idyllic taste of *Obonai Bushi*". They mark performances on a scale of 100 points, cutting the highest and lowest scores before summing up their marks. The youth class only has one round of competition on the second day since there are only about 30 competitors, while the general class has three rounds. All competitors

---

[12] According to the contest's organizers (interviewed in 2017), there were many more participants and much larger audiences when the contest began, but the hall is now too large for this event. The greatest factor of this change may be that the *min'yō* boom faded away in the 1990s, but severe depopulation of this region is another significant factor. Akita prefecture has experienced severe population decline since the 1980s (Akita Prefecture 2015), and has been marked by the greatest depopulation rate in Japan in the past seven years (Akita Sakigake Shimpō 14/4/2020).

[13] Singers are expected to wear formal clothes, in most cases *kimono* on stage. This is another characteristic of the modernization of *min'yō* which Hughes called 'dignification' (Hughes 2008a: 299).

[14] According to an organizer, this is because they cannot concentrate on judging the performance in the hall.

must join the preliminary round held on the first day, 40 of them proceed to the semi-final round and 10 move on to the final round, both of which are held on the second day. All participants are required to sing two verses, the first one as shown above. The second verse can be improvised, but most competitors select the second or the third verse provided in the program pamphlet because they have to sing "accurate lyrics" and these well-known verses are much safer choices than less well-known or original lyrics. The judging process ensures that all of the singers in the final round are technically precise and can sing in an expressive manner.

The contest is managed by an organizing committee. The president of the committee is the mayor of Senboku City. The other 14 executive members are presidents of public organizations or local societies of folk arts, but practical matters are managed by volunteer managers and other public sector staff, including city government officials (mainly civic hall staff and municipal library staff) and local volunteers. The division of duties has changed since the first contest. Now there are 5 sections in the contest management committee, including a general director, manager of general affairs, judgement and ceremony management, stagehands, and administration, and subsections (accounting, stage management, reception, vending goods, recording etc.) under these sections. In sum about 80 staff work together systematically to successfully stage this contest.

As shown above, *Obonai Bushi* seems like a typically modernized *min'yō* when it is sung according to the rules of this contest. The organizing committee arrange the stage settings, performers show their skills to the audience and judges, and their performance is evaluated, ranked and honored. The setting and performance seem typical examples of presentational performance in Turino's framework (Turino 2008).

Participatory music making of *Obonai Bushi* at the party

After closing the contest, the organizing committee hold a party called "*naorai*" for main staff (management directors and some others), judges, the winner and other performers at a Japanese restaurant close to a railway station (five minutes by car from the Civic Hall). I was invited as a researcher and a guest from a university quite far from Akita. They reserve the entire second floor, a typical Japanese style banquet room with a maximum capacity of about 30 people. It is a tatami-floored room with two small alcoves decorated with a hanging calligraphy scroll and ceramic ornaments, with low dining tables set out in three rows with

Photo 2.2 Dancing people in *naorai* in 2017

48   Japanese sitting cushions (*zabuton*) on the floor (Photo 2.2: There is another row of tables behind the camera). This setting allows people to walk around the tables and sit down more freely than common Western style restaurants because people do not have to seek a seat to sit on tatami though these cushions afford to do so, and there is more space to move around the table since they can walk on the cushions (compare with the difficulty of walking on chairs or through narrow spaces between chairs!). Where it differs from the typical Japanese style is that it has a simple audio system with two microphones and two seats for *shamisen* and *taiko* players. It seems like a stage without a riser. This space provides a stage for the MC and singing performances in *naorai*.

In 2017, after starting the party with a toast, the winner, a female high-school student from Oga City, far from Senboku City, was invited to the "stage" to make a short speech. She gave thanks to the organizers and sang *Obonai Bushi* with accompaniment as on stage in the contest. She then left for home with her mother since it was some hours away. Many of the judges also left for home, as most of them came from Akita City, which is about an hour by car or train from Obonai. The remaining guests and staff from not so distant places intermittently sang *Obonai Bushi* again. Other participants joined in by clapping hands and *kakegoe*.

While people were still drinking and socializing, I sat with the chief of a local performing folk arts society. I asked him about the old style of *Obonai Bushi* and the situation of singing. He started recalling old *min'yō* singing at a party in response to my question and said that people sang accompanied only by clapping hands in that situation, and started singing a famous *min'yō* around this region "*Obako Bushi*", and "*Seichō Obonai Bushi*". Hearing his singing, some people were inspired to stand up and start dancing around the tables! After a while, the *shamisen*, *shinobue* flute, and *taiko* joined in, while others (including me) clapped hands and said *kakegoe* (Photo 2.2). This joyful moment involving everyone finished after several verses with laughing and a contented atmosphere. Then someone pressed the MC to introduce and get me to say something. I, still feeling that atmosphere, started singing a short phrase of *Obonai Bushi* (since I did not remember the rest of the song) and shared some impressions from my field research.

In 2018, while many guests (mainly judges) once again left the *naorai* early, others enjoyed singing and dancing. According to my video recording of this scene, the MC (the chief I spoke with the previous year) urged people to sing one after another. It started with a local professional singer who was also an executive of the organizing committee singing *Obonai Bushi* while listeners joined by clapping hands and *kakegoe*. Next was a semi-professional performer who worked in the contest as a *taiko* and *kakegoe* supporting player. After she sang a little bit, two ladies started dancing, answering someone's calling, and others joined in, as they had the previous year. When she reached the second verse, she suddenly got too emotional[15] to continue, and some of the contestants took over without standing. The third singer the MC pointed to was the oldest local lady in the room, an *Obonai Bushi* dance teacher. She sang three verses (the longest of the day), and this time one of the previous dancers and the chief management director started dancing, and others joined in, including this year's winner (a local). When the song finished, the performers were showered with applause and joyful laughter. This performance seemed most lively in this *naorai* performance. There were two more renditions of *Obonai Bushi* and more dancing around the tables before it was finished.

These scenes were improvisational and voluntary. There are many performance roles here, including singing, clapping hands, and playing musical instruments and *kakegoe*. Everyone could voluntarily join in. This is a clear example of participatory performance. What struck me was that they sang *Obonai Bushi* again and again even after hearing it repeatedly for two days, revealing how much they love this local folk song.

49

---

[15] She said that she remembered her husband when singing this.

Different music and different *ba*

Performance on stage and performance in *naorai* are contrasting examples of *ba*. Stage performance is primarily presentational as discussed above, with some elements of participatory performance, just as there are many roles for participants in this contest,[16] and these roles are interchangeable to some extent. The procedure and performance sequence are rigidly arranged in detail by an organizing committee which has more than 30 years' experience of hosting this contest (although many staff change every year). Singers seek to demonstrate their skill for the audience and judges. There is a clear boundary between performers and audience, demarcated by the stage, even though participants become singers on stage and audience on the floor. These characteristics designate that stage performance as presentational.

It is difficult to say that *ba* and agents-in-*ba* co-emerged naturally or improvisationally here (cf. Shimizu 2003), but it is clear that this event would not exist without the singers' performances and the participants cannot be singers without this event. *Ba* of performance in this contest is space setting.

50 Singers on stage are the final and indispensible piece of this setting, after which the stage should be described as "space" as discussed by Low (2017) and in the Introduction. It is not created mainly by singers and performers but set by organizing staff. The setting is embedded in its historical and social context which has run the Obonai Bushi National Contest every year, and competitors fit in to this setting. Their nervousness indicates this situation. They are nervous because they do not control this *ba* and their performance is not for personal joy but for evaluation by others. From a different perspective, this *ba* exerts agency on the participants' behavior and performance, which is thus limited.

In contrast, the *naorai* performance is participatory. This event is much looser and more improvisational than the contest itself, as was suggested by the difference and looseness of the sequence of the parties in 2017 and 2018. The performance atmospheres also contrast. In the stage performance, singers are nervous while the *naorai* is relaxed and enjoyable. Though there is space for singing and playing accompanying instruments, the performance is inclusive and participatory. People can join in the performance in many ways, such as clapping hands, although the singer is nominated by the MC (who is an organizer of the contest). Furthermore, dancing the *Obonai Bushi* – which is missing in the stage performance – makes

---

[16] Christopher Small insisted that the category 'music' should include not only playing music but many other activities like providing performance material and managing an event (Small 1998: 9).

the *naorai* more participatory as Photo 2.2 indicates. This dance has been taught at a local elementary school and performed in the local Bon Dance festival for more than 40 years.[17] Moreover, the dance is relatively easy and quite repetitive, so novices can learn it by watching others, even while the relaxed atmosphere encourages the awkward dancing of foreigners.[18]

Here, *ba* and the agents-in-*ba* obviously co-emerged to be much more improvisational and natural than the stage performance. Though there is a proper setting for *Obonai Bushi* performance like audio equipment, the performance in this room is improvisational and voluntary, especially the dancing. Who will sing is decided by the MC in the moment, who will dance is decided by the *ba*, and everyone can exert their own agency. It was observed that even the leading dancer started dancing not only according to her will, but also as a tacit or explicit expectation expressed by subtle interaction with other people. This *ba* can be figured as *ba* of place making. It is more "place" than "space" (Low 2017: 32, Introduction) and more "making" than "setting" since performers created and dwelled in the *ba* by singing, dancing, playing instruments and clapping hands. This *ba* is made by agents, and involved attendants as participants in *ba*, while their agency formed the *ba* in which they were involved.

Furthermore, this *ba* is fluid and precarious. Much of the time in *naorai* is not for singing but for socializing and chatting. The singing is instigated by the MC and ends with participants' satisfaction or weariness (though it is difficult to identify which is the case from the video footage). When someone is singing, some keep chatting at the table. Participation of this *ba* is not by duty but by will, and maybe the atmosphere of their face-to-face interaction, the force of small *ba* they participate in made them keep talking to each other. This is evidence that *ba* has agency to the agents-in-*ba*.

There is another point to compare. Hanks et al. argued two different levels of *ba*: primary *ba* and secondary *ba* (Hanks et al. 2019, Introduction). As per the Introduction, primary *ba* is featured by non-differentiation, non-separation and wholeness of elements, while secondary *ba* is characterized by differentiation and separation. These two are not dichotomous but all *ba* has these two layers, though there are different extents to which layer is prominent. It seems that the place for participatory performance is deeply rooted in primary *ba* while space for presentational performance is connected more strongly with secondary *ba*.

51

---

[17] The flyer of the 2019 Bon Dance festival is titled "The 49th Obonai Bushi Bon Dance Competition."

[18] Two of the dancers in Photo 2.2 are not from the Obonai region, so they tried to dance by following the native experts. In 2018, they pulled the leading person to the front so they could follow her.

In the stage performances during the Obonai Bushi National Contest, secondary *ba* seems most prominent. As Photo 2.1 shows, performers on stage face an audience on the floor and out-of-sight judges. This solid disposition is maintained throughout the contest. In contrast, in the *naorai* there is no distinction between performers and audience. Roles and *ba* are fluid and the *ba* of place-making dissolves the boundaries between participants. In this scene, primary *ba* comes to the surface, and a sense of wholeness and participation covers over agents-in-*ba*. My unprepared awkward singing of *Obonai Bushi* in 2017 can be seen as the product of the agency of primary *ba*. Field researchers are not immune to the power of the place, not to mention other participants.

While I have emphasized contrasting characteristics, there are some commonalities too. Turino said that the most common element for all musical genres is the social aspect. Participatory music making and presentational events can connect individuals and identity groups, although the two fields differ in the type of engagement, the scale, and the level of intimacy (Turino 2008: 63).

Both stage performance and performance in *naorai* connect people. The competitors from different regions come to know each other through socializing in the municipal gymnasium or in the hall, which gives rise to developing a "cultural cohort" just as old time music and dance does in the Midwestern United States (Turino 2008: chap. 6). Organizers come from different public sector institutions in Obonai to run this event. In the 2017 interview, a retired staffer told me repeatedly that when this contest first began, the whole town[19] enthusiastically worked together to host it. Hughes said "most such [local single song] contests were created by aficionados, not bureaucrats" (Hughes 2008a: 228), but this contest was created by both aficionados and bureaucrats for both economic and affective reasons. *Min'yo* fever has almost gone, but many public sector workers and volunteers still work together, maintaining social networks. Perhaps many of the staff are motivated by a sense of duty to keep this tradition alive, but this is also evidence of the residual power of *ba* where they live (cf. Kawanishi in this volume).

In *naorai* performance, people enjoy making music together so much that it creates a strong affective bond upheld by feelings of wholeness and inclusion. According to Turino, this is a common function of participatory music making:

52

---

[19] Obonai region was the center of Tazawako town at that time, and later merged with Kakunodate town and a village to be Senboku City in 2005.

(P)articipatory music making connects people more intimately and powerfully because of shared interactive engagement among all participants in the actual doing of the activities with each other. This tends to be most effective on a relatively small scale (Turino 2008: 61–62).

This affective power is strongly related to iconic and indexical signs. Turino applied Peircean semiotics to theorizing the communication of emotion and meaning by music and dance (Turino 1999, 2008). He argued:

> Iconic and especially indexical signs tie us to actual experiences, people, and aspects of the environment. Indices are of our lives and experiences and thus are potentially invested with greater feeling and senses of intimacy and reality. Indexical experience plus a perception of iconic similarity with other people and forms of life is the basis for feeling direct empathetic connection. (Turino 2008: 16)

He also suggested that "indices continually take on new layers of meaning while carrying along former associations" (Turino 1999: 235) because "indexical connections are created by experiencing sign and object together, and because we might experience the same sign vehicle at different times and in different contexts" (Turino 2008: 9). He named this feature of indexical signs "semantic snowballing" (Turino 1999: 235; 2008: 9).

53

One of the characteristics of *naorai* is the participants' love for *Obonai Bushi*. A professional *shamisen* player joining this party regularly as an accompanist for the contest said in 2018 that he always feels deep love for *Obonai Bushi*. This deep love is generated by local people's repetitive experience of singing, dancing, and listening to this local folk song. Singing *Obonai Bushi* is a kind of restored behavior for the people in *naorai*. Of course, the performance on stage is also a kind of "restored behavior" (Schechner 1985) since most participants have practiced this song many times as one of the major *Akita min'yō*, and must feel some attachment to this song. But for local people, this song is rooted in their lives in their hometown. *Obonai Bushi* is an indexical semantic snowball for them which gives rise to much deeper affection and sense of identity to this place than amateur singers on stage from other regions. This semantic snowballing and affection based on indexicality catalyze the emergence of *ba*, especially primary *ba* like *naorai*.

Conclusion

On the one hand, the National Obonai Bushi Contest is a good example of the relationship between music performance and *ba*, and the diversity of *ba*. The performance on stage is a typical presentational performance and the contest itself is a typical *ba* of space setting. This type of *ba* is arranged carefully in detail by organizers, and the singers' performances are just a piece of this setting. Performers' agency was limited by this setting. There is affective background of local people and one can observe emergence of *ba* and agents-in-*ba*, but perhaps many of these features of space could be understood without the concept of *ba*, since its emergent phase and affective sense of wholeness and inclusiveness are weak.

On the other hand, the *naorai* of this contest offered evidence that the concept of *ba* is indispensable for understanding performance in place/space. The inclusive and involving power of the performance in *naorai* provides a strong example of participatory performance. Its inclusive atmosphere is a token of the agency of place, in other words, the agency of *ba* that cannot be reduced to individual participants. *Ba* emerges on the spot through the interaction of the participants who participated there as agents-in-*ba* under the effect of *ba*. Affection for Obonai Bushi cumulated by the indexical semantic snowballing fueled this co-emergence in *ba*.

As Hanks et al. (2019) insisted and as argued in the Introduction, the concept of *ba* helps us to focus on the inclusive and non-separated aspect of place and performance. It is easy to understand the validity of this conception to see *ba* of place making like *naorai* where primary *ba* is prominent. Participatory performance is not possible without this layer of place making. At the same time, the presentational performance embedded in the *ba* of space setting can be understood only by the concept of space. And yet it is important to note that the primary layer of *ba* is omnipresent even in the space of presentational performance because it does not exist but is only latent under the secondary *ba* where distinction is evident. No matter what kind of *ba* it is, the performances in this contest showed that music and dance performance create *ba* and are performed in *ba*.

3. Ritual Performance and Agency of *Ba*

Hierarchy and Mood at Ceremonial Feasts in Pohnpei, Micronesia

Masaharu Kawano

Introduction

Although several post-colonial Micronesian and Polynesian societies have curtailed the power and rights of local chiefs, they still enjoy political and social influence over others (Lindstrom and White 1997: 2). Inhabitants "consistently obey their chiefs, share in chiefly status, and accept extraordinary obligations of expenditure in chiefly orchestrated rituals" (Marcus 1989: 196). Ideally, various performances in such rituals are supposed to convey images of a centralized and stratified society to some degree, with rigid rules about honorific language, spatial arrangement, bodily motion, ceremonial drinking, redistribution of goods and so on. But in practice, the rank-order should not be guaranteed by customary rules and social structures. As shown in the *ethno-pragmatics* discussed later, it "must be built, sustained, recalled, fought for" (Duranti 1994: 84) in a ritual process. Thus, chiefly authority and social hierarchy should be maintained and reconfirmed through individual agents' use of semiotic resources, rather than their rule compliance.

However, individual persons are not the only social actors in ritual interactions. Rather, as Kajimaru, Coker and Kazama suggest in the Introduction to this volume, the *ba* itself, which envelops and brings about their performance, is also thought to be a social actor. Therefore, it is necessary to consider how the *ba* emerges in a ritual process and what effects the *ba* has on those persons who participate in the process.

In this chapter, using ethnographic cases of ceremonial feasts from Pohnpei, Micronesia (Fig. 3.1), I will examine the ritual processes through which social hierarchy is actualized by the co-emergence of performances and the *ba*, while illustrating how performances influence and are influenced by the *ba*.

55

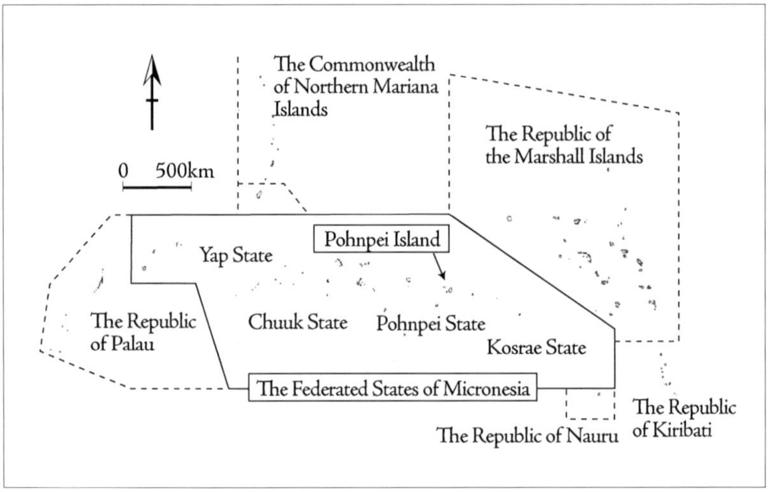

Fig. 3.1 The location of Pohnpei Island in Micronesia
Source: Kawai, Toshimitsu, 2001, *Shintai to keishō: mikuronesia denshō sekai no minzokushiteki kenkyū* (Body and Image: An ethnographic study of traditional worldview in Micronesia). Tokyo: Fūkyō-sha. p. 11

Negotiations over social hierarchy in an interactional process

According to Marcus, chieftainship in contemporary Oceania has become rather ambivalent: both mystified and demystified (Marcus 1989). Marcus considers this ambivalence from the perspective of Kantorowicz's 'the King's Two Bodies.' This concept derives from the Medieval British political thesis that while the king of course has a natural and mortal body as all humans have, he also represents the symbolic and immortal body politic which belongs uniquely to the king (Kantorowicz 1957; cf. Yamamoto in this volume). By correlating the 'two bodies' to the demystified (secular) and the mystical, Marcus finds that Oceanian chiefs also have 'two bodies.' In other words, the chief is both a sacred being, separate from his people, and an exemplary being, respected and admired by his people. Marcus suggests that these two images "must be negotiated situationally" (Marcus 1989: 193) in contemporary Oceania. I contend that this ambiguous duality applies to all titled-persons, since perceptions of them can be separated into a ranked title-holder and an ordinary person.

In order to examine how the double-sided chieftainship is negotiated in a ritual process, it is useful to rely upon anthropological theories of ritual communication, especially the *ethno-pragmatics* approach proposed by Duranti, a linguistic anthropologist. Whereas linguistic pragmatics generally emphasize the connectedness of linguistic forms to the context of their use, *ethno-pragmatics* is defined as the kind of pragmatics which recognizes not only such connectedness but also "the importance of the local level of language usage for an understanding of what linguistic forms contribute to social life" (Duranti 1994: 168).

In social interaction, an established order is often contradicted by different orders, norms or voices, and negotiated through linguistic performances. Thus, paying attention to usage of semiotic resources in ritual communications, it is possible to show "the economy of both centripetal (by reconfirming similar orders) and centrifugal (by offering slight variations or violations) forces in the semiotically constructed political economy of the community" (Duranti 1994: 7). In Marcus' term, the mystified and demystified sides are negotiated not only in political discourse but also through ritual performances.

Keating, another linguistic-anthropologist, also shows how hierarchical relations between chiefs and commoners, between high-ranking and lower-ranking titled persons, are produced and negotiated among participants of various feasts in Pohnpei (Keating 1998; 2000). She draws on Duranti's approach, pointing out that the notion of honor and social stratification are realized through a combination of sign resources, both verbal and non-verbal, including seating arrangements, food sharing, body motion and so forth.[1]

Their insights are useful for showing that hierarchical order is produced and negotiated through actors' interactions, rather than *a priori* expressions of a given social structure. For them, a ceremonial space is assumed to be the setting in which interactions among participants take place, and an arrangement of the space is a useful resource for organizing a ritual event. However, the space is not mere background for each actor. Rather, as Kajimaru, Coker and Kazama powerfully argue in this volume, it has agency which moves participants to some action.[2] In this sense, it can be called *ba*.

---

[1] Keating's approach is important to understanding how a social order is constructed through ritual performances (Keating 1998; 2000). However, she focuses unduly on the semiotic construction of the established rank-order. Therefore, her model of chiefly hierarchy and feasting is not necessarily adequate to grasp the centrifugal forces (cf. Duranti 1994: 7) in the feasting process.

[2] In ritual occasions, there are often opening and closing temporal brackets as well as physically bounding spatial brackets. These brackets are expected to exclude the outside world from the frame of interaction, but, as Bateson and Goffman rightly point out, the frame is always vulnerable (Bateson 1972: 182; Goffman 1986: 247–257). Due to the labile nature of the frame, there are dynamic and continuous framing processes, with ritual order being bracketed and overflowing (cf. Callon 1998). I previously suggested that an interaction-order in Pohnpeian feasts is vulnerable to the day-to-day relationships in ordinary life of Pohnpeians (Kawano 2019). In this chapter, I will show that ritual performances are also vulnerable to the mood of the *ba* in which the performances are taking place.

In this chapter, I will attempt to modify Keating's model of Pohnpeian feasts to recognize that *ba* itself is a social actor, and to show how rank-order is situationally negotiated through co-emergence of performance and *ba* in the feasting process.

Pohnpeian chiefs and title-ranking today

Colonial-era Micronesia, including Pohnpei, was governed by Spain (1885–1899), Germany (1899–1914), Japan (1914–1945), and the United States (1945–1986). When they gained independence in 1986 as the Federated States of Micronesia, Pohnpei became the main island of Pohnpei State. In the process of modernization and administration by foreign powers, Pohnpeian chieftainship significantly changed.

Commenting on Oceanian chiefs in a post-colonial state, Lindstrom and White observe that "political environs of the South Pacific, although freshly populated with presidents, prime ministers, members of parliament, local court justices, and the like, continue to be ruled in many areas by 'custom chiefs'" (Lindstrom and White 1997: 2). In the case of Pohnpei, the chieftainship persists independently of the administrative system of the nation-state, as a result of the historical entanglement of Western democracy and local polity. Although Pohnpeian chiefs today do not necessarily attain public office, particularly at the governmental and state level (Dahlquist 1974: 182), they continue to have great influence over Pohnpeian residents. Pohnpeians call their chiefly system 'the side of custom (*pali en tiahk*)' to distinguish it from the administrative system which is called 'the side of administrative office (*pali en ohpis*)'.

There are five chiefdoms (*wehi*) on Pohnpei (Fig. 3.2): Madolenihmw, U, Kitti, Sokehs, Nett. Kolonia Town, the capital of Pohnpei State, is in Nett chiefdom. Six municipalities including Kolonia Town, are on Pohnpei Island, and others are on outer islands. The chiefdoms are geographically identical with the municipalities, yet politically separated. The chiefdoms are headed respectively by paramount chiefs (*Nahnmwarki*) and secondary chiefs (*Nahnken*) regardless of electoral politics at the municipal level. Each chiefdom is further divided into many sections (*kousapw*) headed by section chiefs in the same manner. Both chiefdoms and sections have a number of people on whom their chiefs have conferred traditional titles.

Most adults are given their ranking-title by their paramount chief or section chief. Each male title has a female counterpart (*mwarepein*). A married woman has the counterpart to her husband's title. The paramount chiefs control hundreds of

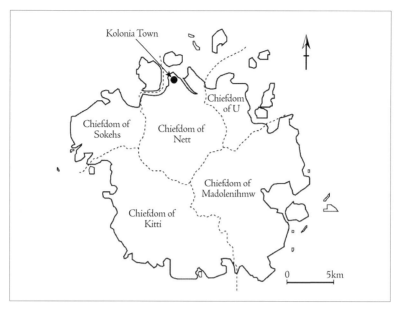

Fig. 3.2 Five chiefdoms and Kolonia Town on Pohnpei
Source: Riesenberg, Paul, 1968, *The Native Polity of Ponape*, Washington, DC: Smithsonian
Institution Press. p. 9.

chiefdom titles (*mwaren wehi*) and section titles (*mwaren kousapw*).[3] Chiefdom
titles are largely divided into three lines: the line of the paramount chief (*oleiso*),
the line of the secondary chief (*serihso*), and the line of honorific titles (*mwar
koanoat*). This division is related to matrilineal clan (*sou*). The title-holders of
the first line belong to the ruling matrilineal clan, and those of the second line
are members of other clans.[4] Paramount chief is the highest-ranking title-holder
in the first line and secondary chief in the second line. The third line has no
connection with clanship or descent. Each title is linearly ranked within each
line (Table 3.1). Though the title of section chief is awarded by his paramount
chief, he controls titles of his section. Section titles are also divided into three
lines, ranked in the same way as chiefdom titles. The title, vacated by death or for
other reason, is usually bestowed on the person who has the next lower ranking

---

[3] The chiefdom titles are more valuable than section titles since the former are not distributed to all
the residents of the chiefdom. In the case of U chiefdom, there are 2,685 residents according to the
census (Division of Statistics, Department of Economic Affairs 2002), but only 185 titles stemming
from three lines according to my fieldwork as of November 2009.

[4] The ruling clan differs from chiefdom to chiefdom: *Dipwinpahnmei* clan in Madolenihmw, *Lasialap*
clan in U, *Dipwinmen* clan in Kitti, *Sounkawad* clan in Sokehs and *Sounkawad* clan in Nett
(Riesenberg 1968: 15).

Ranking	The Line of the Paramount Chief	The Line of the Secondary Chief	The Line of Honorific Titles
1	Sahngoro	Nahnken	Lepen Moar
2	Wasahi	Nahlaimw	Soumaka Mesentakai
3	Dauk	Nahnsahu Ririn	Oun Oare
4	Noahs	Nahnapas	Nahnpei Mesentakai
5	Nahnawa	Nahmadaun Idehd	Souwede

Table 3.1 Top 5 titles in the chiefdom of U

title within the same line. For example, if a paramount chief died, the chiefly title would be transferred to the person who held *Wasahi* (the second-ranking title in the line of the paramount chief). In this sense, the Pohnpeian title system is not necessarily hereditary or genealogical.

This title system changed under the foreign administrations of the previous century. First, the Pohnpeian chieftainship underwent significant changes especially with the German land reforms of 1912. Until the early 20th century, paramount chiefs and section chiefs had great influence over residents through land control. In theory at least, all the land in a chiefdom was owned by a paramount chief and given out to his section chiefs. The sections then contributed to the paramount chief in return through feasting contributions and war efforts. At the section level, the section chief also gave his people the right to use the lands and the subjects reciprocated by supporting the section chief in the same way. However, after the German land reforms, the chiefs lost their claim to the land through which they had ruled their people. From that time on, the chiefs ruled their people through title-giving and the residents were expected to work for their chiefs in return.

Second, the paramount chiefs sought-out those persons who prospered in the cash economy,[5] becoming wealthier than the chiefs, awarding them important titles. In order to give them appropriate titles, the paramount chiefs and their advisors have created new titles by recombining elements of existing ones, or they have rediscovered – from traditions and myths – old titles which had not been awarded for a long time (Fischer 1974: 172). As a result, with population growth has come an increase in chiefdom titles, which is notable especially for the honorific titles or *mwar koanoat*.[6]

60

[5] The present legal and constitutional structure does not guarantee the economic privilege of Pohnpeian chiefs, even paramount chiefs, and they receive no salary for their traditional office.

[6] As Dahlquist reported, the increase in the number of honorific titles was astounding, especially in the 1950–1970s. For example, in the chiefdom of Kitti, traditionally there had only been three honorific titles, but there were 94 during his fieldwork in 1971 (Dalhquist 1974: 189). Similarly, in the chiefdom of U, there had been four honorific titles, but I collected 56 during my research.

Yet, at the section level, as the sections have grown larger, there have not been enough high-ranking section titles to go around. To solve this problem, in some cases, a section has split and new lines of titles have been created and filled (Petersen 1982: 22). In the process, whether at chiefdom level or at section level, "titles have become increasingly important" (Petersen 1982: 23) for the status and the identity of many residents.

Notably, titles do not entail any material rewards or resources. It is only in face-to-face interactions or in feasting events that the ranking of title holders appears in a readily observable way and that social hierarchy among participants is reconfirmed.

Pohnpeian custom of ritual performances and spatial arrangement in a feast

From a local perspective, several performances in a feast are inseparable from the local notion of 'honor' (*wahu*). As Shimizu noted the term *wahu* "may be tentatively translated as honor, prestige, authority or respect according to the context" (Shimizu 1982: 156). 'Honor' is a core-value in Pohnpeian custom (*tiahk en* Pohnpei).

61

Feasts are usually conducted in a 'feast-house' (*nahs*). Today, many households have their own feast-house, which is often adjacent to their house.[7] In everyday life, a feast-house is used for many un-ceremonial activities, such as drying laundry, playing bingo and so forth (Photo 3.1). And yet, when a ceremonial feast is held, the seating arrangement at the feast-house represents the hierarchical relationship between chiefs and commoners. In an ideal plan, paramount chiefs, secondary chiefs, the highest persons in the third line, and their wives are expected to sit on the main platform of the U-shaped feast-house (Figure 3.3). Elderly persons usually sit as an audience on the left and right platforms, whereas other men 'work' (*doadoahk*) organizing the feast. Chiefs and high-persons are labeled 'the person(s) who looks down on' (*sohpeidi*) the persons working in the central ground-level area, from the height of the platform.

The workers are usually engaged in the effort to 'pay respect to' (*wahunuki*)[8] chiefs and high-ranking title-holders and to actualize the social hierarchy of the

---

[7] Traditionally, the feast-house was owned by a section or chiefdom, not by individuals (Shimizu 1987: 134).

[8] *Wahunuki* is a transitive verb of *wahu* ('honor').

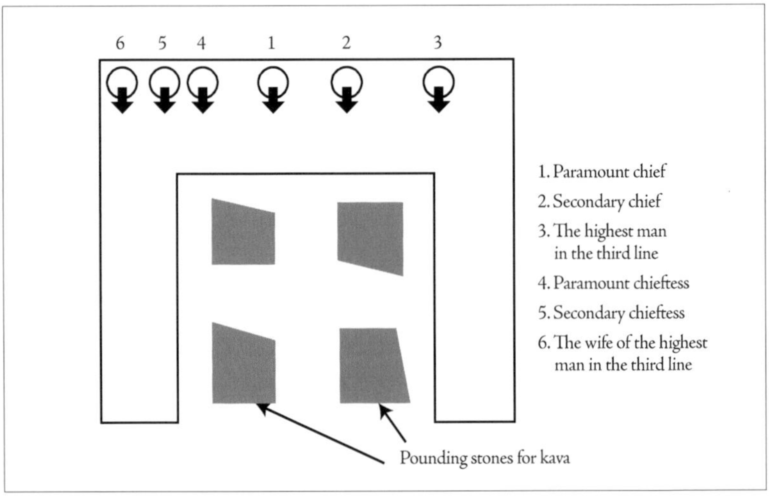

Figure 3.3 The ideal seating arrangement in a feast-house

1. Paramount chief
2. Secondary chief
3. The highest man in the third line
4. Paramount chieftess
5. Secondary chieftess
6. The wife of the highest man in the third line

Pounding stones for kava

62

Photo 3.1 Pohnpeian feast-house *(Left in everyday life; Right at a funeral feast)*

participants. The various ways of making 'honor' visible include: talking to a high-ranking title-holder in 'honorifics'; offering him foods; preparing kava (*sakau*) for him to express respect; serving the kava in the order of the title-ranking; 'lighting a stone-oven' (*saunda uhmw*), 'butchering pigs' (*kamehla pwihk*), 'redistribution' (*nehne*) of pork or yams, and so forth.

Among them, the redistributive performance by distributors or a master of ceremony, who is sometimes a paramount chief's son, most clearly visualizes a linear rank-order of the title holders present. Ritual items such as kava, pigs, yams and cooked foods are redistributed to all the participants through the declaration of the receiver's titles. In this process, the title of each participant is called out in the ranking-order by distributors or a master of ceremony. All the

Photo 3.2 Differentiation of the received meal for lunch by title-ranking
(*Top Left to Right: the meals of the paramount chief, the section chief, and Bottom: the commoner*)

participants other than the highest person receive their portion as a remainder of his precious food. That is, after the collected goods have been symbolically converted into the 'precious food' (*koanoat*) of the paramount chief in a ceremonial procedure, he is served his share, and the rest is redistributed as the 'remainder of [his] precious food' (*kepin koanoat*) to the other participants.

For instance, by calling out "the precious food of *Sahngoro*" (*koanoat Sahngoro*) [the paramount chief of the chiefdom of U], a distributor reconfirms the food of the paramount chief. Immediately after, the second highest person receives his portion of the food with a declaration of his title, followed by the third highest person and on down through the ranking titles. Furthermore, the higher the title-ranking of the receiver, the bigger and more valuable the portion. As shown in Photo 3.2, the precious food of the paramount chief, of the section chief and of the commoner are clearly differentiated in terms of material quality and variety. In sum, temporary ranking among participants is made visible through distributors' performance of announcing the receiver's title in order of rank and to differentiate his received goods according to his rank.

Preventing the ba from being ruined

The way of 'paying respect to' all the participants has nothing to do with the objectives of the feast, the specific context, and some contingent factors. In Goffman's term, framed activities in feasting processes bracket them, and yet the frame is vulnerable. Thus, ceremonial workers should strive to keep un-ceremonial activities bracketed during a ceremonial feast.

Let me give an ethnographic example.[9] On 28 July 2009, a funeral feast was held in the feast-house of my host-family. Benito,[10] a 62 year-old man, is the head of the family and a section chief. In accordance with the funeral custom of Pohnpei, he invited a paramount chief to attend the feast. The paramount chief, secondary chiefs, and their wives sat on the main platform. The platform was not as high as in many other households. I thought this lower platform provided a good opportunity to get an overview photo of a feast. I moved to the back of the platform and stretched to get a shot of the entire feast-house. Benito was shocked by my action. He quickly moved me from behind the platform. I soon learned that, in order to keep the high chiefs 'looking down on' the rest, and to maintain solemn respect for rank-hierarchy, no one could stand behind them. Through Benito's instruction, I learnt that, in Japanese idiom, it was 'ruining the ba' (ba wo midasu) or 'not fitting into the ba' (ba-chigai). From this perspective, strange behavior by an outsider needs to be prevented so that the ba retains its solemn atmosphere.

Moreover, in many cases, whether a visitor's rank is high or low, close relatives and friends, but also distant relatives, uninvited guests and passing foreigners are free to attend a feast without invitation or permission. In addition, guests arrive at a feast at a time that suits them, and ceremonial workers cannot predict who is coming next or what their rank will be. Hence, despite the rigid ceremonial etiquette, there is invariably some confusion or conflict at a feast.

I will provide an example of such conflict. This story was shared by an elderly man. It was about a feast which many high-ranking persons attended. In the morning of the feast, before a lot of participants came, a person with the *Wasahi* title (the second-ranking title in the line of paramount chief) arrived. Immediately, young men began to pound kava on large-stones, preparing to serve him the first cup of kava in recognition of being the highest-ranking person present. But as they gave him the first cup, the paramount chief arrived. Since they were not aware of the arrival of the paramount chief, they continued to serve the second-

---

[9] I conducted fieldwork for a total of 24 months between February 2009 and December 2012.

[10] All personal names in this chapter are pseudonyms.

ranking person. The paramount chief got 'very angry' (*lingeringer*) that he was not dealt with as highest. In this case, their mistake triggered a conflict over rank-hierarchy and destroyed the somber mood of the *ba*. If I had witnessed the chief's anger, I would have felt 'the *ba* frozen' (*ba ga kouritsuku* – another Japanese idiom). There is always potential for such conflicts in a feast. Therefore, the participants of a feast, including the ceremonial workers, must work to ensure that contingent arrivals and other visitors adjust their composure to the solemn mood of the *ba*.

Let me provide an instance of a funeral feast which illustrates such an adjustment. On 9 February 2010, because the deceased was high-ranking, many people with titles participated in the feast. Benito, a section chief, arrived early at the feast-house. As soon as his arrival was acknowledged, he was introduced to sit on the platform as the highest person present. A while later, the paramount chief and his family arrived. When Benito became aware of his presence, he spontaneously gave up his seat for the paramount chief. While a man said "he will be fired [as the person who looks down on other participants]" (*E pahn fired*), his immediate withdrawal, not only altered spatial arrangement, but also made the social hierarchy visible, with the paramount chief increasing the solemn mood of the *ba*.

As Goffman noted, people should get a perception, understanding, or vision of what is going on (Goffman 1986: 2), rather than follow the rule of social hierarchy and ritual courtesy. Putting it another way, it is through participants' understanding of the subtleties of each interaction that the *ba* can emerge or change with their performance. Without such shared understanding, the *ba* can be ruined.

In this way, by adjusting their performance to the changing situations, participants can prevent the *ba* from being frozen. The *ba* emerges with their somber performance, rather than being a result of rule-compliance.

Co-Emergence of chiefly 'thought' and the solemn *ba*

The solemn *ba* is usually inseparable from chiefly authority. The secondary chief is often called the 'oratory chief', as his customary responsibility is to speak on behalf of the paramount chief.[11] In local theory at least, the oratory chief's speech performance is closely linked to the 'thought' (*kupwur*) of the paramount chief. In what follows, I will show how the agency of the *ba* emerges with the agency of

---

[11] On allocation of intention and responsibility among local chiefs, orators and commoners in Samoan *fono* meeting, see Duranti (1993).

the paramount chief, examining an ethnographic case of the ceremonial address by a secondary chief at a feast.

On 24 October 2011, a funeral feast was held. At the feast, close relatives and members of the section to which the deceased belonged are expected to display a large yam, which can increase the prestige of the deceased if it is large enough (Riesenberg 1968: 88). But they could not display large-yams before the section provided both an 'honor feast' (*kamadipw en wahu*)[12] and the seasonal first-fruit rituals of yam to the paramount chief. In order to fulfil the expectations for the yam-display for the deceased without first setting another occasion for an 'honor-feast', the section decided to contribute a large sum of money to the paramount chief during the funeral feast.

In the ceremonial address, the secondary chief stood alone on the platform and delivered a speech for the paramount chief:

> **MC:** Please keep yourselves calms. *Nahnken* is beginning to deliver an oration.

> **The Secondary Chief** (facing the paramount chief): *Soulik* (secondary chiefly title of a section) is presenting a lot of money for your 'precious food' (*koanoat*). This act is appropriate to your 'thought' (*kupwur*). This is because Your Majesty just came here. The tribute is wonderful. He also tributes yam, kava, animal to you. The section is holding 'honor-feast' to welcome you.

> **The Secondary Chief** (facing the ceremonial workers): Bring the tribute here. The chiefly thought is very clear. You should work hard, keeping out of the way of the tribute.

> **The Secondary Chief** (facing the audience): All of the section chiefs, you should give much money as the precious food for 'stone-oven' (*uhmw*). Money is the most important thing. This is since the words of Your Majesty are true... This is why the efforts of this section is appropriate for your 'thought' today. The section is delighted to welcome Your Majesty with a set of things for stone-oven. *Soulik*, please prepare for 'the precious food'.

---

[12] The honor-feast is another legacy of German rule, introduced in 1912 (Petersen 1982: 35) and incorporated into the annual cycle of first-fruit ceremonies of breadfruits and yams. At an honor-feast, section chiefs contributed large-yams to the paramount chief, but today they tend to give him money instead.

And then, the secondary chief of the section walked straight up to the paramount chief and tried to hand over $600, which was wrapped in a banana-leaf. However, the paramount chief got angry and said:

> **The Paramount Chief** (facing the secondary chief): Are you going to do the same thing from today on? I do not prefer it this way. This way is very tiring. Today you should have devoted yourself to the funeral feast. It is the right way.

The secondary chief said "yes, indeed," and instantly prepared to seek his forgiveness (*tomw*). The secondary chief directed two high-title holders to hurry and pound fresh kava by way of apology. According to Pohnpeian custom, the only way to moderate a chief's anger is to pound kava on stones and to give him a cup. After offering the ritual apology, the secondary chief made another speech:

> **The Secondary Chief** (facing the audience): We have prepared kava for apology. This is because of the 'thought' of His Majesty. Obeying his 'thought', we should not commit the same thing in our chiefdom when His Majesty attends a funeral feast. We promise to stop doing this way from today on. The 'thought' of His Majesty is truth for section chief and all the residents in our chiefdom… Your Majesty, here is your money, your kava, your pig. Please check on these 'precious foods' only for you. We are not redistributing these things for other people.

This case indicates that though even the orator chief did not necessarily appreciate what the paramount chief really thinks, he was required to give an oration that supposedly revealed the hidden 'thought' of the paramount chief. In the above case, he made a speech and persuaded all the participants to work hard under the authority of the paramount chief. Corresponding to the ritual act of attributing to the chief the 'thoughts' that he himself interpreted and imagined, he repeatedly spoke of what the chief 'thought'. By making redundant speech at the feast, he could display the chiefly 'thought' to the other people present. But when the paramount chief expressed his anger, the orator found that his interpretation was not identical with the chiefly 'thought'. Thus, he offered a ritual apology and as soon as it was finished, he made another speech to articulate the 'thought' of the paramount chief in a way that corresponded to what the paramount chief had said, and to establish it as truth.

It was only through the temporary deconstruction of the *ba* that this speech act adapted to reorganize the atmosphere of the *ba* appropriate for the new 'thought' of the paramount chief. That is, the orator's speech was influenced by the shifting *ba*. Putting it another way, while he was bound to reveal the agency of the paramount chief under whom he performed, he was also moved by the agency of the *ba*. His adapted oration allowed the sober *ba* to emerge and re-emerge under chiefly authority while revealing the chiefly 'thought' to the other participants. Therefore, it is said that chiefly 'thought' and the solemn *ba* can co-emerge through a ceremonial address and that speech performances can be moved by the changing *ba*.

Ambivalent mood and agency of *ba*

Of course, the emerged *ba* is not always identical with the chiefly 'thought.' This is because the way in which the *ba* appears is not necessarily the same each time. Rather, as suggested in the Introduction in this volume, it is assumed that the *ba* is influenced by and influences an actor's performance. In what follows, I shall examine the relationship between the *ba* and the actor's performance, with a view to the shifting or changing mood of the *ba*.

I will take the funeral feast as an example. In many funeral feasts, a paramount chief is invited to attend in accordance with Pohnpeian custom. Often a secondary chief and many high-ranking title holders take part in the feast. While the men are carefully received by ceremonial workers in the feast-house, women cry and pray in the house for the deceased.

In the feast-house, chiefs are usually introduced to sit on the platform. They are provided a meal for lunch and given several cups of kava to recognize their ranking among participants. Yams, kavas, pork and cooked meals are redistributed in descending order of title-ranking. Although many adult men work hard to represent chiefly authority and social stratification through several performances, the cries of pigs for slaughter, as well as the women's mourning cries and their sacred songs for the dead are always heard in the feast-house. Through these performances in the house, their emotional ties with the deceased are expressed in a funeral feast. In contrast to the formality of customary rule, the funeral *ba* is filled with ambivalent feelings of respect for high-persons and grief over the death of a relative or a friend.

This mixture of feeling often comes to the surface in the redistribution of pork. While an accomplished distributor or a master of ceremonies announces the receiver's title in descending order, he says "family" (*peneinei*) loudly in the middle of redistribution. And thereby, a large abdomen of pork comes to be redistributed to the bereaved family. In another version, for example, as he calls out "Clara's mother" (*nohno* Clara), some quantity of pork is also redistributed to classificatory mothers of the dead. In this moment, he is moved by the ambivalent mood of the *ba*. In this sense, the *ba* can be said to have agency through which some distributors can perform in a different way from that dictated by the hidden chiefly 'thought.'

Between intimate mood and rank hierarchy

The following example is of a small feast among close relatives without a paramount chief, secondary chief or any high title holder. On 27 July 2012, a feast was held at Benito's feast-house. The first objective of the feast was to commemorate the anniversary of the death of Maria, Benito's late wife. The second objective was to celebrate the third birthday of another Maria, Benito's granddaughter, the daughter of Benito's son Kalis. Kalis, Maria and their family lived in Kansas-City, in the United States of America and had temporarily returned home for this feast. The third objective was to congratulate two young men, Gino and Dahker, for their forthcoming overseas-travel. Gino is the son of Jacob, Benito's younger brother, and was going to Hawaii for wage labor. Dahker is Kalis's wife's son from a previous relationship. He lived in Pohnpei and was planning to study abroad in Guam. The kinship diagram of for this group is provided in Figure 3.4.

69

Kalis bought two pigs for $400 from Jacob and slaughtered them for redistribution to the participants, more than 50 people, mainly close relatives. Jacob also slaughtered a pig for the feast.

The procedure of this feast was conducted with the same formality as other feasts. The seating arrangement on this occasion was related to rank-hierarchy, so that as a section chief, Benito sat in the highest position on the main platform. The young men, including Dahker and Gino, worked hard at pounding kava or making the stone-oven, thereby paying respect to Benito and the relatively higher participants. And yet, as a gathering of close relatives, there was a relaxed mood, in contrast to the somber mood described above. Thus, small children sometimes entered the feast-house without constraint. I heard many adults laughing and chatting inside the feast-house.

The order	The name of the receiver	The status or position of the receiver	The receiver's title	What the receiver is called
1	Benito	Section chief	Soulik	Sahk Soulik
2	Sapio	High title holder of another chiefdom	Saudepe	Saudepe
3	Bacardi	Secondary chief of the section	Kiroun	Kiroun
4	Gino	Low title holder of the section	Soumadau en Sowihso	Gino
5	Maria	Granddaughter of the section chief	none	ipwidio
6	Dorelos	High title holder of other chiefdom; Sister of the section chief	Kedinlik Onohleng	Kedinlik Ohonleng

Table 3.2 The redistribution order of pork in top 6 at the feast

Jacob was the distributor of pork, having both a loud voice and a detailed knowledge of the title-ranking among his relatives. The redistribution order of pork in Top 6 is shown in Table 3.2.

He announced Benito's chiefly title first, followed by the high title of another chiefdom. Bacardi, the secondary chief of a section, was absent. Yet, because his son took part in the feast, the son was given pork third, on behalf of the chief. While Jacob continued to call out recipients' titles in this way, he said "Gino" fourth and "the person who reaches her birthday" (*ipwidio*) fifth. In the relaxed atmosphere of the *ba*, he could celebrate two young persons through his performance. However, one elderly man said "you should have redistributed pork to *Kedinlik* before them" in a scolding tone. *Kedinlik* is the chiefdom title which Doroles, Benito's sister, held. He complained about Jacob's disrespectful attitude towards title-ranking. To put it another way, the over-emphasis on intimate mood among relatives threatened the enactment of the solemn *ba* as a chief-centered place. As a result, Doroles became the sixth receiver and got her pork through Jacob's announcement.

The above case illustrates how the ceremonial workers tried to actualize the social hierarchy of the people present, whereas the participation of many close-kin and innocent children and their relaxed interactions produced a comfortable atmosphere within the *ba*. And thus, while Jacob was responsible for announcing title-holders under chiefly authority in descending order, he got carried away with the relaxed and intimate mood of the *ba*. It can be said that his performance was moved by the intimate *ba*. But as the elderly man's critical words prompted the restoration of the honor-oriented redistribution order, the atmosphere of the *ba* was re-shaped. In this sense, especially in kin-based feasting, rank hierarchy and kin intimacy are negotiated through the co-emergence of an actor's performance and the *ba*.

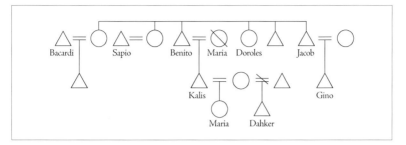

Figure 3.4 The kinship diagram of Benito Family

Conclusion

In this chapter, I have discussed the relationship between an actor's performance and the *ba* in which he participates, at ceremonial feasts in Pohnpei.

From the perspective of an outsider, traditional authority and social hierarchy seem to be maintained by rule-compliance or political ideology. But, as illustrated in the Pohnpeian case, actors do not perform only to reconfirm rank-order under chiefly authority. Rather, they have agency to perform so that the *ba* is not ruined or destroyed. Thus, the *ba* emerges through their performance, making authority and ranking visible.

Chiefly 'thought', which is hidden in ordinary life, can be also made apparent by their speech actions. And yet, they find it difficult to surmise what he really thinks. Therefore, their actions often change depending on his unexpected behavior and speech, turning the *ba* into a place appropriate for his 'thought'. In this sense, both a chief's behavior and other people's actions have the potential to shape and reshape the *ba* which also has agency to move them to guess the chief's intentions and to perform along it.

However, I found that actors in the *ba* have many other interests and values in feast than respect for chiefs and high persons. Especially in kin-based feasts, the solemn *ba* is unstable due to the participants' emotional ties as kinship. Hence, social hierarchy and kin intimacy are often negotiated through the co-emergence of the actors and the *ba*.

In conclusion, while traditional authority and rank-order appear through the co-emergence of the *ba* and performance, the latter is not exclusive to the former. Rather, these co-emergences enable the manifestation of not only formal hierarchy but also the emotional atmosphere through which actors are often moved by the *ba*, thereby actualizing it as the negotiated situation among chiefly authority, rank order and other emotional relationships.

71

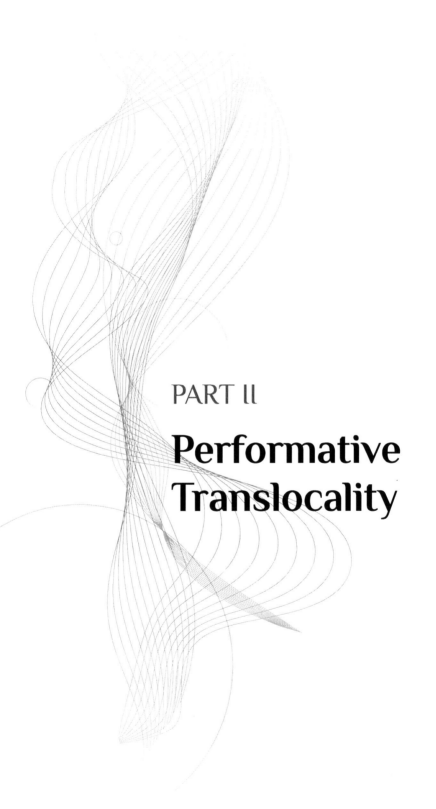

PART II

Performative Translocality

4. Performing Turkish Culture
The Inclusiveness of the Largest Yörük Festival in Contemporary Turkey

Ulara Tamura

Introduction

This paper explores how cultural performativity co-emerges with *ba* through an investigation of the Yörük, a nomadic people of Turkey, and their annual cultural festival, which has recently experienced a revival across the country. Our primary focus is the process through which Yörük culture is being transformed from a "backward vulgarity" into the cherished roots "of the Turks." We will explore this through applying the concept of *ba* (Kajimaru et al. 2021) to an examination of various performances and ceremonies at the largest Yörük cultural festival in Turkey. As William F. Hanks et al. (2019) argued the importance of focusing on the interplay between the *ba* and social actors, I shall analyze the co-emergence of the festival's *ba* and various agencies–both physical and contextual–through performances.

Yörük had been under pressure to abandon their nomadic lifestyle since the Ottoman period and this pressure increased during the Republic of Turkey. Living with livestock without fixed dwellings, they have long been stigmatized as "backward crude people" by both the ruling power of the time and the settled herders and farmers. Recently, however, even as nomadic populations are disappearing across the region, the Yörük and their culture has suddenly come to be praised as the cherished tradition of Turkey. It has become common for domestic political leaders to declare their Yörük origins. Yörük cultural associations, established in various parts of Turkey since the late 2000s, have been central to this transformation, primarily through the annual Yörük cultural festivals, which involve large numbers of citizens and politicians. This paper treats the country's largest Yörük festival, the Ertuğrul Gazi Memorial and Yörük Festival (hereinafter EY Festival) as an example of how the place of the festival itself inspires the claims of integrity and continuity between the Yörük tradition, the Ottoman Empire, and the present Republic of Turkey.

The EY Festival is held annually in early September in Söğüt, a rural town of about 14,000 inhabitants in Bilecik Province, in the Marmara Region of Turkey. Visitors to the event are estimated to number about 100,000 across its three-day program. During the three days of the festival, Yörük cultural associations from across the country provide entertainment, places of exchange and encounter, performances, exhibitions, food and drinks at dozens of Yörük tent booths, as well as performances at four ceremonies by ethnic dance troupes and folk musicians from various regions. Visitors enjoy wandering around the tents and occasional performances, as well as participating in the formal ceremonies.

The formal ceremonies are highly nationalistic moments, as political leaders and the Yörük associations' representatives give speeches, and all participants stand up straight to sing the national anthem. They are to be analyzed as typical examples of cultural performances (MacAloon 1984) where participants accept the historical story that was presented and then reflexively redefine themselves in it (ibid, Takahashi 2005: 19). In this process, the former perception of Yörük cultural backward-ness is dispelled, and the memories of the Ottoman (and later the Republic of Turkey) repression of the Yörük fades and is forgotten. Instead, the "collective memory/social memory" of the people (Halbwachs 1992, Connerton 1989) is transformed as Yörük culture becomes "our foundational culture to be proud of," constructing continuity between the Ottomans and the modern Turkish nation.

In this massive and intentionally constructed "cultural place," various participants appear to be ensnared in the inclusive drive of *ba*. The agency of *ba* in Söğüt emerges primarily from the tomb and the historical origin-story of the Ottoman Empire. Then, as various actors are attracted to this event posing as a memorial service and become more deeply engaged in other activities and performances, the *ba*'s attraction and inclusivity strengthen, attracting even more people. Thus the *ba* and the actors emerge with each other to redefine "our culture."

This paper analyses the micro-scale performances and performativity observed in this *ba*. Earlier performance studies on nationalistic events and ceremonies tend to emphasize the strong unifying effect of performances on the crowd. They seldom present micro-scale analysis of personal experiences and self-reflections. For the participants of the EY Festival, I shall try to describe those micro-scale personal experiences within the festival site. What emerges is a drive towards inclusion into "our own Turkish culture" as participants enjoy the ceremonies and performances; however, how they reflect upon and summarize their experience in Söğüt varies. As a greater variety of cultural performances is offered, there are more opportunities for people to perform and enjoy the jumbles of culture on display.

Ertuğrul Gazi Memorial and Yörük Festival

Ertuğrul Gazi, the person commemorated in this large annual festival, is believed to be the father of Osman, the first leader of the Ottomans. Academic history, however, has only been able to confirm the genealogical record from Osman or later.[1]

In the mid-13th century, the Room Seljuk Dynasty declined as Mongolian forces advanced westwards. After a while, it became subject to the Il Han dynasty. In East and Central Anatolia, there are many small nations governed by monarchs who boast of their lineage to the Turkish nomadic tribes. In Western Anatolia, Turkish and Mongolian knights who had separated from the eastern forces and tribes formed small groups here and there. The Ottomans, in fact, were one of these groups. It was a meritocratic hybrid group in the chaos of the frontier, composed of those who had separated from the tribal army that boasted the legitimate bloodline (Hayashi 2008: 39).

However, when Osman's descendants came to rule a huge empire, a legendary story about the founder became necessary. According to the first Ottoman history, the Chronicles written by Aşık Paşa Zade (1480s): Osman moved to Anatolia when Suleyman Shah Ghazi, the 13th descendant of Oguz, was born. The king of Iran ordered Suleyman to "go and do the holy war (Ghaza) in the land of the Room (Anatolia)." On route to return to his hometown in Central Asia, he died before crossing the Euphrates River. One of his three sons, Ertuğrul Gazi, remained with about 400 nomads' tents. When the Seljuks ruled Anatolia and were fighting pagans, Ertuğrul went west with his three sons to offer support. The king of Seljuks rejoiced and gave them Söğüt as a winter camp, with two mountains as summer camps (see Figure 4.1). A few years after moving to Söğüt, Ertuğrul died and was succeeded by his son, Osman Gazi (Hayashi 2008: 42–43).

According to the leading Japanese Ottoman historian Kayoko Hayashi, one of the four common intentions in the stories of Osman and his ancestors is to incorporate the Ottoman family into the legends of the Oğuzlar, Turkish nomads who originated in Central Asia, in order to claim that the Ottomans are descendants of the venerable Turkish tribes (Hayashi 2008: 44).

Thus, in academic terms, almost nothing is certain about Ertuğrul Gazi. However, the created history (or histories) from the Ottoman era are widely accepted as historical truth in Turkey. The EY Festival we shall explore is entirely dependent on these stories of Ertuğrul Gazi, who came to symbolize the bridge between the Ottomans and Yörüks.

---

[1] Osman appears both in Ottoman and Byzantine historical materials.

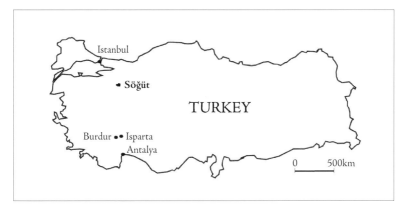

Figure 4.1 The location of Söğüt

Yörük and its cultural revitalization

People who identify as ethnic Turks claim to be descendants of the *Oğuzlar*, who migrated from around Central Asia into Anatolia in the 11th century, in the era of the Seljuq Dynasty. Although they had long led a nomadic life distributed across a wide area near the mountains on the peninsula, from the late Ottoman Empire, they were increasingly pressured to live in fixed dwellings. The pressure intensified after the Republic of Turkey was established in 1923. According to Masatake Matsubara, an anthropologist, the number of nomadic people in Turkey decreased sharply following revisions to the Forest Law (*Orman Kanunu*) after 1960, which banned grazing in national forests (Matsubara 1990). Estimates of the nomadic Yörük population in 1923 vary widely, from three hundred thousand to a million. By 2000, nearly ninety percent of the Yörük were settled and the number of nomadic Yörük continues to decrease. Previously, nomads lived in three areas: from Urfa to Mardin in southeast Anatolia, from Adana to Antalya on the Mediterranean coast, and in an area around Aydın (Matsubara 2004: 16). Today, the residential area of transhumant or nomadic Yörük is limited to the area around the Taurus Mountains in south-central Turkey, west of Mersin.

Nevertheless, Yörük identity continues to exist, and has been sustained in various ways among settled Yörük. However, in rural areas where Yörük have settled near long-established villagers, Yörük identity has been somewhat stigmatized. Nevertheless, expressions like "we Yörük" have become frequently heard at official occasions, especially in the past decade or so. This increased incidence of self-proclaimed Yörük-ness and publicization of Yörük identity is certainly worth analyzing.

77

Yörük associations can be found in various parts of Turkey, playing a leading role in promoting Yörük identity. The first of these associations dates back to the 1980s, with increasing numbers being formed from around 2010. In this paper, various organizations based in Turkey, regardless of the date of formation, which include the word "Yörük" or the name of a particular Yörük tribe in the name of the organization are defined as "Yörük associations" to be analyzed.

From the late 2000s to the mid-2010s, various nomad associations, large and small, were formed in various parts of Turkey. It is estimated that there are now more than 300 such associations (Tuztaş Horzumlu 2017). The more recent of these nomad associations have identified the "inheritance of Yörük culture" as their central purpose, and their primary activity is organizing the Yörük cultural festivals. I will focus here on the various associations' activities in regard to their nationwide solidarity and organizing in recent years.

The following description of the purpose and current status of the Yörük associations is based on an interview (conducted on September 12, 2017) with Mr. Mustafa Küçükyaman (born in 1968; hereinafter, Mr. K), the president of the Toros Yörük-Türkmen Cultural Federation, based in Isparta City. Mr. K is not only the president of the Federation that unites the associations of the Taurus Mountains, which is a center of the Turkish Yörük, but is also the vice president of the nation-wide Yörük-Türkmen Union,[2] an official nation-wide organization under the Presidential Office that binds the confederations and federations in Turkey.

According to Mr. K, the purpose of the Yörük associations is, first, "passing on the declining Yörük culture to the next generation." It also aims to provide support to active Yörük. The actual associations' activities are concentrated in the summer Yörük festivals (şenlikler or şölenler) and winter meetings. Both types of gatherings provide opportunities for developing close horizontal solidarity, as associations cooperate and dispatch personnel to each other's events and hold joint events. There are about forty or fifty summer Yörük festivals, large and small, held throughout the country. Their purpose is to "provide the public and the younger generation with an opportunity to become familiar with Yörük culture, while stimulating awareness to cherish it." Some festivals are very small, while others are very large, with dozens of Yörük associations working together.

The Yörük associations are civic groups that have formed sporadically and spontaneously in various parts of Turkey, organizing such "horizontal solidarity." Depending on their backgrounds and objectives, several local nomad

---

[2] The union is officially known as "Türkiye-Türk Dünyası Yörük Türkmen Birliği", Yörük-Türkmen Union of the Turkic World.

associations come together to form a federation (*federasyon*), several associations join together to form a confederation (*konfederasyon*), and these confederations have come together to form the union – the nation-wide umbrella organization. These organizations and their hierarchical structures are formed in accordance with the law for civil organizations. From the association to the federation and confederation level, all organizations are under the jurisdiction of the Ministry of the Interior, which requires notification from the governors of each prefecture, and the federation is a national organization that requires the approval of the Presidential Office. For example, the Yörük–Türkmen Federation from Isparta province formed in 2004, then joined with federations and associations from various regions nationwide in May 2016 to form the "Turkish–Turkic World's Yörük–Türkmen Union." According to a 2014 pamphlet produced on the eve of the union's formation, 58 confederations, federations and associations were listed as supporting organizations. They were quite active, with frequent meetings. There were more than 80 member organizations in 2016 and, according to Mr. K, there were more than 100 member organizations as of September 2017.

Numerous large and small nomadic associations have been established since the beginning of the 21st century, most of which have the terms "Yörük-Türkmen" in their names. Mr. K explained that "Türkmen moved from Central Asia to Anatolia first and settled on the plains, while Yörük later came to Anatolia to lead a nomadic life. However, the more you examine the genealogy, the more difficult it is to set a clear boundary between the two. So I tried to use the name Yörük–Türkmen when forming federations and other organizations." They proceeded with the formation of the associations, trying to include the groups that settled early after the migration to Anatolia, which, they would have us believe, includes the majority of the Turkish population today.

As mentioned, the activities of the nomad associations, which felt a sense of crisis due to the drastic change to their nomadic lifestyle, have spread throughout the country over the past 10–15 years. They came to unite on a nationwide scale while incorporating local nomadic organizations that had existed for decades. In a word, the associations not only cooperate with one another to strengthen their horizontal connections, but also tried to organize the vertical integration of the horizontal connection. The association formed in the process placed the terms "Yörük-Türkmen" at the front of its name. This could be a development strategy to involve general Turkish people who did not identify as Yörük.

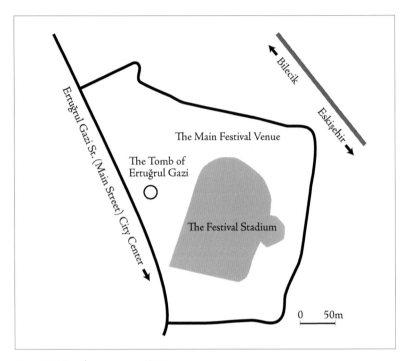

The Main Festival Venue

The Tomb of
Ertuğrul Gazi

The Festival Stadium

Ertuğrul Gazi St. (Main Street) City Center

Bilecik

Eskişehir

0   50m

Figure 4.2 Map of event venues in Söğüt

Ertuğrul Gazi Memorial and Yörük Festival

The "Ertuğrul Gazi Memorial and Yörük Festival (*Ertuğrul Gazi'yi Anma ve Yörük Şenlikleri*)"* is the largest of the Yörük cultural festivals. This festival is held over three days, on the first weekend of September every year in the rural town of Söğüt. It is said that a memorial ceremony has been held annually in Söğüt, Bilecik Province, in the mid-western part of Turkey, where his tomb is located, since the year after his death in 1281. The 2019 festival, in which I participated,[3] was named the 738th.

Söğüt is a small country town with a population of 19,244 (2018). Located 42km from the nearest city, Eskişehir, access to the town is via long, winding country roads. Nevertheless, approximately 100,000 visitors attend the festival every year.

---

[3] I conducted participant-observation and interviews in this festival site in 2017 and 2019. I also collected information from relevant people afterwards as well as news articles online.

During the festival, Yörük associations from all over the country set up tents to entertain, exhibit, and perform. There are several dozen such tents, where visitors enjoy free performances of epic tales, folk dance and music while mingling, relaxing, and sampling various food and drinks.

The official program for 2017 was:

The 1st Day: 8 September (Fri.)

11:00 Offering flower wreaths to the monument of Turks' great ancestors, a silent prayer, chanting "Independence March" (the national anthem), and the governor's opening address

11:15 Folk dance performance

11:30 Visit the Ertuğrul-Gazi Tomb, A ritual offering of şifalı pilav

12:00 Recite Mevlid-i Şerif in the names of Ertuğrul Gazi and Turks' great ancestors

14:30 Symposium

The 2nd Day: 9 September (Sat.)   81

10:30 Welcoming Yörük

11:00 March to the ceremony venue with the Mehter band

11:30 Visit the Ertuğrul-Gazi Tomb

13:00 Visit the Yörük tents

16:00 Jereed (Cirit[4])

20:30 Introduction of and performance by participating Yörük/Türkmen associations, federations, and unions. Fireworks, laser beams and light beam shows.

24:00 Traditional şifalı pilav Lid-Opening Ritual

The 3rd Day: 10 September (Sun.)

9:00 A visit to the mausoleum by government officials and guests

10:00 Silent prayer and singing "Independence March," official greetings (of government officials and guests), folk dance performances and concerts of the Mehter band, parades, şifalı pilav treats

As this official program indicates, the festival is a mixture of various elements: the Ottoman, the Republic of Turkey, the current republic government, Islam,

---

[4] Cirit is one kind of group joust tournament.

Turks, and Yörük. For instance, the recitation of Mevlid-i Serif on the first day is an Islamic ritual, which is widely performed by ordinary Turks at milestones such as the anniversary of the death of a relative and the 40th day after the birth of a child. The Mehter military music, in contrast, is from the Ottoman Empire and is said to have made Europeans tremble at the time. Moreover, the national anthem of the Turkish Republic, the "Independence March," is sung in unison in every ceremony. This mixture of Yörük, Ottoman, and Turkish Republic elements is the outstanding feature of this festival which emphasizes the "one-ness" and "together-ness" of the nation's people. In the next two sections, I shall examine important elements of the events to shed light on the EY festival theme of unity and continuity, the unique *ba*, and the variety of visitors' experiences.

Ceremonies as an explicit *ba* of performances of inclusion

Repeated ceremonies

As we have seen, during the three-day-long festival, there are several ceremonies or ceremonial events held by the festival organizers every day. The opening and closing ceremonies, as well as the "Welcoming Yörük" program on the second morning, are hosted by a loud emotional MC who introduces the many important speakers. The national anthem is collectively sung at each of these events. Compared to folk music and dance performances and parades, these ceremonies convey direct and explicit political messages.

The Turkish national anthem "Independence March" was written by a poet named Mehmet Akif Ersoy in 1921 during Turkey's Independence War after the defeat of the Ottoman Empire in WWI. The lyrics are strongly patriotic and emotional, accompanied by a dramatic marching melody. Here is a translation of the first two verses (out of ten), which are taught in elementary schools and commonly sung in public:

(Translated by Ministry of Foreign Affairs of Turkey)

1. Fear not, the crimson flag, waving in these dawns will never fade
   Before the last hearth that is burning in my nation vanishes.
   That is my nation's star, it will shine;
   That is mine, it belongs solely to my nation.

2. Oh coy crescent do not frown for I am ready to sacrifice
myself for you!
Please smile upon my heroic nation, why that anger,
why that rage?
If you frown, our blood shed for you will not be worthy.
Freedom is the right of my nation who worships God and
seeks what is right.

In discussing the important role of language in nationalism, Benedict Anderson
described what happens in the collective singing of a national anthem:

> there is a special kind of contemporaneous community which language
> alone suggests – above all in the form of poetry and songs. Take national
> anthems, for example, sung on national holidays. No matter how banal
> the words and mediocre the tunes, there is in this singing an experience of
> simultaneity. At precisely such moments, people wholly unknown to each
> other utter the same verses to the same melody. The image: unisonance.
> (Anderson 1990: 238)

Masachi Osawa, a leading Japanese sociologist summarizes the consequential
function of singing a national anthem in a big crowd as such; "unisonance,
singing together becomes a measure of constructing intercorporeal continuation
as emotional unity" (Osawa 2007: 362).

During the EY Festival, the Turkish national anthem is sung with all
participants standing up in the three ceremonies. By definition, it should be
one of the peak nationalistic moments, but when compared to the politicians'
or association presidents' speeches, it seems more like a mundane embodied
ritual for the participants. They just stood up and sang with very small voices,
largely drowned out by the recorded audio blaring from the loudspeakers. From
my observations at this festival, I am skeptical about claims that singing the
national anthem has a strong effect on each participant, but still it is important
to acknowledge that the people do in fact sing the national anthem during each
ceremony of this festival. It is essential for the official program of the festival,
which provides the ba in which collective memory is constructed and reinforced,
to emphasize the continuation of the Yörük, Ottomans and the Republic of
Turkey. While Ertuğrul Gazi is the symbol of the liaison of the Ottomans with

Yörük, this national anthem should be the liaison of the Republic of Turkey with Turkishness.[5]

Official speeches by political leaders

There are two major speech events during the EY Festival. One is in the "welcoming Yörük" program on the second day, where several leaders of large Yörük associations and some municipal governors deliver official speeches. The other is on the last day at the closing ceremony, where several important politicians are invited to speak each year.

This participation by prominent politicians is a recent trend, beginning with Prime Minister (and now president) Recep Tayyip Erdoğan in 2007 and Prime Minister Ahmet Davutoğlu in 2014. It is surprising that the leading politicians in the country, including the leaders of each party, travel all the way to Söğüt for this event, despite its poor access. Every year, big-name politicians make official speeches and pray at the mausoleum. These are reported not only in local newspapers, but also in national newspapers and television.

When I attended in 2017, the prime minister of the time, Binali Yıldırım, identified himself as a descendant of Kayı Boyu, one of the 24 tribes (*boy*), and gave a speech. Kayı Boyu is the clan which claims Ertuğrul Gazi. Since it was the year after a coup attempt, which killed many civilians following a series of ISIS attacks, the speech conveyed that the Turkish people will stand together resolutely against the forces that threaten the nation.

In 2019, several ministers, the chairman and deputy chairman of the Grand National Assembly of Turkey (parliament), and the leader of the Nationalist Action Party (*Milliyetçi Hareket Partisi*, MHB) participated in the festival and gave speeches.

Regardless of their political parties or positions, the messages of their speeches are remarkably similar. They emphasize Turkish unity, how great the Ottomans were, how hard it was to gain this present territory of Turkey in the Independence War, and the importance of solidarity against their enemies. Each of these speeches invoked continuity among the Yörük, the Ottoman, and the Republic of Turkey, whether implicitly or explicitly.

---

[5] Some people might think Mustafa Kemal Atatürk, the first President of the Republic of Turkey, should be the symbol of the liaison of the Republic of Turkey with Ottomans, for he used to be an Ottoman military commander and is a hero of independence. But he evokes a strong image of secularism in modern Turkey (Kemalist, in Turkish "Atatürkçü," means secularist).

Photo 4.1 The closing ceremony at the festival venue (September 2019)

Let us consider part of the speech by Devlet Bahçeli, the leader of the Nationalist Action Party, who seemed to receive the greatest applause from the audience:

> Söğüt is not a mere common part of the country nor just one of the ordinary districts. For the Turkish people, it is the center of gravity and action, the fountain of life, and the jewel of dignity. The Turks came on horseback to this place in Anatolia and settled down. It is a great history and a glorious record that only the 400 tents of Turkmens of Kayı Clan, of Bozok Kolu of Oguzlar, gave birth to the empire that lasted 600 years afterwards. This wonderful fact clearly shows that the Turks have the skills to establish governments and empires at any point in history. (…) We have to wipe (our enemy) out with our own hands and power. None of us fear. (We are to) live completely independently as a descendant of a hero.

This was a poetic and sensational speech, elevating the pride and patriotism of the Turkish people, while frequently referring to historical narratives. Numerous speeches of a similar tone were delivered one after another over about two hours on Sunday morning to a full-house in the huge stadium-shaped ceremony venue (Photo 4.1).

It is a highly nationalistic scene, as can be seen from the program and its contents, as well as audience reactions to the politicians' speeches. If we focus on these superficial phenomena, it is possible to analyze this ceremony as a purely nationalistic and performative unification ritual, as Takahashi (2005) did for the opening ceremony of the Olympics in Nagano. The EY Festival's ceremonies undoubtedly influence the participants to reflect on who they are while emphasizing the authenticity of Turks and Turkish culture. But as I was sitting in the audience, I could not ignore the different reactions of the people gathered there.

I personally found the repeated nationalistic messages exhausting, and was surprised by how patient the audience was, sitting and listening for such a long time. I wondered what was interesting enough to keep their attention. In the 2019 festival, the ceremony venue was filled with perhaps 10,000 or more Turkish people. The ceremony, which was scheduled to start at 10:00, finally started at 10:30. During the speeches of the most prominent politicians, most of the audience listened attentively, clapping at patriotic phrases, while eating sunflower seeds and chewing gum. Peddlers kept coming with food and drinks, selling a lot of bottled water, sunflower seeds, chewing gum and small snacks. Nobody refrained from speaking out to purchase things from the peddlers, and those things were passed along the lines of people sitting facing the central stage.[6]

The series of speeches lasted for more than two hours, with the final ceremony finishing at 13:00, after a parade of nomadic organizations and a dance, lasting about 15–20 minutes.[7] When the MC announced the end of the politicians' speeches, one middle-aged woman behind me spoke out loudly, saying "Finally, here it comes! You guys talked for two and half hours! That's enough!" And then she started enjoying the very short entertainment of marching and dances, clapping her hands along with her family.

It is a wonder that such a huge crowd of people sat through all of that so patiently but at least some, perhaps a majority, were not fully involved or emotionally moved by the nationalistic performances of the speeches. There was an intentionally presented and performed political and nationalistic *ba*, but still the various agents reacted in various ways. In that way, the *ba* was negotiated between agencies even when superficially it appeared to be unified and solid.

---

[6] That scene, with people chit-chatting and eating snacks, shifting their attention back-and-forth between their neighbors and the activities on stage, reminded me of a long and loud Turkish wedding party. They might be culturally attuned to enjoying practical involvement in such a manner.

[7] But the parade and entertainment was too far away to see, for the venue was too large. It seemed to me almost not worth waiting for.

As for the involvement of politicians, a 45-year-old woman who was born and raised in Söğüt recalled:

> it was like another *bayram*[8] for us, the festival used to be more relaxed, enjoyable and have more folk atmosphere. In recent years, ceremonies and concerts have become more and more spectacular, but the whole atmosphere of the festival has been changed because of more and more involvement of politicians. There have been political fights in the venue, and there are so many police, guards and SPs everywhere. I personally prefer our old Yörük festival.

She was not alone. Among those who had experienced the festival one or more decades earlier, many shared with me their preference for the non-political festival of olden days. One 60-year-old lady from Sakarya, who identifies as a Karakeçili Yörük, confessed: "once we saw a fight in the venue because of political issues when President Erdoğan came. It was such a disappointment. After that, we decided to come only for Saturday when fewer politicians attend and have more relaxing and joyful atmosphere."

According to the head of a large Yörük association who has been participating in the festival for 20 years, in the past 10 years or so, government support for the festival has increased, and the present government is definitely more interested in it than its predecessors. Consequently, the festival is becoming more and more official in every aspect and the atmosphere has certainly changed, which raises a question about why the numbers of participants continue to increase each year.

Enjoying the festival through "experiencing our culture"

Jumble marching in the town

On the second day of the festival, just before 10:00 a.m. on Saturday, people began to gather in Söğüt. The vast festival venue next to the Tomb of Ertuğrul Gazi had more than 50 Yörük tent booths. Officially, the opening ceremony was on Friday, and the people from the various associations preparing the tent booths

---

[8] Bayram in Turkish means holiday, but in a narrower specific sense, it means the two major religious holidays of Islam when all the relatives get together.

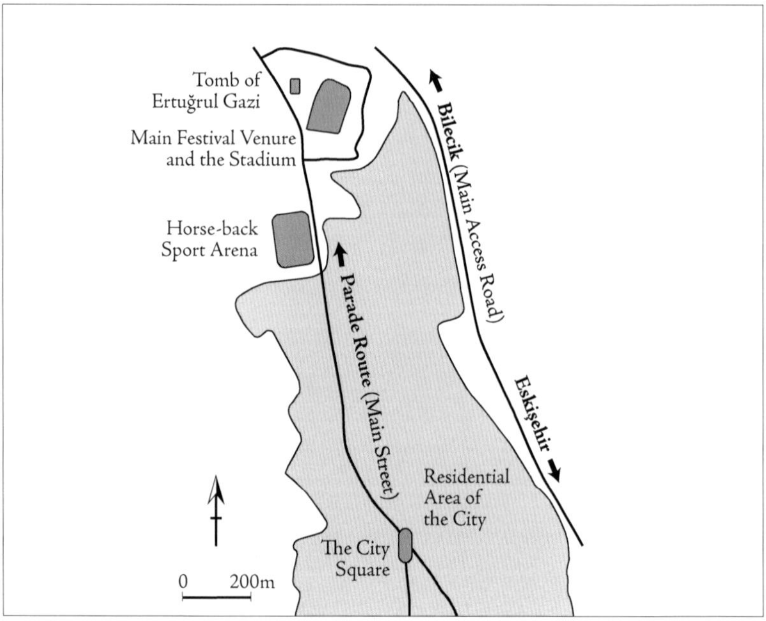

Figure 4.3 Map of the marching street

had been on-site since Thursday, but the general participants, official speakers, and local leaders showed up on Saturday and Sunday when the whole town was filled with people enjoying the festival atmosphere.

Saturday's program began in a square in the town center, far from the festival venue (see Figure 4.3). This was the Yörük welcoming of the official program. There were a number of seats arranged facing the square, where the representatives of Yörük asociations, who gathered from all over the country; the heads of local governments, including the governor of Bilecik Prefecture, and the Mayor of Söğüt were seated as guests.

In a loud and dramatic tone, the MC led the program. The guests were invited to the stage to give speeches after the national anthem, and after commemorative gifts were presented to the association's representatives, the folk dance and Ottoman military music (by *mehter*, the Ottoman military band) provided by various associations and dance groups were performed. In addition to the guests and performers in colorful costumes, many ordinary citizens surrounded the square. From what I heard, there seemed to be not only the locals but a relatively large number of people claiming Yörük identity who came from more than 100km away, regardless of whether or not they were involved in the associations.

Photo 4.2 Marching citizens with a long Turkish flag (September 2017)

Being far behind the official schedule, a marching parade began on the main street of the town just before noon, led by the Ottoman Military Band, heading towards The Tomb of Ertuğrul Gazi, 1.3km away from the square. The *mehter* was followed by a large number of citizens carrying a 100m long Turkish flag in their hands (see Photo 4.2). The march was joined by local citizens, junior high and high school students representing hobby and sporting clubs, many carrying the national flag. Next came members of Yörük cultural associations from across the country, marching with their banners. Many groups marched in ethnic costume, accompanied by a band, performing traditional dances, basking in cheers and applause from the crowds gathered along the road. At the end of the parade was a huge Turkish flag and a portrait of the founding father Mustafa Kemal Ataturk, carried by local officials.

Along the way, there were crowds of onlookers sitting or walking around, journalists taking pictures, as well as people watching and waving from the balconies of apartments along the road. There were also many people watching from cafes and dining rooms along the road (Photo 4.3).

The 1.3km parade was attended by crowds of ordinary residents and officials from all over Turkey, marching with a variety of performances. Some people

Photo 4.3 Marching Yörük association leaders (September 2017)

dressed as Ottoman officers riding fine horses, while others danced cheerfully, cracking wooden spoons to accompany the flute and drums in ethnic costumes. Some children waved their hands smiling along the road while carrying the long national flag. It was a splendid mixture of the Ottoman army, the Republic of Turkey, and Yörük cultural practices from various places. While they certainly depicted the empires established in Anatolia, the land of today's Republic of Turkey, and the people who existed there, the three have been in fact quite separate and hostile. The Ottoman Empire was dominated by elites – simply those fluent in the "Ottoman" language – while Turkish speaking people were regarded as backward. Rulers of both the Ottoman Empire and the Republic of Turkey regarded Yörük as backward and have used a variety of measures to encourage them to settle down. This history was completely unquestioned, while aspects of all three cultures were beautifully expressed in this series of joyful marches purportedly depicting the continuous past of "us, the Turkish people today."

The participants dressed according to their respective "roles" and performed roles such as playing folk instruments or waving Turkish flags. Each person was given a place in "the continuous imagined history" which was directed as an integrated whole. For the audiences who watch the march of the *mehter's* military music, Yörük dances and the Republic's flag along the road, the intended message is that "this is the history and the whole of diverse and proud cultures that connect to us today." This is the underlying message of the festival, which encompasses all of the heterogeneous components as a continuum, condensed in this parade: a collective memory device demonstrating the legitimacy of the Turkish people and its culture.

Visiting the tomb of Ertuğrul Gazi

Commemoration of Ertuğrul Gazi is one of the foremost aims of the EY Festival, as expressed in its name. Most of the visitors[9] of the festival visit the Tomb (Photo 4.4) located adjacent to the festival venue at least once. As the tomb is only big enough for 15–20 people around the coffin, people must wait in a line to visit their "great ancestor" and pray. They patiently wait their turn, then pray in the Islamic way, holding both hands in front by the coffin. When it is time for official guests to attend the tomb, general visitors are excluded from the area. Images of important figures praying by the coffin inside the tomb are always reported in the newspapers and on TV news. When I interviewed general visitors in the festival venue, they said "of course" they were going to or had already visited the tomb for it was important. Even a 14-year-old girl whom I met by the tomb explained "it is important to visit Ertuğrul Gazi for we are proud of our forefather."

Though people show their respect and consider it important to visit him, the praying act takes only about a minute, so it is not time-consuming. Even when the area is very crowded, the flow of people never stops and they can get it done within 15–20 minutes. Many people then take memorial photos with their smart phones posing in front of the tomb and leave the area to enjoy the various kinds of entertainment at the festival.

Yörük tents, folk dances and memories

Yörük-related events at the festival seem to be limited to the hospitality tents, folk dances, the festival competition, and the introduction of their associations. The reports about the festival by various media were largely about the speeches of the most prominent politicians. However, when I participated, the cultural activities of Yörük and Turks seemed to be given greater importance than

---

[9] As the area of his tomb was crowded with people throughout the festival, the locals tend to skip this part of the festivities, as they have ample opportunities in their daily lives.

Photo 4.4 The tomb of Ertuğrul Gazi on the festival day (September 2019)

commemoration of Ertuğrul Gazi by the general participants. It appears that most participants visit the tomb of Ertuğrul Gazi, but the visit itself takes only a short time. Attendees can visit dozens of tents and the tomb at any time during the festival, and can enjoy their favorite performances at their own pace (Photo 4.5). Only time-specific events are described in the official program.

In fact, of the participants I interviewed, the majority who did not identify as Yörük came with the intention of enjoying a day trip to visit the hospitality tents and try to participate in some general events, rather than attending the official program events. When I asked what they thought of the festival, they all looked satisfied and said, "It's very wonderful. It's an opportunity to experience our own culture" (12 years old, female, resident who participates with family every year), "I came here for the first time because I thought it was close as it's about 150 kilometers away (from my home), and it was good to have fun. I am satisfied to show my children our traditional culture" (36 years old, male, joined by a married couple and two children from Adapazarı City). Other common answers were: "The atmosphere of the festival is lively and fun," "You can have a different experience from shopping and ordinary travel," "I want my children to be proud of their wonderful Turkish culture," and "I want them to remember

Photo 4.5 People enjoying a sporadic performance in the tent booth area (September 2019)

our traditional culture." People enjoy Yörük dances, costumes and music as "our culture to be proud of that we want to pass on to our children," including all of the Ottoman military music. Importantly, most of these informants did not identify as Yörük, but came to enjoy "traditional Turkish culture" as "Turkish people."

I also met many people who identified as "Yörük" or as "descendants of Yörük" who participated with a clearer interest. They said they sympathized with the splendor of "Yörük culture" and the need for its revitalization. Though most of these were middle-aged and elderly married couples and friends, there was one young man who came alone. They often went to tents where no events were being held and enjoyed long chats with members of the host nomad association and other guests. They explained their origins as much as possible to one another, tried to identify any common relatives, and exchanged the related information even when they knew that there was no family relation between them. Those who strongly self-identified as and were interested in Yörük, explained to me that this is their largest annual "meeting point (*buluşma noktalarımızı*)." In fact, by repeatedly visiting tents and chatting, a woman in her 50s from Akkeçili Village in Isparta province said she had "discovered" several relatives from places hundreds of kilometers away from the festival and they had been inviting each other to local şenlik and weddings ever since.

In a tent, when I started a conversation with several groups who were taking a break, asking, "Where are you from, are you Yörük?" a middle-aged woman with a family smiled and said, "Well, if it's not Yörük, what's this business for?" One of the other elderly women present responded, "We're not Yörük, but we're here. *After all, it's all our culture,* because we're all Turkish" (emphasis added). This indicates that the festival is a place for those who recognize themselves as Yörük to cherish and enjoy their cultural roots and to discover connections, but for those who don't, it's a place to embrace and enjoy the Yörük roots of their Turkish culture.

Sharing *şifalı pilav*

In the official festival program, "*şifalı pilav*" appears every day: first the ritual sacrificing of animals to be cooked in *şifalı pilav*, then the traditional *şifalı pilav* lid-opening ritual, and finally, its distribution to all the participants of the festival. A literal translation of *şifalı pilav* is "healing pilaf" or "pilaf with miraculous efficacy." The mayor of Söğüt, Mr. Aydoğdu, explained the importance of *şifalı pilav* in an interview with TRT, the national broadcasting company. He said:

94

> Ertuğrul Gazi held *toy* (a festival or a feast) three times a year when he was alive. Decisions related to politics, military, economy, and society were made in this feast. During the decision-making process, people were served food to eat outside of the political meetings, wrestling competitions were held, and a traditional equestrian competition called Cirit was held.
>
> Yörüks and Turkmens from all regions coming to Söğüt in Bilecik Province, not only inherit the tradition of this feast (*toy*) for 735 years, but also make *şifalı pilav* made of their own ground wheat, sheep and goat meat to give it out to the participants of the feast.
>
> They keep the custom of Ertuğrul Gazi, distributing *şifalı pilav* to the people even today, despite hundreds of years after his death. (TRT Haber, 2016)[10]

---

[10] https://www.trthaber.com/haber/yasam/735-yildir-sifali-pilav-dagitiyorlar-271117.html (Accessed on December 15, 2019).

Photo 4.6 Distribution of the *şifalı pilav* (September 2019)   95

The article titled "For 735 years, they are serving *şifalı pilav*" was accompanied by a photo of a cook holding the lid of a pilaf pot. It is apparent that the continuation of the *şifalı pilav* is stressed and its origin is believed to trace back to the "father of the Ottoman founder in Söğüt." This embodies the general theme of the EY Festival which is repeated in many forms; the continuation of Yörük and the Ottomans and the centrality of Söğüt in the context. The pilaf is symbolic of both the authenticity of this EY Festival and the continuity of Yörük and the Ottomans. It is why this simple pilaf is ritualized and displayed everyday (even just to open the lid of the pilaf pot) to the audience.

On the final day, after the closing ceremony, the pilaf is distributed in the park behind the Tomb of Ertuğrul Gazi. There were thousands of people in many long lines to receive the pilaf from many gigantic cooking pots (Photo 4.6). People were sharing and enjoying the pilaf with friends and families sitting on the grass, on the seats of the ceremony venue, and in the tents. For the participants, sharing and eating *şifalı pilav* in Söğüt next to the Tomb of Ertuğrul Gazi is a sensual experience through mouth and nose, imagining the old ancestors enjoying the same pilaf in the same *ba*, that is, in the atmosphere of festivity in the original place of Söğüt.

In the article, the (former) mayor continued to explain how the pilaf has healing power:

> Mr. Aydoğdu considers that the tradition of feast (*toy*) continues and said: "This custom has been kept in the form of remembrance (of Ertuğrul Gazi) and by passing on the tradition. Yörüks used to bring ground wheat, goats and sheep as they gathered from all over Turkey. The sheep were slaughtered here and added to the pilaf. The ground wheat brought from various regions were mixed into the ground wheat from the Söğüt local area to cook the pilaf. The pilaf's miraculous efficacy (*şifa*) here emanates when the selection of ground wheat from all over Turkey (and local wheat) are cooked together. That's why the pilaf here is 'Yörük pilaf.' It is described as 'healing Yörük pilaf' with meat in it." (ibid.)

This explanation, in my opinion, shows the blessing of gathering annually from all across Turkey in Söğüt. Ground wheat and meat are metaphors of Yörüks in the various regions here. Whether they believe in the "miraculous efficacy" of pilaf or not, the act of Yörüks' gathering and enjoying days together in Söğüt is considered to be a blessing for the descendants of Yörüks.

Discussion: Performance and the power of *ba*

Finally, it is worth mentioning the festival's name change as an explicit example of the manipulation of the *ba*. The original festival name was "Ertuğrul Gazi Memorial and Söğüt Festival,"[11] but since 2012, "Yörük" has supplanted the place name and it has become "Ertuğrul Gazi Memorial and Yörük Festival." The background to this change is not yet investigated, but there seems to have been no significant change to the festival content or program. It is conceivable that the change of name reflects the promotion and restoration of Yörük culture in recent years.

As described above, this festival, named in commemoration of the father of the founder of the Ottoman dynasty and the Yörük tradition, repeatedly emphasizes the continuity of Yörük, Ottomans, and the Republic of Turkey. In the process, the festival is a *ba* to unite those three historical narratives.

---

[11] In Turkish, "*Ertuğrul Gazi'yi Anma ve Söğüt Şenlikleri.*"

Takahashi's analysis of the power of performance on collective memory is illuminating in this respect.

> Religious rites or performances produced by a nation reproduce the mythical origin of the nation and the history of community by means of theatrical techniques. At these moments, participants, audience, or TV viewers accept the presented story as embodied memory based on its relationship with themselves... As a result, it reassures communal ideology and the principle of communal constitution, maintains social order and renews constituents' sense of belonging to the community. (Takahashi 2005: 19)

In the EY Festival, people unconsciously dispel the perception of Yörük as backward and renew their collective memory. They express traditional culture as a base culture of the entire Turkish people, with the Yörük association people playing central roles. At the same time, the present Republic of Turkey is performed as continuous with the Ottoman dynasty, in a *ba* to arouse a sense of unity and pride in the nation, the land, and the people.

Thus, the historical narrative around Ertuğrul Gazi as a contextual *ba* emerges and its power is strengthened through material agencies such as the tomb and the *şifalı pilav*. Through performing these various elements of the festival, imagining the *toy* festival of the pre-Ottoman Yörük ancestry, people feel at one with this ancestry and the continuation of those various elements of the history.

97

5. Creating Oceania
Place and *Ba* of the Festival of Pacific Arts

Fumi Watanabe

Introduction

A large and breath-taking international event called the Festival of Pacific Arts (FOPA) takes place every four years, in the same years as the Olympic Games. I first attended this festival at Pago Pago, American Samoa, in 2008, and still remember the unique emotions I felt at the time. I was conducting long-term fieldwork with a group of painters called Red Wave, whose main base was Fiji. Although most of the group were Fijians, their goal was not 'Fijian art' but 'Oceanic art'. No doubt, my impressions of FOPA in Pago Pago were filtered through the pan-Oceanic art atmosphere that Red Wave were aiming for, which I could perceive in every corner of the venue. Each artist and their work presented distinctive features of their countries/territories/states as well as the individuality of the artist, but at the same time, they also shared common characteristics that could only be described as Oceanic. Above all, the sense of unity at the festival, celebrated with pride, formed a place/*ba* characterised by a unique and irreplaceable enthusiasm. The power of such a place and the culture it creates is the focus of this chapter.

FOPA is a quadrennial regional festival in Oceania, a two-week arts and culture festival hosted by the participating nations and territories in turn, which began in 1972. FOPA has received significant attention from anthropologists and Pacific Studies scholars, among others, who have produced studies covering a wide range of topics such as cultural preservation and creation, cultural representation and identity, the construction of regionalism, the relevance of FOPA in the postcolonial situation and decolonisation movements (Na'puti and Frain 2017), FOPA's role as a heritage transaction (Henry and Foana'ota 2015), and intellectual property rights (Harrison 2002).

This paper is also fundamentally focused on the cultural significance of FOPA. In particular, it considers FOPA as a place that foregrounds cultural differences between countries/territories and is oriented towards an awareness of those individually, while at the same time transcending national/territorial boundaries and confirming/constructing cultural continuity in the greater

Oceania region. I will especially focus on the power of *ba* to involve people in the greater community through performance and examine the pan-Oceanic culture that has emerged at FOPA through the lens of Epeli Hau'ofa's concept of 'Oceania'.

The next section will examine the idea of 'Oceania' outlined by Hau'ofa. The following section explains the purpose and philosophy of FOPA, and then considers the context in which the individuality of each country/territory has been recognised and, conversely, the extent to which the cultural continuity between countries/territories has been confirmed. In the subsequent section, I argue, with specific examples from FOPA, that the performances that emerge through *ba* at the festival form a pan-Oceanic culture. I will conclude by discussing the emergence of this culture in relation to Hau'ofa's idea of Oceania.

Envisioning Oceania as a sea of islands

Let us begin by examining the idea of 'Oceania' as it was articulated by Epeli Hau'ofa in support of the decolonisation movement in the region, for it lays the groundwork for understanding the place/*ba* and cultures that emerge at FOPA.

From 'islands in the sea' to 'sea of islands'

Epeli Hau'ofa himself can be best described as an 'Oceanian'. He was born in Salamo, Papua New Guinea in 1939 to Christian missionary parents from Tonga and was educated in Tonga, Papua New Guinea, Fiji, Australia, and Canada. He received a B.A. in History from the University of New England (Australia) in 1965, an M.A. in Social Anthropology from McGill University (Canada) in 1968, and a Ph.D. in Social Anthropology from the Australian National University in 1975. Hau'ofa then served as deputy private secretary to His Majesty the King of Tonga, serving as the keeper of the royal archives from 1978 to 1981, and from 1981 taught sociology at the University of the South Pacific in Fiji. He was appointed Head of the School of Social and Economic Development from 1994 to 1996, then served as Director of the Oceania Centre for Arts and Culture (see below) from 1997 until his death in 2009. He is also an acclaimed novelist. His two novels *Tales of the Tikongs* (1994) and *Kisses in the Nederends* (1995), which depict the postcolonial situation in Oceania with a light-hearted blend of humour and irony, are highly regarded in South Pacific literary circles.

Despite his fame and the important positions he held, Hau'ofa usually wore a faded and sometimes torn t-shirt, a long *sulu* (sarong) and went barefoot. He famously said that paradise is a place where you can walk about barefoot. His strong personality, which combined deeply-held beliefs, a down to earth attitude, and a fun-loving, even eccentric demeanour, has fascinated and was deeply loved by many people.

Hau'ofa's lifelong pursuit of the idea of 'Oceania' is summed up in two articles, 'Our Sea of Islands' and 'The Ocean in Us'.[1] In 'Our Sea of Islands', which has become a slogan of postcolonial activists, Hau'ofa first laments the 'poverty' of the Oceania islands.

> Some of our islands had become, in the words of one social scientist, "MIRAB societies"[2] – pitiful microstates condemned forever to depend on migration, remittances, aid, and bureaucracy, not on any real economic productivity. (Hau'ofa 2008: 29)

With the exceptions of Australia, New Zealand and Papua New Guinea, the Oceania region is extremely small in landmass, lacking in underground resources, physically separated from the world's centres, and has difficulty in establishing a transportation network even between the islands scattered across the sea. If people need money, they have little choice but to go to larger countries for work, and the productive forces within the island region are being hollowed out. Since the government is dependent on foreign aid and remittances from migrants overseas, it no longer functions as a national decision-making body, but merely as the manager of a pool of aid funds. In the process, the bureaucracy that distributes state funds to the people has become so bloated that the private sector cannot grow.

Indeed, this reality had long been described by social scientists, and no solution was in sight. But over the years, Hau'ofa had begun to observe deep pain in the eyes of students at the University of the South Pacific as he lectured about this 'subordinate' situation. Sometimes gripped by pessimism, sometimes perplexed at the thought of turning his back on the conventional wisdom of academia, Hau'ofa continued to ponder the question of whether or not there was a way for the Oceania Islands, which had been completely excluded from world history, to survive. Finally, he came to the realisation that a different perspective was needed, shifting from thinking of small 'islands in the sea' to a vast 'sea of islands'.

---

[1] In this paper, I use the collection of the first published paper with additions and corrections (Hau'ofa 2008) as reference.
[2] Cf. Bertram and Waters (1985).

There is a world of difference between viewing the Pacific as "islands in a far sea" and as "sea of islands". The first emphasises dry surfaces in a vast ocean far from the centres of power. Focussing in this way stresses the smallness and remoteness of the islands. The second is a more holistic perspective in which things are seen in the totality of their relationships. (ibid: 31)

The perception of 'small islands' or 'islands in the sea' is an external perception based on an arbitrary line drawn by the empire. Hau'ofa argued that as long as the denizens of Oceania remain trapped in this perception they will never be mentally or economically independent. Referring to the myths and legends still told on the islands, the history of trans-oceanic traffic as an archaeological fact, and the existence of superior navigational skills such as star navigation, he argues that in pre-colonial Oceania (especially Polynesia[3] and Micronesia) people's perception of the islands was based not on the islands themselves, but on their sea of islands.

Hau'ofa then focuses on the term 'Oceania' and contrasts it with the traditional 'Pacific Islands'. The name Pacific Ocean comes from the name 'Mar Pacifico', implying peace and tranquillity, named by the Portuguese voyager Ferdinand Magellan when he 'discovered' the area in the 16th century. Agreeing with the postcolonial activists who pointed out that the term represented a one-sided view of the peacefulness of the people, and was intrinsic to a colonial idea that sought to tame them, Hau'ofa appealed to the name 'Oceania' as an alternative.

101

> "Oceania" denotes a sea of islands with their inhabitants. The world of our ancestors was a large sea full of places to explore, to make their homes in, to breed generations of seafarers like themselves. (…) They developed great skills for navigating their waters – as well as the spirit to traverse even the few large gaps that separated their island groups. (ibid: 32)

In 'Oceania' people moved around frequently and cultures mingled until the imperialist powers of the 19th century drew arbitrary boundaries. Hau'ofa was especially interested in the exchange community between Fiji, Samoa, Tonga, Niue, Rotuma, Tokelau, Tuvalu, Futuna, and Uvea, from which they ventured to the north and west, into Kiribati, the Solomon Islands, Vanuatu, and New Caledonia (ibid: 33). He claims that '(h)uman nature demands space for free

---

[3] Though Fiji is usually viewed as Melanesia near the Polynesian border, Hau'ofa states that '(f)or geographical and cultural reasons I include Fiji in Polynesia.' (Hau'ofa 2008: 39–40)

movement – the larger the space the better it is for people' (ibid: 35), and argues that the resources for people to nurture their lives should not be limited by the boundaries drawn by the colonial powers. From this point of view, when we examine the social situation in the Oceania region, focusing, for example, on the MIRAB economy, it no longer appears as an unstable entity subordinated to foreign capital, but as a relationship of reciprocity between relatives and friends who have crossed the sea and those who remain on the islands. This perspective allows us to position the present as continuous with the past.

Hau'ofa emphasises that mobility remains a characteristic of the people of Oceania today, and that the sea functions as a connecting link between islands, as a place to live and travel, rather than as a dividing boundary. In order for the Oceania islands to become culturally and economically self-reliant, he argues, they need to be recognised as an integral part of the ocean, not as scattered islands or dispersed nations. Hence, he calls for a strong Oceanic identity:

> The time has come for us to wake up to our modern history as a region. We cannot confront the issues of the Pacific Century individually, as tiny countries, nor as the Pacific Islands Region of bogus independence. We must develop a much stronger and genuinely independent regionalism than what we have today. A new sense of the region that is our own creation, based on our perceptions of our realities, is necessary for our survival in the dawning era. (ibid: 47)

One contentious point in his conception of Oceania as a regional identity concerns the question of Oceania's membership, which Hau'ofa contrasted to the predominant 'Pacific Way' regionalist concept.

The 'Pacific Way' was a slogan associated with the rise of Pacific regionalism in the 1960s and 1970s, at a time when countries were gaining independence in rapid succession, and many were questioning how to secure a voice in international politics for those small countries that had been separated from the patronage of the great powers. It was against this background that Ratu Sir Kamisese Mara, Prime Minister of Fiji at the time, used the term at the 25th United Nations General Assembly in 1970, to give an impression of a 'Pacific region' at the supra-regional level of international politics (Mara 1997: 238). But commitment to the Pacific Way did not last ten years due to the fact that conflicting interests between countries undermined all efforts to develop inter-island transportation networks. The Pacific Way was effective in coordinating joint action for the outside world, but was insufficient to inspire intra-regional cooperation (Ogashiwa 2000: 358–359).

Hau'ofa identified the nationalist spirit as the root cause of the failure of Pacific Way regionalism, and declared the very framework of the modern state to be unfit for the Oceania region. He argues that a fixed unit of reference to geographical boundaries and race which does not take into account the mobility of the people of Oceania is inappropriate to the characteristics of the region. Chaining people to the land in order to demarcate the boundaries of a supposed nation is merely accepting a colonial idea, which is what he calls 'bogus independence'.

By the same logic, he questions the notion of 'the indigenous' in that it only serves the establishment of the modern state. Who is the indigenous of Oceania? Can Indo-Fijians in Fiji be the indigenous Oceanians? Cook Islanders who are citizens of both their own country and New Zealand? French Polynesians and New Caledonians who are French citizens? What about Chinese descendants all over the region? To what degree are these people Oceanians? He continues:

> The issue of what or who is a Pacific Islander would not arise if we considered Oceania as comprising people – as human beings with a common heritage and commitment – rather than as members of diverse nationalities and race. Oceania refers to a world of people connected to each other. (Hau'ofa 2008: 50)

For Hau'ofa, Oceania is not defined in any way by characteristics of its members. Rather, Oceania is about connection itself, and if we dare to define a member, it can only be in terms of this connection. Oceania is not an 'island' but a 'sea (of islands)'.

As we have seen, the 'Oceania' imagined by Epeli Hau'ofa was, first of all, based on specifics of the 'Oceania region'. There was another level to this concept, too: 'Oceania' as a metaphor. Hau'ofa concludes 'The Ocean in Us' with the following words.

> the sea is our pathway to each other and to everyone else, the sea is our endless saga, the sea is our most powerful metaphor, the ocean is in us. (ibid: 58)

The metaphor is extracted from specific characteristics of the Oceania region, and Hau'ofa presents it as connections that are rich in openness and variability. Oceania is not only an expression of regional specificity, but also an indication of a universal mode of relatedness.

Impact of Hauʻofaʻs Oceania

The impact of Hauʻofaʻs 'Oceania' on intellectuals was enormous, and remains so today. Anthropologist Geoffrey White has proposed that although Hauʻofaʻs concept of 'ocean' promotes a recentring of thought and practice in Oceania, his conception of cultural identity was not concerned with declaring differences but was rather 'startlingly expansive and inclusive' (White 2008: 20). David Hanlon, a leading historian of the Pacific region, says that Hauʻofaʻs Oceania represents the area as vast, diverse, fluid, and complex, and incorporating this perspective on the area would contribute to the emergence or re-emergence of indigenous histories and indigenous historical practices (Hanlon 2017: 286). Anthropologist Margaret Jolly contends, however, that the worldview of Oceania is not appropriate for people living in Papua New Guinea or the interior of the Melanesian region (Jolly 2001). Nevertheless, Jolly examined the differences and entanglements between outsiders' and indigenous representations, and highly regarded Hauʻofaʻs Oceania as an alternative vision for the latter (Jolly 2007).

In a more local community-oriented context, SPACLALS (The South Pacific Association for Commonwealth Literature and Language Studies) held a forum at the University of the South Pacific in 1999, followed by a booklet entitled *Imagining Oceania* (SPACLALS 1999). Four of the thirty-five essays referred to Hauʻofaʻs paper, citing it as an excellent example of a way forward for the Pacific Island region. In 2006, the Pacific Epistemology Conference, famous for its serious discussions among postcolonial activists – including writers and scholars, politicians, and artists – was held at the University of the South Pacific. Although Hauʻofa did not personally speak at this five-day event, everyone felt that the entire conference was built on his 'Sea=Oceania' foundation (Prasad 2006).

In this way, Hauʻofa became an important touchstone as the decolonisation movement grew in the Pacific. Above all, it was the Oceania Centre for Arts and Culture (Oceania Centre), founded by Hauʻofa in 1997, that best articulated Oceania philosophy and spread its ideas throughout society. It was also the home of the Red Wave mentioned previously. The Centre, where Hauʻofa acted as Director, is located on the Laucala campus of University of the South Pacific, the largest university in the Oceania Island region, but it was independent of the university's regular program.[4] Hauʻofa believed that art production and learning should occur 'the Oceania way' rather than being based on the modern

---

[4] This discussion refers to the Centre before 2009, when Hauʻofa passed away and changes were made to the Centre's positioning and operating policies.

educational system. The Oceania-style production environment, for instance, is described as 'reciprocity, cooperation, openness to community (in terms of both participation and viewing) and transmission of skills through observation and participation rather than through formal instruction' (Hau'ofa 2005: 8). Furthermore, the objective was not the revival of previous culture, but rather the creation of culture, which Hau'ofa explains in the following way.

> we have to go to our traditions and histories, as well as to our everchanging contemporary social and cultural environments, for inspirations to create images, sounds and movements that speak to us, and speak of us, in our place and our times. (ibid.)

Hau'ofa's goal for the Centre was to embody the idea of Oceania through arts. He found in the arts a set of practices that reflected the unique culture of the region without being closed to anything. The Centre was more of a free-flowing gathering space than an educational institution, where people gathered for the visual arts, dance, and music. The results were tremendous, and the artists who learned there are now at the forefront of the art scene in the Oceania region, especially in Fiji.[5]

105

Oceania, place and *ba*

Thus, Epeli Hau'ofa spent half his life contemplating the genuine independence and autonomy of the Oceania region and elucidating the idea of Oceania.[6] It was a vision of a particular path for the Oceania region to follow, but it was also a vision of a universal culture based on the principles of openness and variability. Hau'ofa thought it was best embodied in the arts. In the next section, we will examine FOPA, the regional festival of the arts, and the world of Oceania as it emerges there. Before that, though, let me briefly summarise Hau'ofa's Oceania philosophy.

In the first place, Hau'ofa's idea of Oceania was based on the region as a geographical entity. He was strongly convinced that the development of Oceanic arts and culture had to take place in the concrete geography of the Oceania region, and that the cornerstone of the struggle for decolonisation was to not let go of this concrete nature. To make this point, Hau'ofa often repeated the saying

---

[5] Red Wave, a group of painters who have been based at the Centre, is discussed in detail in Watanabe 2014.
[6] Various obituaries and memorial essays were published on Hau'ofa's death, most notably Wesley-Smith (ed.) 2010 and Hereniko 2010.

'Muhammad didn't go to the mountain. The mountain came to Muhammad.' Muhammad, here, represents the artist and the mountain represents the (Western) world. His point is that people should transport themselves to Oceania to see the paintings or dances, rather than the artists and performers traveling to the Western world in search of an audience. The deeper point is that the art of Oceania is generated and nurtured in a place with a particular context, in contrast to Western art, which is detached from context. Oceania cannot be performed in a place remote from the Oceania region, nor can it be 'somewhere' that does not have a place-ness. Oceania is not a colourless, implantable physical space, but a place that is contextualised and meaningful. This was explicitly articulated in Hau'ofa's essays.

Based on this premise, Hau'ofa's Oceania had four key characteristics of concern in this paper. First, he argued that in pre-colonial Oceania, the sea was a place of passage connecting islands, not a boundary between them, presenting a vision of Oceania as a unity based on the sea rather than the land. This view is based in historical fact, but there is also an ideological dimension rooted in postcolonial thought. Second, Oceania's constituency cannot be defined, but instead emerges through connections. That is, belonging to Oceania is not defined by lineage or traditional land ownership; but by participation and practice. Third, the environment of the Oceanic production was understood in terms of openness to the community (the boundary between producer and receiver is ambiguous) and the transmission of technology through participation and observation (experiential and physical learning). This productive environment, Hau'ofa claimed, was what made arts and culture so Oceanic that it should not deviate from such a concrete place. Finally, the culture that Hau'ofa sought to create was one that reconciled traditional cultures and histories with the present cultural environment.

When viewed in this way, Hau'ofa's Oceania has many characteristics as a place as well as *ba*. While the place exists apart from the subject and is the object that the subject acts upon, as described in the Introduction, *ba* can emerge only through the interaction or inter-performance between agents. Rather than a solid physical state, it is more like a mood that co-emerges with the agents who participate in *ba*, encompassing and driving everything within it. From this perspective, its affinity with Hau'ofa's conceptualisation of Oceania is clear. For example, the requirement for Oceania's membership was to have 'a common commitment', which overlaps with the principle of *ba*, where members and Oceania (*ba*) emerge simultaneously, rather than prior members (subjects) creating the world. In the context of Oceania's production, the ambiguity of the boundary between producer and receiver, and the experiential nature of the learning process, correspond to the characteristics of *ba* where actors co-emerge through participation. Furthermore, the nature of openness, variability, and fluidity in Oceania's unity is the very essence of *ba*.

The next section examines the context of FOPA as a place and considers how it overlaps with Oceania as a place. In the following section, I will focus on the ways *ba* emerges from place and eventually reinforce the place. I will then argue how the world that rises from the fluctuations of place and *ba* coincides with the world of Oceania as described by Hau'ofa.

Representing nations: Context of the place

This section identifies three major contexts in which FOPA has been embedded. First, it was established in the postcolonial context, where a cultural revival was essential not only for constructing people's identity but also for stabilising the political and economic situation. Second, it is a context in which delegations are representatives of their respective countries' indigenous cultures. Third, the countries represented also have much in common, including institutional backgrounds that promote regional identity. These three contexts are the 'place'-like features of FOPA.

Formation of FOPA: Postcolonial cultural revival

This section first clarifies the background and purpose of FOPA and then contextualises it in terms of both the differentiation of national cultures and its opposite, regionalisation. As mentioned, FOPA is a quadrennial regional festival that began in 1972 and is hosted by a different participating country/territory each time. During the two-week period, delegates live together in the host venue and present a variety of performances and works, such as: 1) performing arts (traditional song and dance, contemporary music and dance, drama, fashion shows, opera, and films), 2) exhibitions (modern art, books, photography, artefacts, and postage stamps), 3) festival village activities (informal cultural performances, tattooing, carving, craft-making, traditional cooking, tasting, and souvenirs) (Yamamoto 2006: 5–6). The venue consists of a space with a stage or galleries and a 'festival village'. The festival village comprises rows of huts from different countries and territories, displaying and selling their specialties, demonstrating production processes. It also provides space for the delegates to just hangout, creating a variety

Festival Number	1	2	3	4	5
Year	1972	1976	1980	1985	1988
Hosting Country/ Territory	Fiji	New Zealand	PNG	French Polynesia	Australia
1 American Samoa	x		x	x	x
2 Australia	x	x	x	x	x
3 Cook Islands	x	x	x	x	x
4 Federated States of Micronesia				x	x
5 Fiji	x	x		x	x
6 Guam		x		x	
7 Hawai'i		x	x	x	
8 Kiribati	x	x	x		
9 Marshall Islands			x	?	
10 Nauru	x	x	x	x	x
11 New Caledonia	x	x	x	x	x
12 New Zealand	x	x	x	x	
13 Niue	x	x	x		x
14 Norfolk Island	x	x	x		
15 Northern Mariana Islands (CNMI)				x	
16 Palau			x		
17 Papua New Guinea	x	x	x	x	x
18 Pitcairn Island	x	x	x		x
19 Rapa Nui (Easter Island)		x		x	
20 Samoa	x	x	x	x	x
21 Solomon Islands	x	x	x	x	x
22 Tahiti, French Polynesia				x	
23 Taiwan					
24 Tokelau	x	x	x	x	x
25 Tonga	x	x	x	x	x
26 Tuvalu				x	
27 Vanuatu	x	x	x		x
28 Wallis and Futuna	x	x	x	x	x

Table 5.1. Participating countries and territories

of interactions. The 12th FOPA, held in Guam in 2016, welcomed more than 2,700 official delegates from 25 countries and territories. The host nations and participating countries/territories from the first in 1972 to the twelfth in 2016 are listed in Table 5.1.

The idea for such a festival first arose in 1965 when the Fiji Arts Council proposed a regional celebration of the Pacific community. This proposal was

6	7	8	9	10	11	12
1992	1996	2000	2004	2008	2012	2016
Cook Islands	Western Samoa	New Caledonia	Palau	American Samoa	Solomon Islands	Guam
x	x	x		x	x	x
x	x	x	x	x	x	x
x	x	x	x	x		x
		x	x	x		x
x	x	x	x	x	x	x
		x	x	x	x	x
		x	x	x	x	x
	x	x	x	x	x	x
				x		x
x	x	x		x	x	x
x	x	x	x	x	x	x
x	x	x	x	x	x	x
x	x	x		x	x	
x	x	x	x	x	x	x
		x	x	x		x
		x	x	x	x	x
x	x	x	x	x	x	x
x		x		x		
		x		x	x	x
x	x	x	x	x	x	x
x	x	x	x	x	x	x
		x	x	x	x	x
		x	x	x	x	x
x	x	x		x	x	x
x	x	x	x	x		x
		x	x	x		x
x	x	x		x	x	
x	x	x	x	x		x

Festival numbers 1 to 11 are largely based on Sullivan 2014: 8, Stevenson 2012, and my observation. Festival number 12 is based on my observation and research.

109

considered as a formal agenda item by the South Pacific Commission[7] in the same year. A common concern was identified that traditional art forms in the Pacific region were in danger of disappearing. A consensus was formed that they needed

---

[7] Renamed the Secretariat of the Pacific Community (SPC) in 1997, it had 26 country and territory members as of July 2020.

	Year	Location	Theme
1	1972	Suva, Fiji	Preserving Culture
2	1976	Rotorua, New Zealand	Sharing Culture
3	1980	Port Moresby, Papua New Gunea	A Celebration of Pacific Awareness
4	1985	Pape'ete, French Polynesia	My Pacific Home
5	1988	Townsville, Australia	To promote the maintainance of indigenous cultures of the Pacific regions
6	1992	Avarua, Cook Islands	Seafaring Pacific Islanders
7	1996	Apia, Western Samoa	Tala Measina (Unveiling Treasures)
8	2000	Noumea, New Caledonia	Words of Yesterday (Paroles d'hier), Words of Today (Paroles d'aujourd'hui), Words of Tomorrow (Paroles de demain)
9	2004	Koror, Palau	Oltobed a Malt - Nurture, Regenerate, Celebrate
10	2008	Pago Pago, American Samoa	Su'iga'ula a le Atuvasa: Threading the Oceania'Ula
11	2012	Honia,ra, Solomon Islands	Culture in Harmony with Nature
12	2016	Hagatna, Guam	What we own, what we have, what we share, united voices of the Pacific
13	2021 (planned)	Hawai'i	"E kū i ka hoe uli" Take hold of the steering paddle
14	2024 (planned)	Fiji	TBA

Table 5.2. Themes of the festival (Stevenson 2012: 10–15).

to be preserved and developed by creating spaces where islanders could meet, share and celebrate their cultural heritage with each other. After the 9th South Pacific Conference decided on Fiji as the first venue, a special committee for the Festival was set up in the capital city of Suva in 1970. In 1972, the first FOPA was held in Fiji soon after its independence, with approximately 1,100 delegates from 15 countries and territories[8] participating. In 1975, a special workshop was held in Noumea and the South Pacific Arts Festival Council,[9] consisting of representatives of all the participating countries and territories, was formally established in Niue.

With the exception of the cancellation of the fourth festival in Noumea in 1984 (held the following year in French Polynesia) due to political instability, and

---

[8] Australia, Nauru, American Samoa, Fiji, Tonga, Solomon Islands New Caledonia, Cook Islands, New Zealand, Tokelau, and Western Samoa (Samoa in 1997), New Hebrides (Vanuatu in 1977), Norfolk Islands, Papua New Guinea, and Tahiti (Yamamoto 2006: 7).

[9] When the festival's name was changed to the Festival of Pacific Arts in 1985, the committee was renamed the Pacific Arts Council. The committee is in charge of the overall planning and operation of the festival, including the determination of the venue. Although it is considered an independent organisation, it receives financial support and advice directly from the SPC (Yamamoto 2006: 6–7).

the postponement of the thirteenth in Hawai'i in 2020 due to the COVID-19 pandemic, FOPA has remained a quadrennial celebration to this day. The evolution of each theme in each session is shown in Table 5.2.

The 15th meeting of the Pacific Arts Council in 1998 confirmed the following expected outcomes or objectives, with minor modifications to the original, and no fundamental changes have been made to date.

> We, the indigenous peoples of the Pacific, assert our cultural identity, rights and dignity. We do so, mindful of our spiritual and environmental origins, through our dynamic art forms and artistic history and traditions. As indigenous peoples, we share the following objectives:
>
> + Encourage awareness of a collective voice
> + Foster the protection of cultural heritage
> + Explore the creation of dynamic new arts
> + Cultivate global awareness and appreciation of Pacific arts and cultures
> + Promote our traditional languages
> + Value the wisdom of our elders
> + Support the aspiration of our youth
> + Advocate a culture of peace through dialogue with the cultures of the Pacific
> + Promote cultural development within the social, economic, and political development of our countries
> + Encourage the indigenous peoples of the Pacific to continue their efforts for recognition
>
> (Leahy et al. 2010: 26)

111

In the workshops and committee meetings at each festival, the question of what constitutes the common denominator of the Pacific region often arose, which invariably led to a discussion of tradition. After much discussion, it was decided that tradition is the work of the people who have continued to support it, rather than a fixed art form. This allows both 'valuing the wisdom of our elders' and 'supporting the aspiration of our youth'. These statements also reflect a shift toward encouraging 'dynamic new arts', innovation and change.

Moreover, they emphasised that art is an intrinsic part of culture. Dance, music and crafts, the foci of the festival, certainly do not constitute independent fields of art in Oceania, but are closely related to everyday life and rituals, so it is not surprising that art and culture are perceived as inseparable. The contribution of culture to the 'social, economic, and political development' of the countries of the Pacific has also become more apparent. It is also congruent with the SPC's strategy of utilising culture as a resource for economic development, and will make it easier for FOPA to receive financial support from international organisations such as UNESCO and the EU.

As we have seen above, FOPA was established under the auspices of SPC with the aim of promoting the cultural sector in newly independent countries as they sought economic and social stability and development. Therefore, rather than encouraging a distinct or separate field of art, a continuum of art and culture has been promoted, with the aim of reviving and preserving traditional cultures lost during colonialism, as well as encouraging new artistic and cultural activities that reflect the contemporary world. FOPA is a product of the post-colonial period in Oceania, when the region was comprised of newly independent states.

Representing nations

One of the highlights of FOPA has been the opening ceremony, usually held in a large venue, with delegations entering in alphabetical order, as per the Olympics. A placard bearing the country's name announced their entrance. Most of the delegates were attired in team uniforms tailored especially for FOPA. Upon entering the venue, each group paused the parade for an allocated time to stage a spectacle of music and dance. In recent years, delegations have ritualised giving a gift to a representative of the host country. This practice, which is unique to the region where the culture of gift-exchange remains prominent in public affairs, has been a true spectacle, and was carefully performed in a manner that showcases the donor country's traditional culture, including the items gifted and methods of exchange. Some venues had a stage, while in others performance took place directly on the ground. Either way, the venue was filled with delegates and other participants, and performances were met with great cheers and enthusiasm. Thus, through the important ritual of the opening ceremony, the delegates were made keenly aware of the fact that they were representatives of their respective countries and that every delegation represented a different culture.

Furthermore, the two weeks of the event typically have many moments that heighten awareness of cultural and national differences. For example, while spending time with the Fijian delegation at the 10th FOPA, the first one I attended, it seemed to me that the Fijian delegates were very good at determining where the people around them were from. This might be because many Islanders live in or visit Suva, Fiji's capital city. Delegations typically include veterans of previous festivals, though, during which time they have gotten to know the other delegates and thus may have learned how to distinguish country of origin. However, when I asked what they looked for, a number of distinguishing markers were clearly identified by many people, including traits such as face, body, and skin colour, as well as language spoken, clothing and adornment. Clothing and adornment included not only the traditional costumes worn on stage, but also everyday items such as shirts with the name of the country printed on them, sarongs, hair ornaments, shoulder bags or hats. The main venue, the festival village, is lined with huts from each country. Delegates hang out and indigenous crafts and cultural practices are presented throughout the day. At the same time, there are performances by delegations from all over the Pacific on various stages and venues from early morning until late at night. In short, there are many national markers around the venue, and there is a strong atmosphere of mutual flaunting of these markers throughout the festival.

Reportedly, the Guam delegation's participation in the fourth FOPA in Tahiti in 1985, led them to realise the extent to which they had lost their indigenous dances, songs and chants, and thus their distinctive identity. This experience triggered a cultural revivalist movement that investigated and rebuilt their culture so that the Chamorros (indigenous people of Guam) could be recognised. Today, those efforts continue to be sustained by participating in FOPA (Islands Society website; Bevacqua 2017). As we can see, FOPA's atmosphere of reviving and preserving traditions has the power to heighten participants' awareness of their own unique histories. Furthermore, as will be discussed in the next section, there are many examples of FOPA being a catalyst for decolonisation and supporting independence movements. On a related note, it is worth considering that FOPA often uses not only national flags, but also ethnic and provincial flags (e.g. Australian Aboriginal, Guam, Hawai'i, Rapa Nui, Republik Maluk Selatan, West Papua).

In recent years FOPA has been attended by nearly 3,000 official delegates. The FOPA space is full of opportunities to speak self-consciousness, and functions as an arena for expressing and creating differences between self and other. Furthermore, with FOPA broadly focused on culture, rather than the more limited domain of art, the participants are positioned as representatives of their respective cultural groups rather than as individual artists. This tends to give the delegates a strong sense of pride, as well as a sense of responsibility for carrying their country's culture on their shoulders. Thus, FOPA is an arena in which participants have opportunities to become more aware of their own culture and to celebrate it.

113

FOPA and regionalism

Another highlight of FOPA is the arrival of the canoes, sailed for days from the islands of Oceania. This usually precedes the opening ceremony and is recognised as the actual opening of FOPA. Seafaring is understood to be an essential symbol of Pacific Islander identities and was directly featured in the theme of the sixth FOPA in the Cook Islands (Yasui 2009: 451–454). The practice of voyaging has been one of the most remarkable aspects of Oceania's culture in FOPA. In a region with a history of thousands of years, where the first settlements began with voyages and where voyages have formed a network of islands, no other subject can evoke such a sense of community.

This arrival ceremony symbolically confirms the growing sense of pan-Pacific unity. This unity, which can be felt at FOPA, is perceived to be more important to FOPA than the cultural differences between countries mentioned. In fact, as the festival has evolved, the idea of Pacific regional integration has become more prominent. Secretariat of the Pacific Community (SPC) stated that FOPA has made a significant contribution to the development of Pacific Island identity and, by encouraging the celebration and respect for each other's culture, has promoted the integration of the region. SPC also noted that the Festival has enhanced political and economic stability in the region by promoting communication between the cultures, and thus deepening the sense of unity among the geographically dispersed countries.

FOPA's development coincides with the growing independence of the countries of Oceania. In this process, these newly independent, territorially small and geographically isolated countries have sought regional solidarity to establish a position in the international community. The discourse of reviving lost cultures has responded well to this need, with a regionalism formed at FOPA based on a common thread of art and culture. In short, FOPA was founded on the idea that music, dance, crafts and other cultural production are fundamental to the culture of the Pacific region, and that their revival and celebration by the countries of the region will create a sense of community, which might in turn lead to mutual political and economic development.

Just like seafaring culture has been noted as the foremost Pacific culture, 'the emphasis of arts festival is primarily on the revival of art forms of earlier times, to look back at the past rather than look ahead to the future' (Hereniko 1994: 424), and the regional identity of the Pacific has certainly been strengthened by focusing on the commonality of the artistic heritage of the past. However, especially since the eighth Festival in Noumea in 2000, some efforts have been made to shift to a more future-oriented direction. As reflected in the theme 'Words of Yesterday, Words of Today, Words of Tomorrow', the festival's policy shift aims to secure greater social, economic and cultural vitality by strengthening the category of contemporary art (Leahy et al. 2010: 76).

One of the particular challenges of pursuing this new policy, though, is that there is no unified definition of the term contemporary art at the Festival.[10] Nevertheless, it is clear from the use of the term in the SPC and Arts Council reports. It is used to refer to the art style from temporal period of today, in contrast to the traditions of the past, rather than in accordance with the Western art historians' category 'contemporary art'. It is specifically defined by the form of expression. Painting in general, some sculptures, photography, film, and literature (including poetry readings) are usually classified as contemporary art, but in the case of forms where the medium itself has traditionally existed, such as sculpture, the boundaries of what is 'contemporary' are sometimes blurred and the choice of nomenclature is left to the individual artist. For instance, I was at the 10th FOPA in American Samoa, where a Fijian sculptor was participating in a show in which he carved a canoe in front of a crowd, jokingly saying 'Today I am no contemporary (artist)', but the organisers named the show contemporary art. Also, a Maori tattooist told me in an interview that 'depending on the designs you use tattoos can be a modern art or a traditional art'. This blurring of the boundary between traditional art, which is relatively restrictive, and contemporary art, which allows for relatively free expression, serves as the basis for the creation of a pan-Oceanic culture, as will be discussed in the next section.

This section has identified three major contexts in which FOPA has been embedded. First, it was established in the postcolonial context, where a cultural revival was essential not only for constructing people's identity but also for stabilising the political and economic situation. Second, it was a context in which delegations represented the indigenous cultures of their respective countries. Third, it was a context in which the countries all had a great deal in common, and shared institutional backgrounds that promoted regional identity. These three contexts illustrate the features of FOPA as a 'place'. In the next section, I will examine the power of FOPA as *ba*, and consider the cultural creation that takes place in such a place or *ba*.

115

---

[10] This is inextricably linked to the question of what constitutes an authentic tradition of a country or region, and therefore the committee left the issue to the respective countries/territories (Leahy et al. 2010: 72–74) and has avoided expressing a unified view. However, it is also pointed out that the FOPA guidelines refer to contemporary artists as professional performers and that traditional artists usually cover carvers, weavers, storytellers, tattooists and traditional healers (Leahy et al. 2010: 62).

Beyond representing nations: *Ba* and place

Festival and culture

The importance of 'festival' in Oceania's culture has been stressed repeatedly in scholarly research. Karen Stevenson, for example, points out that feasting traditions are associated with almost every cultural practice in the region and that festival is an underlying structure that could unify Pacific cultures. She also explains that this is why SPC decided to create a festival to encourage the traditions and cultures of the Pacific (Stevenson 1999: 29).

Though FOPA is one of the largest festivals in the region, there are numerous other festivals for promoting arts and culture, organised both domestically and regionally. Festivals continue to play an important role in Oceania, and modern cultural festivals such as FOPA should be treated as cultural events, rather than as commercial or tourist pastimes.

In New Zealand, where many Pacific Islander immigrants reside, there has been a progressive development of Pacific festivals reflecting the origins of various immigrant groups, with the 1990s seen as a crucial point of 'festivalisation' (Mackley-Crump 2015: 45). What is intriguing about this phenomenon is the creation through festivals of a new culture based on Pacific-ness, which plays an important role in helping immigrants form a sense of place in their new homeland. Mackley-Crump points out the central place of the 'Pacific' in this migrant identity formation.

> Because the festival is constructed as a Pacific space, a celebration of Pacific communities, the performances that take place within it are viewed as representative of those communities; performances become "Pacific" by virtue of the space they appear within. (ibid: 141)

What we see here is a dynamic in which a festival is composed of spaces that embody the culture celebrated there, and the performances and works presented are seen as representative of that culture. This makes it possible for performances such as rock, hip-hop, and reggae, for example, to be presented alongside the traditional music and dance styles, and to be embraced as Oceanic performances. Mackley-Crump discusses this in contrast to staged authenticity. MacCanell's (1973) discussion of staged authenticity in tourist settings, assumes Goffman's front-stage versus back-stage distinction. MacCanell argues that tourists feel a greater sense of authenticity back-stage, so, by incorporating a device front-stage that gives an illusion of revealing the back-stage, tourists can be led to believe they have had more authentic experiences. However, while MacCanell assumes that performances are constructed specifically for the festival, Mackley-Crump argues that performances at Pacific festivals do not have that artificial front-stage-back-stage mechanism, and are thus fundamentally the same as those staged within community contexts (Mackley-Crump 2015: 15).

Among other things, FOPA has eschewed tourism promotion, being instead a celebration of a gathering of delegates, officials, and others involved in staging the event. More importantly, in Oceania, cultural performance does not occur in a binary relationship between showing and looking. As we have seen, Hau'ofa had already made a similar point to Mackley-Crump: the line between the producer and the audience of an artistic practice is nebulous in Oceania, and it would be inappropriate to assume that performances are experienced in terms of a front-back dichotomy. Even where a modern stage has been built and the different roles of presenting and observing are clearly defined, the people involved invariably transgress the boundary between performer and audience. Performative participation occurs, or conversely, the performers tend to seem to forget that they are on stage, or a performance emphasises its continuity with everyday life, and so on. In many cases, the events that occur at these *ba* are reflected in the performances on stage (see the next section).

FOPA's continuity with everyday life is also evident in the overall ambiance of the festival. For example, one of the key venues, the festival village, is intended to be, as the name suggests, a village. Delegates sit around and chat in the huts, making it look like a village of houses. There are also a number of factors that encourage delegates to identify and act as a group rather than as individuals. For example, delegates share accommodation provided by the host country, often in a public school building, where they sleep rough on mats and pillows in the classrooms. Breakfast and dinner are served as a group. To get from the accommodation to the venue, small vans, trucks, and buses provided by the host country are used, so people travel in groups at fixed times and along fixed routes. Apart from delegations from relatively wealthy regions such as Australia, New Zealand and Hawai'i, it is highly unusual to see an individual act in a Pacific Islander delegation. Notably, more recently, host countries have begun to provide a means of communication. Mobile phones with local SIM cards were given free to delegates in Solomon in 2012 and local SIM cards were given free to delegates in Guam in 2016. Rather than to push them to act as individuals, this enabled the delegates to stay in close contact, to work together, and to deepen whatever new contacts arose.

In sum, FOPA should not be regarded as a commercial or tourist event separate from everyday life and culture, but rather as an important cultural place/*ba* that is continuous with everyday life. With this cultural embedding, as Mackley-Crump argued, FOPA functions as both creator and monitor of Oceania-ness. The next section examines how a pan-Oceanic culture is formed within the dynamics of place and *ba*.

From place to *ba* ...to place to *ba*

We have seen in the previous chapter that FOPA consciously promoted a regionalist perspective. However, a major evaluation in 2010 found the festival had been relatively less successful in promoting artistic collaboration and building an international and cultural network than comparable activities such as organising handicraft workshops (Leahy et al. 2010: 59–63). On the other hand, respondent from Palau, for example, who participated in the 2004 FOPA, stated:

> (Non-formal collaboration) always happened at meal times. We could not miss it. The Cook Islander started it and then we all joined in. It became a non-schedule event that we all looked forward to and enjoyed so much. (Leahy et al. 2010: 60)

This suggests that although FOPA may have fallen short of its goals for formal collaborations, informal artistic collaborations are an important part of its contribution to the creation of a pan-Oceanic art and culture. An example of this informal creation occurred in 2008, when I attended the 10th FOPA in American Samoa, and was part of the emergence of a collaborative work entitled *Pacific Tree*. There was a single coconut palm towering over the venue at Utulei Beach. A Tahitian tattooist jokingly carved in relief a heart shape and some tattoo motifs on that coconut palm. A Samoan carver saw it the next day and began working on it. As more and more people joined in, eventually the words 'Pacific tree needs no officials' were scrawled on the trunk of a completed collaborative work. This work can be seen as a manifestation of collective frustration with FOPA's failure to promote artistic collaboration, an assertion by the artists that they could collaborate without official support. This reiterates Hau'ofa's point that Oceanic artistic production needs a non-formal context.

Whether it's dance, music or drama, performers usually repeat the same performance multiple times during the two-week period, but the performance can vary markedly over the course of the festival, depending on the audience's response.

For example, at the 11th FOPA in the Solomon Islands in 2012, Fijian dancers had prepared a formal stage performance of contemporary dance based on traditional Fijian *meke* dances. However, the audience was not very receptive and it was difficult to get them to participate. Observing that the audience included many Polynesians and Caucasians, they improvised, introducing *hula*-like steps and hip swings that anyone could dance to, and the audience participation immediately increased. The crowd became more animated, and the choreography was hastily changed to accommodate it. Over subsequent performances they improvised, sometimes transforming in a frenzy on stage, and sometimes dancing with the Tahitian delegates in their spare time. In the process of drastically adapting their choreography, a dance fusion of *hula* and *meke* was born.

Another example is the twelfth FOPA in Guam in 2016, where young Kanak (indigenous people of New Caledonia) dancers and musicians came with a sophisticated hip-hop performance. The audience reaction to the performance at the opening ceremony was rather poor, despite the extreme skill demonstrated by the breakdance with several large backflips. The next day's stage performance also lacked excitement, with the audience standing still. The following day's performance was entirely transformed: a fusion of the original hip-hop with reggae music and dancing. The plaza in front of the stage was soon filled with an enthusiastic crowd of dancing Islanders.

I asked one of the performers for the backstory. First, he said, when he saw Rapa Nui's dance performance with a large crowd, he felt the sense of unity that he wanted to create. He recognised that their hip-hop was difficult for the crowd to participate in, and suddenly blended hip-hop with reggae on stage. The other performers very smoothly and pleasantly adapted to accompany him. The audience's response was so positive that they kept the new blended style. He explained,

> They like hip-hop ok, but they are here to dance. Our hip-hop is too hard to follow, I think. Somehow it was reggae (that) come up. They can dance good reggae. We all love it you know, it's a Pacific music.

First, what is common to both *hula* and reggae here is the way in which '*ba*' arises, generated by FOPA as a place. The emergence of *ba* might be the moment a Kanak performer leans in to put in his first reggae step. Or it could be when the bassist started tapping out a reggae rhythm. Or maybe when the crowd started swaying their hips. Either way, those sounds and moves begin to resonate with each other, and amid the swirl that surrounds them, *ba* appears and drives people.

119

There is no musical score or plot there. Since the actions are driven by *ba*, the reasons for action can only be explained as 'somehow'. It is impossible to explain explicitly why it was reggae. But the ongoing reggae rhythms made the bodies sway, new lyrics were sung, and people kept flocking to the stage, reflexively completing a huge reggae scene. The same goes for *hula*.

Importantly, the performances created in these *ba* are not just spontaneous eruptions that then dissolve away entirely on the spot. As Mackley-Crump has argued, because FOPA as a place is made in an Oceanic way, the festival stage functions as a device to approve Oceanic culture, and variations that occur on stage are seen as new and authentic Oceania culture rather than anomalies. *Hula* is not Hawai'ian/East Polynesian, and reggae is not Caribbean, they are embraced and institutionalised as being Oceanic/Pacific.

Let me consider just one more case study. At the 12th FOPA in Guam in 2016, the Kanak delegates performed at Dededo. Since it was a grassy plaza with a flat stage, it was even easier for the excited audience to join the performers. As the performance was coming to an end, the Kanak delegation began their final 'dance for independence'. The performance was centred around the elders who continuously chanted into the microphone, with other performers encouraging participants to join in a whirling circle, chanting, clapping and singing. The bamboo percussion instruments continued to strike a monotonous rhythm. The harmonica played a monotonous melody. The chanting continued to urge the crowd to join the circle for independence. More and more people joined the circle, which grew larger and larger, as a light state of intoxication from dancing in circles encompassed the people.

I learned from interviews with participants that not all the people who joined the circle agreed with the idea of independence. Nevertheless, as I was myself, they were called in by the sounds, the whirlwind, or the heat emanating from the assemblage of bodies, and before they knew it, they were joining the circle. In short, the body resonates as it is thrust into *ba* and begins to make the gestures of 'dance for independence' without knowing it. The idea does not come first, but it will follow. A young Chamorro man, a local resident who participated in the performance, told me that, for the first time in his life, he began to think about the independence of Guam. Another Chamorro artist said his participation in the performance inspired him to learn more about the Kanak indigenous movement, and through the influence of Kanak friends he made here, he became involved in the Guam independence movement after FOPA. This highly nationally contextualised movement was experienced as a regional matter, part of the decolonisation of Oceania.[11]

The chants, the monotonous repetitive percussion, the swirling motion, the heat, and other elements of the performance are filled with affectionate devices. With the performance, an affectionate *ba* emerges, which draws new subjects into the performance, which reinforces *ba*. But affections are not enduring in nature. *Ba* dissolves with the convergence of performances. However, the residual of what emerged in affectionate *ba* (here the idea of an independence movement) will remain even after *ba* dissolves, because it reconnects to the place. Furthermore, in the context of the particular place (FOPA), it will be institutionalised in a way that is neither Guamese nor New Caledonian, but rather Oceanic, and will become a resource for next social movements.

In this way, after *ba* emerges from a place and dissolves away, the co-emerged Oceanic performance will be carried over to the place, institutionalised, and remain as culture. This is because *ba* is destined to dissolve away, while a place aims to endure. Through re-performance, the institutionalised and preserved performances in a place function as a source for the emergence of the next *ba* and the birth of the next Oceanic performance.

Creating Oceania: Discussion and conclusion

Finally, I will conclude by discussing the placeness of FOPA and *ba* that emerged from it in light of Hau'ofa's Oceania philosophy.

First, as we have seen, the basic concept of Oceania as a region integrated by the sea provides the underlying context shaping FOPA as a place. In particular, FOPA's postcolonial positioning, its aim of constructing regionalism, and its use of voyage imagery to provide a basis for regional unity, have much in common with Hau'ofa's Oceania concept.

However, as indicated by the fact that FOPA was called 'Pacific' rather than 'Oceania', the underlying idea was rather nationalistic. FOPA is very much an international event, and the delegates are representatives of their countries. The registration of delegates by country of origin defines FOPA's membership much more rigorously than Hau'ofa's vision of Oceania in which membership

---

[11] There was a sensational moment at the closing ceremony when a group of Guam delegates held up two banners that read 'Decolonize Oceania' and 'Free Guåhan'.

emerges through connections. Furthermore, FOPA's orientation towards the differentiation of national cultures is contrary to Hau'ofa's idea of Oceania. For FOPA, Pacific regionalism is envisioned as a cooperative relationship between countries with independent identities. By contrast, in Hau'ofa's Oceania, the shared and interconnecting sea (Oceania) is pre-eminent. For Hau'ofa, the islands in the sea result from the connection of the sea, in contrast to FOPA's prioritizing of islands (countries).

And yet, as we have seen in the previous section, the defining characteristics of Oceania emerged within the context of FOPA, and this was discussed as the emergence of *ba*. In particular, even though Hau'ofa did not directly commit to the operation of FOPA, we can see that FOPA unintentionally (but perhaps inevitably) manifested the characteristics of the Oceania that Hau'ofa imagined, and it was this environment that supported the emergence of *ba*. The principle of 'openness to the community', for example, blurs the boundary between producer (performer) and receiver (audience), which in turn blurs the subject/object dichotomy. It is not the Fijian dancers, Kanak performers nor the audience that created the *hula* or reggae performances. They co-emerge with *ba*, from the participation of all the actors. However, although the performances that appear (*hula* and reggae) are ephemeral and essentially dissolve with *ba*, they are installed in a place as a residual. Because the context of Oceania's production is based on the principle of participation, there is room in the social place to accommodate them. In other words, the process of artistic production through participation covers both a principle of place and a principle of *ba*.

When understood in this way, *ba* in FOPA does not emerge from nowhere. The place precedes and is embedded in the context, and *ba* emerges from that place. Since *ba* is driven by the affectionate principle, it has the nature of dissolving, and what is born in *ba* is essentially one-time, though with a residual. The residual will be installed in a place through institutionalisation: in a place, which aims to be rational and to endure, it will be repeated/re-performed and acts as a resource for the next *ba* to emerge. In this way a place and *ba* are established among wavering flows, requiring each other. And Hau'ofa's idea of Oceania encompasses both this principle of place and the principle of *ba* (see Figure 5.1). Hau'ofa is right in stating that cultural creation requires both traditional (repetitive performance) and contemporary (ephemeral performance), and that it is never created out of nothing.

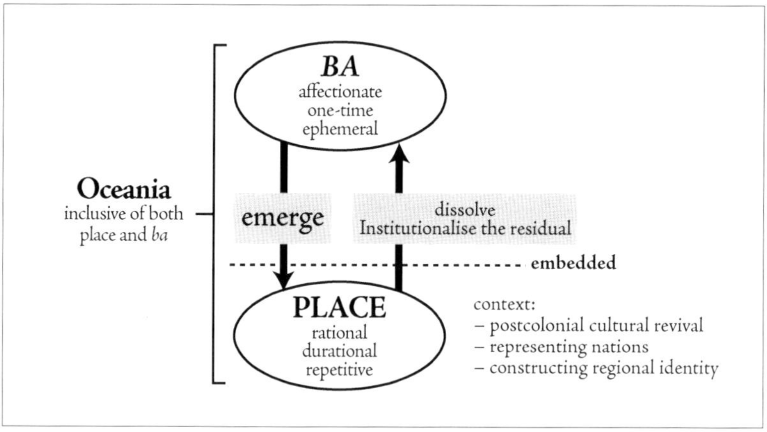

Figure 5.1. FOPA as place and *ba*

Thus, this paper has focused on the sense of unity that arises at FOPA and the pan-Oceanic culture that emerges within that sense of unity, by recognising the characteristics of FOPA as a place and *ba*, and considers them in terms of Hauʻofaʻs Oceania philosophy. Though Hauʻofa did not directly envision or operate FOPA, he was right in foreseeing that 'Oceania' arises in the artistic context, and we can see its emergence in FOPA. Especially it was important to understand that the wavering flow between place and *ba* shaped the creative aspect of FOPA and the world of Oceania. FOPA is not just a political arena nor tourist pastime, but is an essential part of Oceanic culture.

123

6. Performers' Two Bodies/ Double Consciousness

Performers and Traditional Repertoire in Tibetan Refugee Society

Tatsuya Yamamoto

Aims of this chapter

This chapter attempts to clarify the Tibetan performers' ambivalence towards policies to preserve and promote Tibetan traditional performing arts which seek to reproduce pre-1950s Tibet in Tibetan refugee societies.[1] Tibetan performers born and raised in India and Nepal have experienced a tension which splits their lives into conflicting temporalities of pre-1950s Tibet and contemporary India. Ambivalence about this has two effects. On the one hand, it has led Tibetan performers to make productive compromises between perceptions of pre-1950s Tibet and contemporary life in India, developing 'new' traditional repertoires and incorporating 'new' gestures into traditional repertoires. On the other hand, it has also functioned to blur their sense of identity as Tibetan refugees. In order to understand the mechanisms which bring both creativity and ambivalence to Tibetan refugee performers, this chapter focuses on the development of Tibetan nationalism within the Tibetan refugee societies and policies to preserve and promote Tibetan traditional performing arts as media for constructing Tibetan identity. It then analyzes the discourses and practices of Tibetan performers expressing such developments and policies on stages and in their daily lives. To better elucidate the diasporic antinomy bringing creativity and ambivalence among performers, this chapter combines Ernst Kantorowicz's 'two bodies' theory with Paul Gilroy's 'double consciousness' and explores what the antinomy brings to Tibetan performers and their lives. Analyzing and clarifying the diasporic antinomy embodied through their performances reveals how the 'co-emergence' of performing subjects and *ba* impacts on undetermined and uncertain processes of lived antinomy specific to Tibetan refugees.

---

[1] In this paper, pseudonyms are used for interviewees' names.

General information

Tibetan refugees have been fleeing to south Asian countries such as India, Nepal and Bhutan, and to Western countries since the (14th) Dalai Lama fled Tibet in 1959. According to the 2009 census, there are 127,935 Tibetan refugees in the world. Among them, 94,203 live in India and 13,514 live in Nepal. Tibetan refugees can be roughly classified into three clusters: Tibetans in the first wave leaving Tibet from 1959 to the end of the 1960s; the second wave leaving Tibet from 1979 to the beginning of the 1990s; and the third wave leaving Tibet since 1996. Sixty years since the first wave began in 1959, it is not uncommon to find Tibetan refugees in the first wave living together with third generation refugees. Although classified as Tibetan refugees, almost all the Tibetans born in India and Nepal have never been to Tibet and only know it from the discourses and images via various media and what 'new comers' bring to Tibetan refugee societies in India and Nepal.

His holiness the Dalai Lama established the Tibetan Government in Exile (TGiE)[2] as an institution to unite and govern Tibetan refugees after his exodus to India. To date, no country officially recognizes the TGiE; its international status is that of a pseudo-state. 125

The TGiE has emphasized the preservation of Tibetan culture. For instance, it says

> The purpose of the Tibetans in exile is two-fold, via., to seek justice for our homeland and, to preserve our identity and language by practicing our culture and traditions. The first purpose is dependent on many factors including international situation, political changes within China etc. that are beyond our control... [while] the second purpose is not dependent on external factors and can be fulfilled by every Tibetans [sic] in exile, irrespective of gender, age, and education, whether lay or monk/nun. (CTA 2003: 6; Roemer 2008: 67)

This clearly outlines the TGiE position and attitude towards Tibetan identity and culture. The TGiE has situated Tibetan culture as a core of Tibetan refugee identity in order to bind Tibetan refugees and resist 'cultural genocide' by the Chinese government. It has attempted to justify their political claim that Tibet was an independent country before the Chinese invasion in the 1950s by

---

[2] Although its official name is the Central Tibetan Administration (*dbus bod mi'i sgrig 'dzugs*), most Tibetan refugees use the Tibetan government (*bod gzhung*). Following their usage, this chapter uses the TGiE.

contrasting Tibetan culture against Han-centric culture in China, as Goldstein calls this situation the 'confrontation of representations' (Goldstein 1997: 56). For the TGiE, authentic Tibetan culture is the pre-1950s Tibetan culture which Tibetan refugees have been preserving outside Tibet; culture in Tibet under Chinese domination is regarded as inauthentic and unwanted.

As a governmental institution, the Tibetan Institute of Performing Arts (TIPA, *bod gzhung zlos gar tshogs pa*) has engaged in the cultural policies of the TGiE since 1959. It was originally called the Tibetan Music, Dance and Drama Society, but changed to the present name in the 1980s. According to its website, the TIPA "aims to preserve and promote Tibetan musical heritage and associated arts". It insists that "dance and music are integral parts of Tibetan culture and tradition".[3] The TIPA has committed to preserving the pre-exilic repertoire of Tibetan dance, music and drama as condensing Tibetan ways of life, and to promote such performing arts to awaken Tibetan identity among refugees. Especially, it has sought to attract the attention of Tibetan youth who are more enthusiastic about Bollywood music and Western pop than with traditional Tibetan culture. It has also called for the unity of Tibetan refugees through performing the traditional culture repertoire, and for disseminating information about Tibetan issues to audiences both within and outside Tibet. It had 51 performers, 31 male and 20 female in 2008. Forty-six of the 51 were born in India or Nepal. As civil servants, they are salaried employees, but their income was relatively less than other civil servants such as teachers and office workers in the TGiE.

The TIPA's performance is roughly classified into several clusters like the traditional program, the contemporary program featuring their group the 'Aakama', the Tibetan Opera (Ache Lhamo) performed in Shoton (*zhos ton*) every March or April, and the summer festival called 'Yarkyi' (*dbyar skyid*) in August. Additionally, TIPA's performers tour Tibetan refugee settlements in South India and foreign countries and participate in events such as arts festivals in India. Through these activities, the TIPA has attempted to teach Tibetan refugees the importance of preserving and promoting Tibetan culture, and to incite their sense of responsibility to help do so. This chapter focuses on the traditional program and performers' recollections after their stage performances.

126

---

[3] https://tipa.asia/about/introduction/

Photo 6.1 TIPA stage performance

TIPA's traditional performances:
Making the present 'the past'

127

As the TIPA aims "To preserve and promote the age-old folk music, opera and dance tradition of Tibet", its performers explained to me that they have been preserving the authentic repertoire of pre-1950s Tibetan culture. In order to preserve and perform authentic Tibetan dances and songs in front of an audience, performers must learn and practice the traditional repertoire. Tibetan residents in Dharamshala generally recognize TIPA's performers, and the performers are aware that they are seen that way.

As mentioned, the traditional program constitutes TIPA's main activities. While this program is addressed to foreign supporters and tourists, including Indian citizens, it is also performed in the lunar new year for Tibetan settlements in India. They usually perform for around 150 minutes including intermission. The program includes diverse songs and dances from different Tibetan areas. If you ask them about their program, they will confidently answer that it is an opportunity to touch authentic Tibetan culture.

However, these songs and dances are not performed under the same setting as they were in pre-1950s Tibet. For instance, there was reportedly no clear division between performers and bystanders in Tibet, and the repertoire was deeply embedded in everyday life. However, after 1959, the situation drastically changed: TIPA now performs the repertoire on stages in India and foreign countries using modern microphones and lighting. The modern equipment has become indispensable to their performance. By combining modern tools with the traditional repertoire on stages, these performers invite their audiences to experience "the age-old folk music, opera and dance tradition of Tibet".

The backdrops with images of scenes in Tibet – such as the Potala palace, which was the Dalai Lamas' residence; the Jokhang temple, built by Songtsen Gampo, the founder of the Tibetan empire; Norbulingka, the Dalai Lamas' second house; and Mt. Kailash – play an important role in TIPA's modern stage settings. By putting these images of Tibet on the stages, TIPA's director and performers attempt to visually convert the venues for their performance into 'Tibet'. Although almost all of these songs and dances from different areas in Tibet gathered in the traditional program had never been performed in front of the Potala Palace and Jokhang temple, performers 'Tibetanize' each venue for their performance by linking the traditional Tibetan songs and dances from different areas to symbolic and visually representative places in Tibet. The process of 'Tibetanization' turns out to whitewash the traces of each place and transform the concrete places into an abstract 'Tibet' which never existed. In this sense, while they attempt to 'Tibetanize' each venue for their performance, the process makes each place a 'non-place' (cf. Auge 1995).

128

Furthermore, this 'Tibetanization' process makes pre-1950s Tibet the temporal venues for the performance. On the stages, TIPA's performers perform traditional songs and dances which TIPA claims preserve the authentic repertoire of pre-1950s Tibet, free of Chinese influence. The audience is welcome to admire this supposedly authentic pre-1950s Tibetan culture visualized on the stage with the backdrop scenes of Tibet. The temporality that performers produce by performing the repertoire of authentic pre-1950s Tibetan culture is both the present when Tibetan refugees live outside Tibet and a past which had never existed in Tibet. As the process of 'Tibetanization' makes the places 'non-place', it also makes the time for their performance 'non-time'. Therefore, TIPA's traditional performances visually and aurally 'Tibetanize' each venue.

While their past-oriented performances manifest abstract 'Tibetanization', separating cultural and substantial meanings from concrete places and times, it also 'Tibetanizes' the performers themselves. Their pre-1950s-oriented repertoire basically has no space for individual creativity and subjectivity. The performers are instructed to be true to the prescribed forms of the repertoire and to reproduce it. Each performance must be performed in the same way regardless of who the performer is. For instance, the court music 'Nangma' and folksongs from Toe area 'Toeshay' are the most basic among TIPA's repertoire and have a notation book written by an instructor of TIPA for Tibetan guitar players. Every TIPA performer has been trained to play every song in this notation book in the prescribed way. Although each player's personal technique is somehow observed, the instructor's playing style is regarded as correct and the closeness to his style and taste is appreciated as correct and good performance. These normalized songs and dances are performed on stage as ideal and authentic for the audience.

Additionally, performing collectively tends to negate individual idiosyncrasies. Because many performers sing and dance on the stage together, it is quite difficult for audience members to identify individual performers and recognize their idiosyncrasies, except perhaps family and friends. For most of the audience, the performers on the stage become anonymous through this setting. And these anonymized performers are substitutable due to the normalized format of the traditional repertoire. Conversation between male and female performers featured on the stage clearly shows the substitutability of performers. To depict typical scenes from everyday life in the Tibet of memory, performers have added conversational pieces to the program. The lines of dialogue are scripted to be true to 'authentic' Tibetan conversation, and each performer repeats the normalized dialogue. Thus, normalizing the repertoire and performers has been the most important method in TIPA.

129

The eradication of idiosyncrasy from performers on stage has played a crucial role in preserving the songs and dances of the pre-1950s Tibet. The anonymized performers in front of the backdrop with symbolic scenery can serve as a medium to awaken the targeted Tibetan audience to their responsibilities for preserving and promoting authentic Tibetan culture. Its faceless substitutability enables Tibetan audiences to picture themselves in the anonymized performers' place, because both performers and audience are Tibetans, and both are committed to achieving their two-fold aims of seeking justice for their homeland and preserving their identity and language. TIPA's stages are always oriented to the pre-1950s Tibet and simultaneously 'homogeneous empty space and time' (cf. Anderson 1983) without any ground of 'when', 'where' and 'who'.

Situation of performers engaged in traditional performance

While the performers are anonymized and rendered substitutable through the preservation and promotion of pre-1950s Tibetan culture, they were born and have grown up in the contemporary world, far from the abstract time and space of 'pre-1950s Tibet'. Once they finish their daily training or stage performance, they appear as substantial persons who are different from the anonymized and homogeneous performers preserving and promoting Tibetan culture. Performers in their twenties or thirties with whom I am familiar loved singing and dancing but did not necessarily show much enthusiasm for traditional Tibetan songs and dances. As mentioned, most of them were born and have grown up in India and Nepal as second- and later-generation Tibetan refugees who have not experienced Tibet firsthand. Thus, while they undoubtedly know much about Tibet, their understanding is based on indirect information through tourists' remarks, articles in the media and knowledge provided through school education. For instance, when I arrived at Dharamshala via Tibet in 2006, some performers asked me to show them pictures taken in Tibet and to talk about my impressions of Tibet. In this sense, Tibet has been an indispensable, albeit imaginary, part of their lives.

While performers experienced a disjuncture between themselves and Tibet, India's influence has been apparent. Having been born in India, most performers demonstrate a strong attachment to Indian popular culture. For instance, one of the common topics among them was the latest Bollywood movies and they occasionally went to clubs to dance to Bollywood tunes. Generally speaking, Tibetan songs and dances do not have space in their everyday lives. The hobbies and topics they were familiar with were not much different from those of local Indian youth.

Furthermore, Indian food culture has had a strong influence on their taste. If I went out with performers, they were likely to order Indian dishes such as tandoori chicken or chicken curry, not Tibetan cuisine. If I said I wanted to eat Tibetan food, they immediately rejected my demand, or reluctantly agreed because they knew I had not had a chance to have Tibetan dishes in Japan. Thus, their preference was basically for Indian food over Tibetan food. Recently, restaurants serving Chinese dishes have been increasingly numerous in Dharamshala and have also attracted performers. In the early 2010s, during an outbreak of self-immolations, both in Tibet and in exile, there were calls for 'patriots' to participate in the Lhakar movement, which made claims on Tibetan cultural fundamentalism and demanded that Tibetans eat vegetarian Tibetan dishes. As civil servants, many performers participated in the movement and told me that they do not eat meat on Wednesday. However, they did not hide their preference for Indian non-veg dishes even then.

Indian influences also appeared in their verbal communications. We can easily find Hindi phrases within our conversations in Tibetan. For instance, these performers used Hindi phrases like *chutti* (holiday), *chappal* (sandal) and *aaloo* (potatoes) and rarely replaced them with Tibetan phrases. They also unintentionally repeated 'Indian' gestures like ways of nodding the head and making a fool of others. Those 'Indian' gestures became quite common and natural for them.

Thus, when we look at the everyday lives of performers, it is apparent that they have embodied both Tibetan and local Indian tastes and practices. While they attempted to create 'homogeneous empty time and space' on stage by performing pre-1950s Tibetan dances and songs, their everyday lives in India reveal a 'heterogeneous time and place' (cf. Chatterjee 2004) based on their substantial experiences of living together with others from different backgrounds.

Performers' two bodies/ double consciousness

To elucidate the duality that these performers have lived, let us consider Kantorowicz's theory of 'the king's two bodies' (Kantorowicz 1957) alongside Paul Gilroy's 'double consciousness' theory (Gilroy 1993). As Kantorowicz said, kings in medieval Europe lived two bodies, that is, a 'body natural', a monarch's corporeal and mortal body and a 'body politic' an immortal political body. The former is the substantial body of each individual; its death means the king changes. The latter is the status of the king and its body never dies. The 'body politic' doesn't entail any substantial idiosyncrasy, is abstract, and somewhat anonymous. According to Kantorowicz's understanding of these two bodies of medieval European kings, the 'body politic' was superior, filled as it is with mysterious powers that ameliorate the imperfections of mortal human nature (the 'body natural').

131

Kantorowicz's conception of the king's two bodies is useful in considering the bodies of nations/refugees living under the nation-state order (cf. Malkki 1995). National belonging is passed onto descendants through reproduction although every substantial individual is destined to die. In this case, each individual body is the 'body natural' and the body with a nationality is the 'body politic'. While only certain subjects manifested two bodies in medieval Europe, the subject with 'two bodies' became ubiquitous under the modern nation-state system.

Gilroy's argument about double consciousness is a response to a Black self-consciousness constructed through the Atlantic slave trade. Du Bois was the first to note the Black's double consciousness, but Gilroy rearticulates it, saying "I want to suggest that Du Bois produced this concept at the junction point of his philosophical and psychological interests not just to express the distinctive standpoint of Black Americans but also to illuminate the experience of post-slave populations in general" (Gilroy 1993: 126). Gilroy says,

> Double consciousness emerges from the unhappy symbiosis between three modes of thinking, being, and seeing. The first is racially particularistic, the second nationalistic in that it derives from the nation state in which the ex-slaves but not-yet-citizens find themselves, rather than from their aspiration toward a nation state of their own. The third is diasporic or hemispheric, sometimes global and occasionally universalist. (Gilroy 1993: 127)

For Gilroy, the term double consciousness refers to the fundamental diasporic antinomy of being both Black and American. Focusing on being either Black or American fails to explain the self-experience; on the contrary, subjects have to encounter a "doubling effect" which cannot be resolved by assimilation in either side (Gilroy 1993: 159). Gilroy's idea of double consciousness can be attributed to other diasporic individuals and communities who have found themselves living as both a member of a diasporic community and of a host country.

As we have seen, Tibetan refugee performers also experience two bodies and double consciousness. Those born and raised in the 'heterogeneous time and place' of India have been simultaneously embodying and generating the 'homogeneous empty time and space' of pre-1950s Tibet. These performers have lived two bodies: 'an idiosyncratic natural body in contemporary India and a substitutable national body pinned to the abstract past,' and a double consciousness: 'recognizing the fact that they were born and grew up outside Tibet and that they are Tibetan.'

At this point, we need to focus on Gilroy's remark on the "doubling effect". He says that the dichotomy brings about everlasting conflict based on the fundamental antinomy for each diasporic individual. If one aspect becomes prominent in self-consciousness, the other immediately appears and existentially confuses the subject. Thus, the substantial individual is required to sit on the fence of the two bodies and double consciousness. This position can provide the individual with space for creativity, or it can be alienating and generate difficulties that the individual cannot handle alone. From the performers' perspective, their engagement in the traditional Tibetan repertoire may provide opportunities to demonstrate their creative potential, and simultaneously lock them into a dilemma, the state of 'no way out'. Tibetan refugee performers born in India and Nepal have been living these two bodies and double consciousness with the diasporic antinomy appearing as creative and ambivalent in the Tibetan refugee way of life.

Effects of two bodies/double consciousness

These performers have lived contemporary 'heterogeneous time and space' while simultaneously living and performing the abstract 'homogeneous empty time and space' of pre-1950s Tibet. This antinomy has enabled them to create something new in their own ways. As noted above, because of their aim to preserve and promote pre-1950s Tibetan culture, performers are expected to not revise or transform the traditional repertoire of Tibetan songs and dances. Nevertheless, performers have attempted different approaches to the repertoire without changing the format and content. For instance, when four male performers played a song 'dramnyen shaptro' for foreign tourists in Dharamshala, one performer suddenly urged the audience to clap their hands and the audience complied. Although I had never previously seen such a direction in this song on the stage, encouraging the audience to clap their hands subsequently became a standard part of the song's performance. When I asked the performer to tell me why he urged the audience to clap their hands, he said 'I just wanted to attract their attention. Then that idea came to my mind. It worked well, didn't it?'

As with the instance above, in order to attract an audience's attention, performers have made myriad adjustments, such as translating the lines of scripted conversations on stage. For instance, they performed for a group of Japanese during my stay in Dharamshala. Before the performance, one of the performers asked me to translate the conversation into Japanese, which was warmly appreciated by the Japanese audience.

Simply speaking, these instances of creativity contradict their original aim of reproducing the time and space of the pre-1950s Tibet. As mentioned, most songs and dances performed by TIPA did not originally presume a clear division between the performers and audience but were embedded within everyday life in Tibet. Hence, performers' efforts to attract the audience's attention appear to be intrinsically deviant because they do not conform to the pre-1950s Tibetan scheme, as some audience members have told me. In this sense, such efforts are incompatible with the 'Tibetanization' of time and space on stage.

Furthermore, while TIPA's performers don't make changes to the existing repertoire, the logic of preservation could be shaken when they 'unearth' songs and dances. TIPA's performers are divided into two group and compete with each other every August. In this competition, they uncover an as-yet-unknown traditional song or dance and perform it on stage in front of TIPA's director and other members of TGiE. For a month, these performers go to visit older generations of Tibetan refugees in Dharamshala or other Tibetan settlements in order to discover unknown songs and dances.

However, this annual challenge is increasingly difficult, as the competitors' predecessors have already discovered most traditional songs and dances, and because the first-generation Tibetan refugees on whom they depend are getting older and fewer in number. Under these circumstances, some performers choose the pragmatic option. If they could not find a complete version of an unknown traditional song or dance, they combined the fragmented information about it with the existing repertoire. After interlinking the existing part to the unknown one, they perform it as pre-1950s Tibetan culture in front of TIPA's director and other members of TGiE. For instance, a group of performers got fragmented information about a song from the Kongpo area. They decided to perform it for this year's competition but could not find a complete version of it. After some discussions, they decided to combine this fragment with the existing repertoire from Kongpo. Their performance in front of the guests was highly appreciated and was the winner that year. Since then, the song has been presented to Tibetan refugees and foreign audiences as traditional (pre-1950s) Tibetan culture.

Beyond the narratives above, there are multiple justifications for recreating songs and dances in the name of the pre-1950s Tibetan culture. For instance, Tashi said to me, 'As you know, TIPA says that we have been preserving the pre-1950s Tibetan culture. But I believe that every traditional culture is indispensably destined to be mixed with the contemporary and different culture. No way to avoid it. I think that the pre-1950s Tibetan culture must have also gone through different transformations by encountering other cultures.' As a Tibetan who has lived both the contemporary 'heterogeneous time and place' and the 'homogeneous empty time and space' of pre-1950s Tibet, Tashi analogically interlinks his experience on modifying Tibetan culture in India to the pre-1950s Tibetans' experiences. Through this analogy, he confirms the changes TIPA's performers have made as unavoidable and somehow denies the validity of the TGiE and TIPA's logic to pin down traditional Tibetan songs and dances to pre-1950s Tibet.

Thus, performers engaging in preserving and promoting pre-1950s Tibetan culture cannot stay within the 'homogeneous empty time and space' of pre-1950s Tibet because they have lived the 'heterogeneous time and place' outside Tibet. To performers, the traditional Tibetan songs and dances are objects to be performed in the substantial time and place. These songs and dances sometimes demand a limited creative input from the performers, too. Performers' creative practices like urging handclapping and translating dialogue into different languages result from interactions between performers and an audience in a particular time and place. Recreating unknown songs and dances is a sign of creative decision-making in the face of limited and fragmented information, and competition time limits. In a sense, the tension between obligations to pre-1950s Tibet and living in contemporary India has led performers to be productively self-reflexive of what they can do creatively under restricted conditions.

Unresolved ambivalence of two bodies/ double consciousness

The gap between the 'homogeneous empty time and space' and the 'heterogeneous time and place' does not promise positive results for diasporic performers, thrown into the antinomy of living two bodies/double consciousness. Let us now explore how this antinomy has been negatively experienced.

First, we should examine the ambivalence performers feel about living with two bodies/double consciousness. As performers of TIPA, they have focused on what the performing arts groups in Tibet are doing. As the TGiE has been promoting Tibetan culture and making political claims both inside and outside the Tibetan refugee societies through TIPA's activities, the Chinese have also been attempting to justify their policies on ethnic minorities in China and their claims to Tibet through government-run performing arts groups. All of TIPA's performers consider songs and dances by these groups to be Sinicized. For instance, when we watched Tibetan cultural programs on TV together, they pointed out Sinicized elements of the songs and dances performed by the government-run arts group. By saying 'what TIPA has been preserving and promoting is the authentic Tibetan culture', they attempted to differentiate their performances from the state-run Tibetan performing arts groups.

At the same time, the fact that they have never been to Tibet undermines confidence in the claim that they are guardians of authentic Tibetan culture. For instance, when I joined some senior performers to watch the Chinese government-run Tibetan performing arts group on TV, after commenting that their performance had been Sinicized, one of them stated 'Although their performance is inauthentic, I think there are authentic and as-yet-unknown songs and dances in Tibet'. Other performers agreed, saying: 'There are more songs and dances in Tibet than we know. I am sure our performance is based on the authentic Tibetan culture but the songs and dances we have recognized are just a part of all the songs and dances in Tibet'. The recognition that there would be more authentic songs and dances in Tibet brings some sense of inferiority to their claim of authenticity. The fact that they do not have access to Tibet forces recognition that their claims to authentic knowledge of Tibetan culture are unavoidably limited. The disjuncture between regarding themselves as protectors of authentic Tibetan culture while recognizing the limits of their knowledge of Tibetan culture highlights the difficulties these performers face.

The ambivalence of living with two bodies/double consciousness affects not only their engagement with the repertoire, but also their sense of belonging. Tenzin, a junior performer, exemplifies this dilemma. Tenzin was born in Dehradun, India, as a second-generation Tibetan refugee and grew up in TIPA's dormitory. He is highly inquisitive and a voracious reader. When I went on tour with TIPA, I had numerous opportunities to talk with him because my mattress in the dormitory was next to his. After other performers went to sleep, Tenzin took me outside to talk about a variety of themes. Midnight chats outside the dormitory became a daily routine.

After a performance in the Kollegal Tibetan settlement, he asked whether Tibet will be independent of China. I tried to answer his question honestly, but then he declared 'I can't have a strong sense of being a Tibetan'. He said that he felt uncomfortable and found the other performers' strong sense of identity as Tibetan refugees difficult. He also said that because he was born in India and didn't know much about Tibet, he couldn't identify himself with Tibetans in general, which made it difficult to concentrate on his role in preserving and promoting the pre-1950s Tibetan culture, although he is employed as a performer in TIPA. The 'heterogeneous time and place' where Tenzin has lived always intrudes on the 'homogeneous empty time and space' of pre-1950s Tibet pursued by the TGiE and TIPA. This reality made him uncomfortable when he talked about Tibet or heard narratives of longing for it. Tenzin felt alienated from the 'homogeneous empty time and space' of pre-1950s Tibet although he has engaged in Tibetanizing time and space on stage for audiences.

Tenzin's anxiety about his Tibetan refugee identity often emerged in public. After a show in Kalimpong, West Bengal, local Tibetan refugees offered us dinner. I shared a table with Tenzin and some friends. We drank many glasses of Tibetan rice beer and went to the toilet before leaving the dinner. Then we found Phuntsok coming from the toilet. Phuntsok was born in Tibet and came to India in the late 1990s. Suddenly Tenzin pushed him behind the toilet's door. He started shouting 'I am not like you, the newcomer!' and kicked the door repeatedly. A few of us managed to get him to stop and calm down, after which we all decided to head back to the guesthouse.

After a few days, I talked with Tenzin about his outburst towards Phuntsok. Tenzin began to talk about how newcomers behave differently from Tibetans born in India. Although Tenzin has been engaged in constructing Tibetan refugee identity through cultural performance, he felt compelled to exclude newcomers from the fold, even while feeling alienated from that fold himself.

Tenzin's case might appear exceptional if we rely on his perception that other performers were more self-confident in saying 'I am a Tibetan refugee'. However, some performers are discomfited by the tension between the preservation motive that locks them into pre-1950s Tibet and the fact that they live in contemporary India. They were all reluctant to share these feelings with each other, as far as I could tell. For instance, Samrap told me 'I am like a leftover. I couldn't fit into American way of life and decided to come back to India. I couldn't take advantage of my political status as a Tibetan very well. I can't behave like other Tibetans.' He also said 'I know I should not say this because I have been employed by a governmental institution. But, for the future generation including my son, sticking to Tibet won't result in a successful future. Tibet will be too tight shoes for them.' Another performer who moved to the U.S. also spoke to me of his ambivalence to take advantage of his Tibetan nationality. While it has benefited him, he has also been frustrated by the demands of Western supporters to conform to ideal images of Tibetan. He said 'I was born in India as a lay Tibetan. But some Westerners want me to behave like a Tibetan monk from Tibet! They don't regard me as a Tibetan living contemporarily.' It appears that these performers were more comfortable speaking about these things to me, an outsider to the Tibetan refugee communities, and were reluctant to talk about personal impressions and conflicts with their Tibetan friends because such statements might be interpreted as evidence of their lack of loyalty to Tibetan issues. These remarks are intended to highlight their ambivalence: feeling that they cannot be exemplary Tibetans because they were not born and raised in Tibet.

Thus, for Tibetan performers living two bodies/double consciousness, their diasporic antinomy appeared both positively and negatively. Engaging in a cultural and political campaign proclaiming their authenticity as Tibetans although they have never been to Tibet has negatively impacted their self-confidence in claiming to be guardians of authentic Tibetan culture. Performers like Tenzin and Samrap, who confessed ambivalence about the ideal Tibetan identity, illustrate the hardships of living the antinomy of two bodies/double consciousness.

Conclusion

This chapter explored the antinomy of Tibetan refugee performers, focusing on their practices and narratives. The performances on which this chapter focused are based on Richard Schechner's argument which treats stage performances and everyday practices in the same way (Schechner 2003). This chapter attempted to describe reflexive movements between stage performances by performers and their everyday practices. Performers in TIPA not only concentrated on their own performances but also paid attention to and reflexively interpreted others' behaviors and narratives on or behind stages. These reflexive movements have constantly built up their subjectivity. The 'performing subject' is emerged in *ba* as the event where these reflexive movements have been substantiated. 'A performer demanding an audience clap their hands,' 'a performer mixing different songs in the name of the Tibetan tradition,' 'a performer violently differentiating himself from a newcomer performer' exemplify the 'performing subjects' emerging from each concrete *ba* where they lived.

And these 'performing subjects' reflexively produce *ba* a little behind the emergence of *ba* which produced these 'performing subjects.' The *ba* where the audience clapped hands in response to the performer's demand, the *ba* which the audience produced by qualifying the performer's reconstitution of authentic Tibetan tradition, and the *ba* which became awkward by discriminating Phuntsok show how the *ba* reflexively emerged through the performances by the 'performing subjects.' At the concrete time and place, performing subjects and *ba* reflexively co-emerge.

In addition, these co-emerging *ba* and performing subjects live in a sustaining temporality. Performers' two bodies/double consciousness matters on this issue of temporality. Since their birth in India or Nepal, their ancestors and the TGiE have repeatedly told the performers that they were originally rooted in Tibet. They have created the 'homogeneous empty time and space' of pre-1950s Tibet through preserving and promoting Tibetan culture on stage, and the performers have been expected to identify themselves with the history of Tibet in exile. However, these performers were born and raised in India and Nepal in their own 'heterogeneous time and place.' In this sense, at the concrete *ba*, performers have experienced each event as splitting them between a vector commanding preservation and authenticity and one demanding self-transformation. As a Tibetan refugee, each performer is destined to act in the concrete *ba*, and incidents in this *ba* are experienced as occurring somewhere in the middle of 'homogeneous empty time and space' and 'heterogeneous time and place.' If the 'heterogeneous time and place' took precedence over 'homogeneous empty time and space', a creative performing subject emerged with the specific *ba*. If the 'homogeneous empty time and space' took precedence, a subject suffering from ambivalence emerged with the *ba*. They have been stuck somewhere in the middle of 'homogeneous empty time and space' and 'heterogeneous time and place' because they cannot fully belong to either. This indeterminate diasporic antinomy has substantially formed the Tibetan refugee-specific way of life.

The Introduction to this volume notes that *ba* appears and is experienced as uncertain and contingent. Hence, *ba* is substantially interlinked with uncertainty and contingency. However, the cases in this chapter show that uncertainty and contingency can appear in different ways. In the case of Tibetan refugees, uncertainty and contingency appear as a diasporic antinomy based on two bodies/double consciousness, the antinomy between the 'homogeneous empty time and space' and 'heterogeneous time and place'. This chapter suggests that anthropologically exploring the matters of *ba* will lead us to consider the multiple ways that *ba* and performing subjects co-emerge.

139

7. Conflicts Create *Ba* and Agency

How E.A.B.I.C. Rastafarians Occupy the World

Shuji Kamimoto

Introduction

Some people have been violently deprived of their territory and their history. This is hard to imagine for others who are fortunate enough to accept the fiction that their history has evolved continuously in their region with little difficulty (Furuya 2001: 53). In this chapter, I will discuss how *ba* arises and agency co-emerges among people who share a particular diasporic mindset. This study focuses on the Ethiopia Africa Black International Congress (Hereinafter referred to as E.A.B.I.C.), a denomination of Rastafari in Jamaica.

Jamaica has a pyramid-shaped social hierarchy with a small number of white people at the top. Poor Blacks near the bottom of this hierarchy are the main adherents of Rastafari. Rastafari is a religious and ideological practice that developed among people living in the slums of the capital Kingston in the 1930s. A practitioner of Rastafari is called a Rastafarian (in short, Rasta). Rastafari's core belief is that Haile Selassie 1st (Rastas call him Haile Selassie I), the Ethiopian emperor crowned on 2 November 1930, is a savior for Black people. The idealization of Africa and the desire to return to Africa are widely shared by Rastas because most Black ancestors were slaves forcibly brought to Jamaica in the Atlantic slave trade. More importantly, the Rastas saw African diasporas as akin to the people of Israel in the Bible and have created a unique African ethos that can be practiced in everyday life. This was a challenge to Jamaican society, where British norms were highly valued. However, Rastafari does not have an originating Scripture. Instead, Rastas have created their ethos by adding their own interpretations to the Bible, daily events, and world history. Therefore, although there are beliefs and assertions that they generally share, there is no consensus. Likewise, there is no over-arching organization that governs Rastafarian groups.

Simpson (1955) and Smith et al. (1960) are pioneering studies on Rastafari. These studies based on fieldwork revealed Rastafari's ideas, beliefs, and assertions, which had been unclear until then. While Simpson analyzed Rastafari as one of many Black cults in the West Indies, Smith and his colleagues tried to understand it as a social problem of urban poor people. They concluded that "the movement is rooted in unemployment" (Smith et al. 1960: 28) and insisted that the government should take care of this situation (Nettleford 1970: 73).[1] As a result, the government asked several African countries to accept Rasta's 'returning', but none were interested, because most Rasta's were unskilled workers.

Since the 1960s, Rastafari's status in Jamaican society has changed. Before independence in 1962, Jamaica needed a new nationalism that would unify its people. As can be seen in the national motto declared at the time, "Out of many, one people," creole nationalism was accepted to unite the diversity of the ethnic and racial groups. In this way, selected Afro-Jamaican practices – intensive and secular rituals, speech patterns, food, musical forms, and dance associated with the rural peasantry – were legitimized, at least to some extent, by the state (Thomas 2004: 4–5). In 1968, the Black Power movement was growing at the Mona campus of the University of the West Indies and activists embraced Rastafarian ideology. Subsequently, Rasta's activities in reggae music and arts such as painting and sculpture have come to prominence, and Rastafari practices and attitudes towards Africa have inspired mainstream society. As a result, Rastafari has changed from social outcast to bearer of Jamaican popular culture (Edmonds 2003: 126). As Rastafari's status has grown and solidified in Jamaican society, and with Jamaica's independence from British colonialism, the passion for returning to Africa which had peaked in the 1950s dissipated and most Rastas changed their objective to "Africanizing" Jamaica (Barrett 1997 (1988): 117).

141

What I want to highlight here is the fact that for Rastafari, Africa has always been an important symbol and object for interpretations as biblical, historical, and everyday events, all of which is interwoven in their beliefs and practices. Although Rastafari has become a "part of the taken-for-granted landscape" of Jamaican society (Callam 1980: 43; Edmonds 2003: 126), its perception of time and space is totally different from others'. The implications of these differences will be discussed in this paper. As Clifford wrote, "peoples whose sense of identity is centrally defined by collective histories of displacement and violent loss cannot be 'cured' by merging into a new national community" and "Positive articulations of diaspora identity reach outside the normative territory and temporality (myth/

---

[1] Nettleford, one of the authors of the University Report, wrote "The process of becoming Rastafarian is still regarded by the wider society as one of mental deterioration and the recent embrace of the creed by the young educated high school and university graduates is seen as an urgent matter for the psychiatrist" (Nettleford 1970: 56).

history) of the nation-state" (Clifford 1997: 250–251). That is, Rastafari is not confined to the normative territory and temporality of Jamaica, and the conflict between Rastafari and opposing forces is a key factor in Rastafari's survival. Hence, the questions in this paper are: Where Rastafari clashes with the normative territory and time of the nation state, what kinds of *ba* and agencies are emerging?

Outline of survey sites and objects

According to Jamaica's 2011 census, of its 2,683,707 population, Black people accounted for 92.11%, mixed race for 6.06%, Indian (South Asian) people for 0.75%, Chinese people for 0.19%, white people for 0.16%, and 0.72% report identifying as "other". As for religion, 67.54% identify with one of the Christian sects, while only 1.08% identify as Rasta (Statistical Institute of Jamaica 2014: xiv–xv). However, since for many "Rastafari is not a religion but a way of life", it is likely that some proportion of Rastas were included in the 21.32% who answered they had no religion.

E.A.B.I.C. is based in the Bobo Shanti commune, located in the hills of the coastal town Bull Bay in St. Andrew Parish, the most populous city in Jamaica. St. Andrew Parish is next to Kingston Parish. Bull Bay used to be a fishing village, but today most residents commute to work in Kingston, about 14 kilometers away. The Bobo Shanti commune began in the early 1970s and now occupies 40,000 square meters. Members of the E.A.B.I.C. are generally called Bobos.

Bobos worship the founder Emmanuel Charles Edwards, and Marcus Garvey, a national hero and the founder of the Universal Negro Improvement Association (UNIA), as well as Haile Selassie 1ˢᵗ. In a sense, as the founder of E.A.B.I.C., Emmanuel is a priest while Garvey is a prophet, and Selassie is the king of OAU (Organization of African Unity) – but they share the same soul and the mission to save Black people. They are called the holy trinity of E.A.B.I.C. The E.A.B.I.C. textbook, *Black Supremacy in Righteousness of Salvation*, calls Emmanuel "The Lord Servant""The Black Christ in Flesh""The Man of Justice in Flesh""Creation Crown Champion of Human Rights""Founder, Leader, President, God and King of the E.A.B.I.C." (E.A.B.I.C. 1978: 36 D) and "Freedom Fighter for Black People at Home and Abroad" (ibid: 70). What kind of person was given such titles?

Emmanuel was born in 1909 or 1911 to parents of the syncretic religion, Pocomania (Revival, which now claims 1.35% of Jamaicans as practitioners) the Black River of St. Elizabeth Parish in western Jamaica. He moved to Kingston in 1933. It seems that he initially practiced Pocomania but gradually became Rasta while living in Kingston. Emmanuel earned a living by working as a painter, a baker, and selling shaved ice and glacés with a few colleagues, until around 1941 when he began working as a carpenter for the Jamaica Defence Force (Newland 1994: 3; van Dijk 1993: 117).

He organized an island-wide convention at Ackee Walk in Kingston where his camp was first set up on 1 March 1958 as a Rasta calling for a return to Africa. This was about the time that Ghana gained its independence from Britain, led by President Kwame Nkrumah who had expressed sympathy for Marcus Garvey. At this time, the British colonies in the Caribbean began agitating for a new federation. Around the world, expectations for liberation from colonialism were rising. Emmanuel's three-week convention was the biggest repatriation convention ever, making him one of the most famous Rastafari leaders. Chevannes wrote "following the convention, Prince's [Emmanuel's] followers became more sectarian." and "They began to attribute divinity to him and separated themselves from other Rastafarians by wearing the turbans and the robes" (Chevannes 1994: 173).[2] Emmanuel kept headquarters of E.A.B.I.C. in Ackee Walk until they were evicted in a slum cleanup in 1968. After that, they kept moving in search of a suitable place for their headquarters. In October 1969, the headquarters was set on fire, and 36 members living on a mountain in the suburbs were arrested on charges of squatting.

Construction of the present commune began in 1972. Bobos worked hard to build relationships with local residents. Bobos first built the palace and tabernacle for Emmanuel, and then gradually built communal quarters for the congregation and rooms and houses for individuals. They wanted to be self-sufficient to some extent. Chevannes says that in the late 1970s beans and leafy vegetables were planted inside the commune (Chevannes 1994: 173). Although the E.A.B.I.C. and Bobo Shanti still exist, the death of Emmanuel in May 1994 marked a major change in the way E.A.B.I.C was managed. After Emmanuel's death, the administration of the commune was left to a 33-member committee headed by priests and a 14-member parliament. However, many people left the commune after his death. Some ex-bobos built a small commune on the hill next to Bobo Shanti. Since the mid-1990s, the name E.A.B.I.C. has become widely known inside and outside Jamaica by dancehall dee-jays trained in the Bobo Shanti, such as Sizzla and Capleton.

143

---

[2] In 1959, Emmanuel invited Claudius Henry, the leader of African Reform Church, to hold a convention at Colonation Market in Kingston on 1 August and prophesied that the repatriation would take place on 5 October. At the convention, 57 people were arrested in a fight with police and many Rasta's dreadlocks were cut (Smith et al. 1960: 14–16).

Photo 7.1 External appearance of Bobo Shanti

Become an African in Bobo Shanti

At the root of Emmanuel's teaching is that African diasporas are elected people who have been promised salvation. As a result, categories such as Africans, Ethiopians, and Blacks in E.A.B.I.C. are often identified with the Israeli people in the Bible with its religious implications. Emmanuel has made various efforts to realize the belief, one of which is the 1958 repatriation convention. In their discussions about repatriation, Africa variously refers either to the continent of Africa or to a specific country or place on that continent. However, referring to the Exodus, it is sometimes said that Jamaica today is Egypt, and that Bobo Shanti is reproducing the life of the African past. In my research there was no consensus on the meaning of the word Bobo Shanti, but in Ethiopian Amharic, it means "a child of Shanti" (Ashanti).[3]

---

[3] Ashanti or Shanti here refers to the Ashanti kingdom on the Gold Coast (Ghana), West Africa. The family of fugitive slaves (Maroon), Kujo, Johnny, Aconpon, Kuaco and Kofi, are all Ashanti. Other interpretations of the word Bobo Shanti I have heard are "black love", "humble Ethiopia", "righteous warrior", "life and love." Their practice is not to fix the meaning but to embrace multiple coexisting meanings.

Photo 7.2 Nameplate of Bobo Shanti   145

The place where Bobo Shanti was built is also meaningful. Its history of government persecution has been likened to biblical descriptions. According to Chevannes, the Ackee Walk was described as Nazareth where Jesus Christ grew up, Harris Street as Galilee, Eighth Street as Capenaum where Jesus was during the Galilean mission, Ninth Street as Bethlehem, and Bull Bay is akin to Mount Teman where God is said to have appeared (Chevannes 174: 1994). In other words, the concepts of time and space used in E.A.B.I.C. are different from those of Jamaica in the same period. And E.A.B.I.C. is actively trying to keep a distance from Jamaican society. In fact, in Bobo Shanti, the United Nations flag is hoisted to declare extraterritoriality, outside the control of the Jamaican government. They refer to Bobo Shanti as the Embassy of Ethiopia in Jamaica (Egypt) for a similar reason. This will be discussed in more detail later. Ethiopia is not simply a geographical area but also an abstract idea. Inside Bobo Shanti, the Ethiopian Embassy, the buildings are painted with the Ghanaian flag, because Kwame Nkrumah was a Garveyite. Bobo Shanti also has a number of other roles, according to *Black Supremacy*, such as "Melchizedek Righteous Kingdom" "Black Supremacy Government for the Poor and Have-Nots" "Ethiopia Poor

People National and International Freedom League Government""United Black Sovereign Nation" (E.A.B.I.C. 1978: 64).[4]

An overview of the bobos of E.A.B.I.C. as of August 2006 is as follows: 174 persons were registered in the office of E.A.B.I.C. However, because it is unusual for Rasta to commit exclusively to a particular denomination, not all individuals who claim to be E.A.B.I.C. members are necessarily registered. The 174 followers also include those currently living abroad and those based in Bobo Shanti who have not returned for long periods of time. Therefore, 174 is not an accurate number. During my fieldwork in August 2006, I could speak with about 70 members who spent more than a month there (some have houses on the Bobo Shanti property). Most of them can be regarded as pious members because they were keeping Bobo Shanti order and insisted that E.A.B.I.C. is the only true Rastafarian teaching. Most of them, about 80%, were men. Male members are divided into prophet, leading prophet, acting priest, and leading priest. Prophet is the lowest stage of spirituality. As for nationality, most were Jamaican, but members from other Caribbean, North American, and South American nations were also present. I was the only Asian. As the Jamaicans were the majority, the Jamaican creole language (Patwa) with Rastafari vocabulary was dominant.[5]

As stated above, Blacks are the majority in Bobo Shanti. However, going back one or two generations, we find that many Black Jamaicans have Indian and Chinese relatives. There were also whites of European descent as well as descendants of indigenous peoples from South America. That is to say, it is unusual to find 'pure' African descent in Bobo Shanti. People who have diverse backgrounds are learning and practicing the teachings of E.A.B.I.C. as Africans and as Blacks. My body, for example, is marked by Asian characters, but some tried to include me by commenting "You are Black because you have dark eyes." Others attempted to excuse members with Caucasian features by saying "Their hearts are black." In addition, as racial and ethnic minority group members often said "All of us are originally Africans" based on the fact that the roots of modern humans are in Africa. In short, it is possible to include people from

---

[4] In E.A.B.I.C., the world dominated by European values that they try to leave is called the "X world". This "X" implies death of Jesus Christ on the cross. In contrast, the bobo's ideal world is called "R world". This "R" is said to mean things such as "righteous" and "Rastafari."

[5] It is commonly called I-talk. For example, they use I&I which is a fusional phase of Rastas and try not use the words with "cri-" or "cre-" because they have negative or oppressive nuance. Instead "creation," they tend to use the word "iration."

diverse categories who are eager to join E.A.B.I.C. even if their racial or ethnic characteristics are different from most members.[6]

In any case, Bobo Shanti is a space where various bobos can acquire and practice the Africaness and blackness of E.A.B.I.C. Practicing these characteristics is a way to distance oneself from the modern world, including Jamaica, and a way to earn salvation in this life. Africaness and blackness cannot be strictly separated, but E.A.B.I.C. tends to classify concrete practices as Africaness and mindset or worldview as blackness. In particular, Africaness, the practices of living, refers to unique ways that are different from non-Rasta Jamaicans and other Rasta sects. The following sections provide examples of the African practices of E.A.B.I.C.

Rastafari in general see Jamaican society today as shaped by an ideology that justifies a capitalist economic system which developed under colonialism and slavery. Most Rastas are trying to break away from that society. They criticize Christianity and white supremacy for their justifications of colonial rule and slavery. Christianity was criticized for teaching false saviors and using the concept of the heavenly afterlife to make slaves more willing to endure hardship in real life. Christianity is thus regarded as a teaching about death. On the contrary, Rastafari is regarded as a way of life that realizes salvation in this lifetime. White supremacy, meanwhile, is associated with British norms that prevailed in Jamaica during and after the colonial period. In contrast, the E.A.B.I.C. encourages people to "live (like) black, talk (like) black, eat (like) black" (E.A.B.I.C. 1978: 13).

In practice, this means that, for example, when they talk about the body, they mention that Black features such as skin color and frizzy hair have been considered inferior in Jamaican society. Hence, where straight hair is favored, growing their hair to make dreadlocks became a symbol of rebellion among a group called Youth Black Faith in the 1950s (Chevannes 1994: 152). Growing dreadlocks was justified using the Bible,[7] but the origin of the idea is unknown. It may have been influenced by the Mau Mau of Kenya, who fought an anti-colonial struggle, or by Indian Sadhus.

When they become leading prophets, bobos distinguish themselves from other Rastas by wearing turbans and robes. Chevannes claims that Emmanuel wore a turban to make the aggressive nature of the dreadlocks less visible (Chevannes 1994: 187). While this explanation is plausible, the practice is also

147

---

[6] Nevertheless, typical usage of Africa(n) and Black in Rastafari is essential, and physical characteristics are sometimes mentioned to divide minorities.

[7] "They shall not make bald patches on their heads, nor shave off the edges of their beards, nor make any cuts on their body" (Leviticus 21: 5), "They shall not shave their heads or let their locks grow long; they shall surely trim the hair of their heads" (Ezekiel 44: 20).

common among Pocomania followers. Bobos wear white turbans and robes on Sabbath days, outfits quite similar to those of Pocomania and the Ethiopian Orthodox Church. Males do not remove their turbans in public. Males are expected to wear shirts in their pants so that they do not look sloppy in everyday life. Female members are required to wear skirts, no pants. Although the dreadlocks and turban are unique features of Rastafari, both men and women are expected to look traditional and conservative. They also have a conservative attitude to their bodies, which can be seen in criticism of the "Satanic music" popular in dancehalls, with its sexy costumes and aggressive language. In contrast, Bobos tend not to speak loudly or touch bodies. These practices differ from the norm of Jamaican society and are regarded as humble.[8]

According to the E.A.B.I.C., correct ways of earning a livelihood are also determined by Africaness. Broom manufacturing has been a major E.A.B.I.C. economic activity since its headquarters were located downtown in the 1950s. Although some members receive money from relatives who have emigrated or who engage in paid labor, making brooms is an important activity understood to be related to their roots. Using straw to make brooms, is related to descriptions of the Israelites using straw to make bricks in Egypt (Exodus 5). Waged labor is seen as "an extension of slavery", whereas collecting materials in and around the hills and neighborhoods behind Bobo Shanti requires no capital and has no bosses; thus, broom making makes it possible to remain somewhat independent within the capitalist system they call Babylon. It is widely known that E.A.B.I.C. members make and sell brooms because they peddle the brooms. Their brooms are often cheaper than plastic products sold in supermarkets and are also purchased by non-Rasta Jamaicans. On the Sabbath, which starts at 6 PM on Friday, they avoid all economic activities. Whatever economic activity they engage in, they are expected to tithe one-tenth of their income to cover the costs of operating the communes.

As we have seen, when they refer to particular practices as African, the contrast is with European or Jamaican. In short, Bobos idealize an 'African' way of life that is psychologically and physically distinct from the mainstream Jamaican way of life. By sharing these lifestyle formats, they build empathic relationships among the community.

148

---

[8] Famous dancehall dee-jays, who call themselves E.A.B.I.C. members, sing about both secular subjects and the teachings of Rastafari and E.A.B.I.C.. Economically successful dee-jays also provide financial support to E.A.B.I.C. However, the secularity of this music is basically subject to criticism in the context of E.A.B.I.C. Therefore, if the dee-jays want to become priests, they must quit the dancehall.

Photo 7.3 A picture in Bobo Shanti. Upper left is Selassie. Center right is Emmanuel. Lower right is Garvey on the Black Star Liner.

Logic of repatriation

I have already mentioned that the call for a return to Africa was deeply enshrined in the E.A.B.I.C.'s origins. They call for a return to Africa not only as a critique of the Atlantic slave trade and colonial rule, but also in reaction to incongruities in mainstream society's understanding of the emancipation of slaves in 1838. E.A.B.I.C. has explained that repatriation is a legitimate right with the following logic and story.

According to E.A.B.I.C., emancipation in 1838 was not emancipation in a substantive sense. Emmanuel argued that the return to Africa was the first step toward the emancipation of slaves, and that financial compensation for the African diaspora, the descendants of slaves, and for underdeveloped African countries should be part of this process. As discussed, E.A.B.I.C. links Jamaica to Egypt, and the return to Africa is, for them, the "Exodus" described in the Old Testament. Emmanuel stated that he was the leader of the entire African diaspora and Rasta and that "When Haile Selassie I, visited Jamaica in 1966, He left documents considering the Right of I Prince Edwards and my people. Such documents state that all slave-children is to be handed over to I Prince Edward and sent home to Black Africa" (E.A.B.I.C. 1978: 36 C) to justify promoting the return as a "Black Moses."[9] However, it would be unrealistic for Emmanuel alone to promote the return to Africa. Emmanuel has insisted that the realization of repatriation is a global issue and has called for a heteronomous return.[10]

He called on "The head of the U.N. Sec. Gen, and all the heads to see it that Black Man get back his Right" [sic] (ibid: 33) based on the 1948 UN Declaration on Human Rights. He argued that the promotion of the return of African diasporas was essential "to protect fundamental human rights" and cited that "Everyone has the right to freedom of movement and residence in the borders of each state." "Everyone has the right to leave any country, including his own, and to return to his country" according to Article 13. "Everyone has the right to a nationality" and "No one shall be arbitrarily denied of his nationality nor denied the right to change his nationality" as per Article 15 of the Declaration on Human Rights to justify their return (ibid: 56–57). He also says, "I Prince Emmanuel nationality is Ethiopia Black Africa, our nationality, I could not afford to affect to change my nationality" [sic] (ibid: 57). The term "Ethiopia Black Africa" is not restricted to a specific country, but may include, for example, Ethiopia, Ghana, Nigeria, Sierra Leone, Liberia, Uganda, etc. as mentioned elsewhere in this book (ibid: 28, 31).[11] Although not slaves themselves, according to Emmanuel, they are reincarnated slaves who died in Jamaica under slavery (ibid: 35).

Throughout the 1970s and 1980s, Emmanuel and members of E.A.B.I.C. sent telegrams and letters to the United Nations, the International Court of Justice, Queen Elizabeth, the Governor General of Jamaica and others requesting their return. In July 1988, Emmanuel filed a complaint in the Supreme Court against Hugh Shearer, Deputy Prime Minister and Minister of Foreign Affairs demanding compensation for slavery, but the case was never heard (van Dijk 1993: 324). Furthermore, they continue to explain the necessity of repatriation

150

---

[9] During my fieldwork, many members reported that Selassie I had continued visiting Bobo Shanti since his visit to Jamaica in 1966 and Selassie I had consulted with Emmanuel on how to return.

[10] Rastafari are among the most prolific contemporary advocates for the repatriation of people of African descent and reparation for slavery and colonialism internationally (Zips 2006: 132).

[11] Although the true intent of the reference to these countries in *Black Supremacy* is unknown, the following reasons can be assumed. Ethiopia was ruled by Selassie I, and Ghana was founded by Nkrumah. Many slaves were shipped from what is now known as Ghana or Nigeria. Sierra Leone had developed a free town as a haven for emancipated slaves amid the growing movement to abolish slavery. Liberia is where Garvey planned to build a Black nation. Emmanuel considered Idi Amin, who launched a coup in Uganda in 1971 and became the Chair of the Organization of African Unity in 1975, to be a reincarnation of Garvey.

to African politicians who travel to Jamaica.[12] In February 1991, eight members of the E.A.B.I.C. visited Ethiopia, Nigeria, and Ghana to rally support for a plan to repair to Africa (van Dijk 1993: 326). E.A.B.I.C. received a grant of land from the local chief at New Tafo in Ashanti Region, Ghana (Zips 2006: 155). By the time I conducted my fieldwork, the following information was shared among the members.

First, all diasporas, including Bobos, do not return as immigrants. No passport or visa is required, as one follower said, "We were taken without passports, so we went home without passports." Procedures for leaving Jamaica will be carried out at the embassy, Bobo Shanti. They will use the Black Star Liner, a ship of Marcus Garvey's company. The cost of building it will come from the £20 million that Queen Victoria paid in compensation to the colonies, as well as from countries that profited from colonial rule and the slave trade.[13]

Thus, it appears that the demand for repatriation is essentially a religious practice and a continuation of the practice of daily rituals for salvation and observance of various norms related to food, clothing and shelter, although it is full of political language. Therefore, they cannot easily give up their worldview. In other words, such claims are at the level of belief and do not lead members to the practical means of finding compromises with outsiders to realize their demands. It is therefore difficult to say that sufficient consideration has been given to solutions to issues such as how to live and learn languages after returning to Africa. When they discussed repatriation or Africa, Bobos would say things like, "I want to make a space like Bobo Shanti and live there" or " I want to pray to Selassie I and Emmanuel in Lalibela", but they remain vague. Their demand for return reveals a disagreement with the mainstream society's view of the world.

151

Emancipation Day march

August 1 is Jamaica's national holiday, Emancipation Day, but the E.A.B.I.C. does not see it as a day to celebrate. Instead, they have marched in protest on this day each year since 1999. This section discusses part of the march in 2006. The

---

[12] In 1989, Emmanuel reportedly asked the Foreign Minister of Nigeria for assistance, which he readily granted. Newspapers also reported that in 1997 the E.A.B.I.C. welcomed the president of Ghana at the airport (Jamaica Gleaner, 5 August 1997), and petitioned UN Secretary-General Annan, who visited the University of West India in 1998 (Jamaica Gleaner, 7 April 1998).

[13] Also written in Black Supremacy p.33.

Photo 7.4 Police and Bobos

number of participants changed over time, but it started with about 25 people and eventually exceeded 50.

On July 31, the night before the march, I went to the office of E.A.B.I.C. to see one of the leaders of the march to get permission to participate. When I asked him about the march, he explained that the purpose was to hand a petition to the Governor General of Jamaica and to let general Jamaicans know that slavery is not over yet. And he told me that some believers living outside Bobo Shanti marched on that day. He continued to call me a journalist even after we had known each other more than a year, he added, "Take a lot of pictures and deliver our opinions not only to the Japanese people but also to the president." After leaving the office, several members gathered in the royal restaurant, writing messages with magic markers on cardboard, taping cardboard to the ends of strips of wood to make placards for use in the march. The placards said: "FREEDOM, REDEMPTION, REPATRIATION" "AFRICA = YES, JAMAICA = NO" "FREEDOM OF MOVEMENT" "THE UN IS RESPONSIBLE FOR ALL THE RIGHT AND TO SEE IT DONE NOW [sic]" "AFRICA FOR THE AFRICAN" "REPATRIATION NOW".

Photo 7.5 A leading priest interviewed by local media

The march was to begin downtown Kingston, with the members scheduled to join the procession at various times. The E.A.B.I.C. hold a ceremony at 6 AM every morning, and since people were not allowed to go out until the ceremony was over, it was around 9 AM when the members who participated in the march gathered at the entrance to the commune. Both men and women wore white robes or T-shirts, and many wore black turbans or headdresses. Some wore black cloaks. This style of wearing a black item over a white costume is said to visually symbolize "black over white (Black supremacy)". Also, many of the men wore stoles instead of cloaks. Some wore Rasta tri-colored (red, yellow and green) stoles and others wore the light blue and white of the United Nations flag. Some wore Rasta colored turbans and others wore the UNIA tri-colored (black, green and red) turbans instead of black ones. When the participants gathered, the members chanted sacred verses and began to walk towards the foot of the mountain where the cars were waiting, holding placards, ceremonial drums, the United Nations flag, the E.A.B.I.C. flag, and the UNIA flag.

The participants, including me, rode in a minivan to St. William Grant Park, the starting point of the march. The park is a legendary place for the E.A.B.I.C. because Emmanuel is said to have lowered the Union Jack that was hung there and hoisted the Ghana flag in its place at the 1958 repatriation convention. On the way to the park, the members were singing hymns, some about repatriation to Africa. The minivan arrived at the park around 9:45. The members unloaded drums, flags, placards, and other items, and started to pray for about an hour facing east, toward Africa. Then the march began. After walking around the park seven times, they turned towards King's House (the governor's residence). Walking around seven times is modeled after the Israeli "Battle of Jericho" (Joshua 6: 1–27) led by Moses' successor, Joshua.[14] At that time, this march became more lively with a group of members from Bobo Shanti joining in from the back of a truck.

After about two hours, the group passed through the Cross Roads, one of the most important transportation points, and reached the Half Way Tree. The streets, which are usually jammed with cars and crowded with peddlers and passersby, were empty on this day. Gradually, the number of sweaty members increased and the parade of marchers grew longer. The group, crossing the Half Way Tree, began to move north towards King's House. Soon they were stopped by police motorcycles for about five minutes, but when the leaders politely told them the march was "a march for peace" and had no intention of disturbing public order, the policemen allowed them to resume the march.

We arrived in front of King's House shortly after 1 PM. There were policemen waiting in front of the gate. The faces of the marchers had become more tense. When three leaders told the policemen that they intended to visit the Governor General and requested a meeting, they were rejected because "requesting a meeting on behalf of the deceased (Emmanuel) is improper as a procedure". In response, the followers told the policemen that he should be supporting them, since he is also an African like them and began to explain "the will of God to return." Some followers began to curse the policemen. While the argument continued, other members lined up drums on the sidewalk in front of the hotel diagonally across from King's House and began to play. There was a large crossroad in front of King's House, and the members blocked the crossing. Police officers with rifles began to drive the members to the hotel for obstructing traffic. As a result, members faced King's House and the police across the intersection. There were some members who waved flags and danced to the sound of drums, and some members eloquently expressed their opinions to the policemen in front of them. Some were watching anxiously to prevent overly excited members from wrangling with the police.

---

[14] On their way to the Promised Land, Joshua and his followers reached the fortified city of Jericho and walked around the closed gates of Jericho for seven days. When the conch was sounded, the walls collapsed, and Joshua and his companions invaded Jericho.

After hearing the noise, guests from nearby hotels and restaurants came out to see what was going on. I explained the members' opinions and asked the onlookers for their opinions about their return to Africa, many of them answered, "I don't want to go back to Africa because I like Jamaica" and there were not many favorable responses to the marchers' opinions and actions. At about 3 PM, the members started preparing to leave.

After two ceremonies at Half Way Tree and Spanish Town Road, the members returned to Bobo Shanti around 8 PM. At various places in Bobo Shanti, there was talk about the events of the day. One member told me how he stood up against the brutal police. Another expressed his hope that the appeal on the day would gradually awaken people's minds. Thus, different members had different feelings about the march and what they felt from it.

Black members from the United States and Trinidad and Tobago participated in the march, but none of the white members from Latin America participated. In recent years, however, there has been an increase in the number of E.A.B.I.C. members in Latin America, and a new phase has emerged in the movement as minority E.A.B.I.C. members began calling for their return. In Chile, a white priest, Rodrigo, is actively campaigning. The Chilean movement is summarized in three reports: Report of the Mission to the U.S. Human Rights Office in Chile (March 2009), Report of the Interview of the E.A.B.I.C. with the Ambassador of South Africa in Chile (December 2009), and Report of the E.A.B.I.C. Mission at the Department of the Inter-American System of Human Rights of the Ministry of External Affairs of the Chilean Government (May 2010).

Three priests and a female member visited the United Nations Office in Chile. They had requested a meeting with the High Commissioner, Margarita Uprimny, but she was not present, and her secretary met with them instead. The theme discussed was "Reasoning about our Freedom, Redemption and International." Rodrigo and his colleagues called for a return to Africa in the manner allowed by the headquarters. While acknowledging the authority of the Jamaican headquarters, they are increasing their presence by working together on global issues. In the 2010s, the news of such movement started to spread around the world through not only TV news and newspapers but also social networking services and video sharing services. As a result, the Emancipation Day marches organized by E.A.B.I.C. members have been held in other former British colonies as well. Other denominations of Rasta also joined the 2013 Emancipation Day march in the Bahamas.[15]

---

[15] Police destroyed the commune in the Bahamas on 19 August 2005, suggesting that police control of Rastafari is stricter in the Bahamas.

Conclusion

In this article, I focused on the diaspora consciousness of the E.A.B.I.C. members. Specifically, I have discussed how they are building relationships with Africa, creating daily life practices and trying to recover their places of origin.

The terms African and Black used in E.A.B.I.C. context were polysemous. For example, Emmanuel's desire to strengthen ties between Ethiopia, where Selassie 1ˢᵗ appeared, and Ghana, where Nkrumah appeared, is reflected in his seemingly unprincipled style of using Ethiopia as the group name and respecting the Ghana flag pattern. If we recall Furuya's words quoted at the beginning of this chapter, we must address the fact that some people cannot build a positive identity without using methods that are considered unprincipled by mainstream society. In any case, Emmanuel has tried to use his original logic to create positive fiction for the African diaspora, and the fact that E.A.B.I.C. has survived to date underscores the appeal of his fiction. It was not only Black Jamaicans who were attracted to the fiction. Minorities such as myself and white Europeans can be accepted as Black and African because Emmanuel did not choose an exclusive direction that limited the meaning of the words Black and African. By wearing a turban, making brooms, and learning correct behavior, people with diverse backgrounds nurture not only an identity as Africans in the context of E.A.B.I.C. but also empathic bodies to build *ba* together.

The reason E.A.B.I.C. longs for Africa is the slave trade. They have demanded actual return to Africa as part of compensation. Emmanuel argued that the emancipation of slaves in 1838 was unilateral, not as they wanted it to be. Not surprisingly, the process of emancipation they want differs from that of other Rasta and Jamaicans. The peculiarity of their assertions is that the term "Embassy" and the "United Nations Declaration of Human Rights", which are deeply related to the concept of a modern nation-state, are central to the E.A.B.I.C. worldview, which gives them new meaning. Imitating the Battle of Jericho's legacy in the course of the Emancipation march and attempting to deliver a letter to the Governor of Jamaica on behalf of the deceased Emmanuel demonstrates that they sometimes confront the world outside of Bobo Shanti with their own logic.

The explicit purpose of the Emancipation Day march was to deliver a letter to the Governor General and to let general Jamaicans know their desires for repatriation. But perhaps the implicit purpose was that each member embodies the experience of being a bobo. The march on 1 August was the eighth march since 1999 which means most of the members, including the leaders, must have understood that it was impossible to meet the Governor General by this method. The members know a lot about repatriation. But to deepen that knowledge, it is important to take action. By walking around Kingston, singing hymns, dancing, and confronting the police, the participants gain E.A.B.I.C. devotion. This process was necessary to update the E.A.B.I.C. world view. The confrontation between the members and the police in front of King's House was planned, but there could be unforeseen consequences. Depending on how the bobos and police feel and act in the moment, the atmosphere of *ba* can vary greatly. My honest feeling was sadness when I saw the oppressive exclusion of the members, and yet I felt protected by great beings when I heard their hymns on my back. Each of the members in front of King's House must have had various feelings like me. The leaders who were behaving politely, the members who were concerned about avoiding violence, and the police who were in a position to confront them, would have experienced the march in different ways. Forefront of conflict was a *ba* which inspired the agency of those present. Such experiences are not unique to E.A.B.I.C. in Jamaica. The case of Chile and the Bahamas shows that as the members perform their own visions as Africans in their respective lands and their information is shared, new elements and senses are added to the Africaness of E.A.B.I.C. 157

8. After Fieldwork

Vestiges in/from a Fieldworker

Eriko Kawanishi

Introduction

> A long-time fantasy among Anglo-American anthropologists has been that someday there would be Trobriand, Bororo, or Ndembu anthropologists who would come to the United States and provide a reciprocal critical ethnography (as Tocqueville is conventionally said to have done) from the point of view of a radically cultural other. (Marcus and Fischer 1986: 156)

I am an anthropologist from Japan who conducted ethnographic fieldwork in Glastonbury, UK. This pattern, a non-Western anthropologist studying Western informants, is unusual in the history of anthropology, where traditionally a Western anthropologist works with non-Western informants. Thus, my work might contribute to fulfilling the "fantasy" that George Marcus and Michael Fisher describe above, a "cultural other" researching Westerners. This chapter begins with a discussion of how it relates to *ba*, the theme of this volume. Then I discuss autoethnography as a research method and previous anthropological studies of Europe. Finally, I outline two cases from my fieldwork on the Goddess movement and Sufism in Glastonbury and present a conclusion.

All the chapters in this volume engage with the concept of *ba*. According to the Introduction, whereas place is treated as container, *ba* "is often what moves people, allowing or hindering their actions, and thus guiding the formation of an actor as an individual in the first place" (See p.2). *Ba* co-emerges with people and helps people to notice something. In fieldwork, the researcher is affected by *ba* as well as the local people. We can discuss this in terms of the relation between informants, fieldworker and field.

This chapter considers how my agency as a fieldworker co-emerges with my field, and what "vestiges" are left inside and outside the field from interacting with my informants. How has my performance, which emerges from the interaction with my informants in the field, affected them and changed me?

Here, the word "vestige" refers not only to my influence on other people, but also theirs on me: what I left behind, and what I took away from Glastonbury. The *Oxford Dictionary of English* (2005) defines "vestige" as "a trace or remnant of something that is disappearing or no longer exists." According to the Introduction, "*Ba* carries a residual aspect of *ba*, a vestige of the past *ba*, which will be used as a resource (Schechner's "restored behavior") for the next performance from which will emerge a new *ba*" (See p.12). In this chapter, the word: vestige" refers to the performance that was influenced by a *ba* and emerged from a distant *ba* as well as the same *ba*.

Autoethnography

Autoethnography is a research method in which the anthropologist's personal experience is analysed. According to Tony Adams, Stacy Holman Jones, and Carolyn Ellis, autoethnography:

+ Uses a researcher's personal experience to describe and critique cultural beliefs, practices, and experiences.
+ Acknowledges and values a researcher's relationship with others.
+ Uses deep and careful self-reflection – typically referred to as "reflexivity" – to name and interrogate the intersections between self and society, the particular and the general, the personal and the political.
+ Shows "people in the process of figuring out what to do, how to live and the meaning of their struggles."
+ Strives for social justice and to make life better.

(Adams, Jones, and Ellis 2015: 1–2)

Autoethnography is a self-reflexive practice that requires ethnographers – people who write fieldwork-based ethnography – to analyse their personal behaviour, experiences and how they have changed. Some autoethnographers research their own society, while others become a member of the group they study, but in either case, they must objectify themselves. The ethnographer is not the only "self" visible in autoethnographic texts. Autoethnography is an attempt to humanise informants who are "other" for the ethnographer.

Autoethnography is a response to the *Writing Culture* shock of the 1980s, a method for removing the ethnographer's authority.[1] The term "auto(-)ethnography" was already used in the 1970s,[2] but "the move to include personal experience [was] *implied* rather than explicitly embraced" (Adams, Jones, and Ellis 2015: 16). The *Writing Culture* "shock" refers to the impact of James Clifford and George Marcus's argument that ethnographic writing was not objective description but rather a representation which imposed the ethnographer's authority over the informants. Since *Writing Culture* was published (1986), ethnographers have been required to rethink their research methods and relationships with informants.

The issue here is about the agency of both the informants and the ethnographer, as well as the importance of considering *ba*. Karsten Paerregaard (2002) said, "In recent years, a growing number of anthropologists have rejected traditional notions of ethnographic data as objective social facts that only need to be observed or 'picked up' by the fieldworker" (Paerregaard 2002: 330). Referring to Barth (1995), he continued:

> (C)ultural knowledge is regarded as consisting of constructions produced and reproduced by social agents who constantly negotiate and contest existing forms of wisdom. (...) The idea that anthropological knowledge emerges from an insight acquired by the fieldworker through his or her personal interaction with the people under study rests on the assumption that the ethnographer and his or her informants recognise each other as self-conscious social agents, and their relationship thus is humanised. (Paerregaard 2002: 330)

The first of the case studies I will discuss here concerns my interactions with Pagans. Ethnographers studying Paganism typically inform their informants that they are attending ceremonies or events as researchers. Some ethnographers become members of the groups they study; other times, practitioners decide to study their existing groups.[3] Jone Salomonsen, who studied Reclaiming Witches in the US, says "in Witches' rituals, covens and classes, there is no outside where

---

[1] Adams, Jones, and Ellis explain "three interrelated concerns and considerations about social scientific and qualitative research contributed to the formation of autoethnography: (1) new and changing ideas and ideals about and ideals for research, a recognition of the limits of scientific knowledge, and an emerging appreciation for personal narrative, story, the literary and the aesthetic, emotions and the body; (2) a heightened concern about the ethics and politics of research practices and representations; and (3) the increased importance of social identities and identity politics (2015: 8).

[2] Anderson (2006: 375–378) explains the history of autoethnography.

[3] See, for example, Bado-Fralick (2005); Greenwood (2000); Magliocco (2004); Pike (2001); Rountree (2004); and Snook (2015).

an observer can literally put herself" (Salomonsen 2002: 17), and labelled her own approach as "a method of compassion," designating "an attitude in which belief is taken seriously, both cognitively and emotionally"[4] (Salomonsen 2002: 18). Thus the borders between researchers and their informants become blurred during fieldwork, affecting the perspectives and behaviours of all parties.[5]

Most of the people I met through fieldwork – not only the Pagans – were interested in alternative values and lifestyles which are (by definition) different from "traditional" or "mainstream" British culture and Christianity. Examples include: New Age, Paganism, Goddess movement, Sufism, Buddhism, indigenous cultures (especially Native American), Indian philosophy (such as Hinduism), alternative therapies, divination, vegetarianism, veganism and Earth mystery. Regardless of ethnic background, everybody is welcome to experience and accept these teachings and worldviews. Something new might be created from the interaction between me and my informants. This is quite different from fieldwork in tribal communities, which anthropologists traditionally researched.

From this perspective, both my informants and I are social agents who interact with each other in a field. This field is not a mere container to hold an anthropologist and her/his informants, but a context which affects their performance. *Ba* is thus an important concept for analysing the performance of agents in the field, since this performance emerges not only from the relation with their informants, but also from their field, *ba*.

161

Anthropology of Europe

Anthropology originated as a study by white male scholars of "exotic others" who lived outside Europe. Thus, it eventually was accused of Orientalism. According to Susan Parman, an American anthropologist,

> Europe exists as a conceptual contrast, as a vehicle of occidentalism, to define and enforce the boundaries and hierarchical inequalities of Occident and Orient (West and non-West). (Parman 1998: 2)

The image of Westerners thus produced was a mirror image of "exotic others."

---

[4] Elaine Lawless (1993) studied ordained women ministers in the US. She worked with her informants reflexively in that she readily acknowledged her presence in the research, and reciprocally in that she and her informants have established a working dialogue about the material. She called this approach "reciprocal ethnography," which she also called "a method of compassion" (Lawless 1993: 60–61).

[5] See Blain, Ezzy and Harvey (2004) and "Special Section – Paths into Pagan Studies: Autobiographical Reflections," *The Pomegranate* (Ezzy et al. 2015).

Although Japan is not a Western country, it is quite active in the field of anthropology. Japanese anthropologists have conducted fieldwork in Asia, the Middle East, Africa, South America and Oceania. At the same time, Japan has been extensively studied by Western anthropologists.[6] It has been unusual, however, for Japanese anthropologists to study Europeans and North Americans of European descent.

Europe has been endlessly studied by scholars in other disciplines (eg. historians and sociologists). The Mediterranean, Celtic and Alpine regions have all been studied as exotic or non-mainstream outliers, but the anthropological study of the politically and culturally dominant countries only began in the 1980s. Akiko Mori, a Japanese anthropologist, explains this was a result of anthropology becoming increasingly interested in the world-system from the late-1970s, when the "exotic non-Western (savage) others" were located within the same world-system with anthropologists, and differences between Europe and its others were relativised (Mori 2004: 9–10).

However not many Japanese anthropology PhD students choose to study Europeans or North Americans of European descent.[7] Therefore, the relation between researching and researched is unbalanced. Papers written in Japanese typically use analytical concepts that originate from English, French or German thinkers. Any paper not using such concepts would probably not be well-received because it has not adequately engaged the existing literature. Meanwhile, non-Western concepts are rarely used except in the analysis of the cultures or societies from which they originate.

The recent ethnographic research on Westerners in the West, which long considered itself to be the cultural, political, and economic "centre" of the world, is a reflective response to the Orientalist critique, which aims to dissolve the self/other dichotomy. The relationship between an anthropologist and her/his informants in Europe is rather different from the conventional ones. Two cases of anthropologists and their informants in Glastonbury will suffice to illustrate this.

---

[6] Many Western anthropologists have published ethnographies of Japan. For example, significant before WWII are Embree (1939), *Suye Mura: A Japanese Village* and Benedict (1946), *The Chrysanthemum and the Sword: Patterns of Japanese Culture*. Later, we find Smith (1974), *Ancestor Worship in Contemporary Japan*, Dore (1978), *Shinohata: A Portrait of a Japanese Village*, and more recently Hendry (1993), *Wrapping Culture: Politeness, Presentation and Power in Japan and other Societies*, and Bestor (2004), *Tsukiji: The Fish Market at the Center of the World*.

[7] Ethnographies which are based on PhD dissertations about the dominant culture in North America, the UK, France and German speaking regions by Japanese anthropologists include: Mori (1999) (a parish in Carinthia, Austria), Suzuki (1999) (US), Sakai (2015) (Northern Ireland), Shioji (2003) (Cotswolds, UK), Takahashi (2013) (Archipelago town in southwest Finland) and Terado (2006) (Lourdes, France). They are all female scholars.

The New Age in Glastonbury (2000), written by two British anthropologists, Ruth Prince and David Riches, is an ethnographic study of the Alternative Community in Glastonbury which analyses the New Age movement based primarily on Prince's fieldwork from October 1989 through December 1990 (Prince and Riches 2000: ix). She explains her fieldwork in the preface:

> (M)y field location was a few miles from the village where I spent my childhood, and with a group of people whose way of life arrived in Glastonbury, in the late 1960s, around the time I was born. (…) My own personal beliefs and attitudes were not so far removed from the Alternative Community; I had been a vegetarian for a number of years and was interested in environmental issues and in experimental forms of lifestyle. (Prince and Riches 2000: ix)

She notes that "'similarity' made access to the place of study quite easy" (Prince and Riches 2000: x) and:

> I made a point of telling people I was an anthropologist, but as a young woman in her twenties I passed for a New Ager at a superficial glance. Unlike what anthropologists more normally face, my presence as intruder was not immediately apparent through language barriers or obvious physical differences. (Prince and Riches 2000: x–xi)

She also says:

> (U)nlike the white anthropologist in a developing country, I was able to become fully a 'part of the furniture'. Yet for all this, and not least on behalf of my own psychological well-being, I remained apart. Thus, for me, the familiar remained foreign. (Prince and Riches 2000: xii)

In short, Prince studied her familiar society as an anthropologist, sharing the language, physical features and cultural background of her informants. The only significant difference was their beliefs and engagement in New Age matters. She blended in easily.

Adrian Ivakhiv, a Canadian anthropologist, studied Earth's "power places," conducting research for three years in the mid-1990s, attending meditation retreats and psychic fairs, group visualisations and ritual circles, watching mediums perform, dowsing with copper rods and visiting several sites that have

163

become gathering places and travel stops for New Age and ecospiritual pilgrims (Ivakhiv 2001: 14–15). In *Claiming Sacred Ground* (2001) he mentions that:

> I could, and often did, fit into the role of participants. This role came easily to me, as I had had contact with certain streams of these alternative cultural movements for well over a decade prior to taking on this research, and I remain sympathetic to the urge infusing the quests of many of their participants. (Ivakhiv 2001: 15)

Unlike Prince, Ivakhiv did not stay in Glastonbury for a long time, but they both became familiar with alternative cultures, were native-English speakers, and had no obvious physical differences, such as skin color, from their informants. Thus their presence did not disturb the community.

These ethnographers could easily "disguise" their positions as researchers. Their relationships with informants were relatively equal. They met their informants as New Age practitioners, rather than as researchers.

Of course, this is not the case for non-Western anthropologists who study Westerners. Although non-Westerners visited Western countries for many centuries, their cultures and political systems were typically considered to be "behind" and their intentions were assumed to be to learn the West's "superior" cultures and political systems. For the people who were studied by Western anthropologists 50 years ago, Europe and North America were too far away and too expensive to conduct ethnographic research. However, these regions are now accessible for people from some non-Western countries. A few non-Western anthropologists have begun to study Westerners. Their relationships with Western informants were rather different to the relationships of Western anthropologists with non-Western informants.

Tomoko Sakai (2011), a Japanese anthropologist who studied the Northern Ireland conflict, for example, discusses the power dynamics between researchers and informants in interviews by second language. If the social status of informants is higher than the researcher, or if the researcher is not familiar with the field, the researcher is often situated in a subordinate position to her/his informants. These situations arise for anthropologists who study in non-Western countries, too, but while they are typically able to relativise the values of field-site by taking their data home for analysis, non-Westerners who study in the West are not always so able to relativise the Western values they encounter in the field and can find themselves entangled in them during the analysis (Sakai 2011: 95–96).

Sakai also notes that while English is a global language today, non-native speakers often find themselves in a subordinate role, even academic researchers (Sakai 2011: 95–96). This can, perhaps counterintuitively, be beneficial for the research – because the interviewer is at a disadvantage, the informants can comfortably assume the role of teaching, leading to fruitful and informative interviews (Sakai 2011: 98). This means, however, that if the anthropology of Europe aims at relativising Europe and its values, it is not always successful.

This was the situation I confronted as an anthropologist conducting fieldwork in English as a second language who could not become 'part of the furniture'. In the next section, I briefly outline Glastonbury and my experiences with the Goddess movement and Sufism.

My first visit to Glastonbury was November 2005, as a graduate student. I returned again in 2006, 2008 and 2009–2011 for my MA and PhD research. I have returned four times since, in 2017, 2018, 2019 and from January to March 2020. I conducted this research using semi-structured interviews and participant observation.

Glastonbury – an alternative community

Glastonbury, a country town in the County of Somerset, is in southwest England (see Fig. 8.1), with a population of 8,932 in 2011 (Somerset Intelligence 2012–2013). Agriculture and sheepskin products were its traditional industries, but both have declined due to the relocation of factories to low-labor-cost countries. Like many small communities today, educated young people typically leave town in search of better-paying work and opportunities.

Glastonbury became known as a centre of contemporary spirituality from 1967, when hundreds of hippies were drawn to its local legends (Hexham 1981: 11): the Celts, King Arthur, Joseph of Arimathea, and Jesus Christ (Bowman 1993, 2000, 2005, 2008). However, 'they mostly went away'; 'only a few dozen "hippies" (…) had settled down to live' there by 1977 (Garrard 1989: 5). In the 1980s, though, people who were more interested in spiritual life than material matters began moving from the cities to Glastonbury, at a time of increasing economic depression in the town as its factories relocated. The migrants opened spiritual goods shops and healing centres, making Glastonbury even more attractive to spiritual people, and the town revived. Although 92.5 percent of its residents are white British, the proportion of residents who do not identify with one of the UK's top six faith communities is twelve times the national average

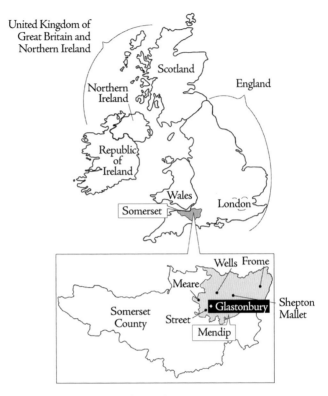

Fig. 8.1 Location of Glastonbury

(Somerset Intelligence 2012–2013). Many locals did not like these changes initially, but later came to welcome spiritual seekers because they are harmless and can bring economic benefits (Kawanishi 2013). Various faith groups exist in Glastonbury; from the traditional to New Age and alternative, such as Church of England, United Reformed Church, Methodist Church, Catholic, Gospel Hall, Jehovah's Witness, Grace Community Church (evangelical church), Taizé community, Sufi groups, the Goddess Temple, Druid groups, Buddhist groups, Indian philosophies and meditation groups.

Some Japanese people know Glastonbury as a sacred "power place" with the highest energy in the UK. The intentions of Japanese who visit Glastonbury often differ by gender. Women tend to be interested in spiritual matters, such as healing, divination and "energy," while the men are more likely to be hippies, travellers or backpackers. There are many more women than men.

Avalon, another name of Glastonbury, frequently appears in Japanese pop culture, in animations, films and video games (See Table 8.1).

Genre	Creator/Sales agency	Title/Character names	Submitted	Notes
Gamebook	Herbie Brennan (Irish, author)	*GrailQuest*	1984–87 translated and published	Arthurian legend, eight volumes
Animation, Film	Mamoru Oshii (Japanese, filmmaker)	*Avalon*	2001 released	
Computer game	TYPE-MOON (Japanese game company)	*Fate/stay night UBW (Unlimited Blade Works)*	2004 distributed	Arthurian legend, Animation and comic are also distributed
Comic	Harold Sakuishi (Japanese, comic artist)	Avalon Festival in *BECK*	2004–05 serialised	Glastonbury Festival is the model of Avalon Festival
Game application	GungHo Online Entertainment, Inc. (Japanese video game developer)	Guardian dragon of heaven "Avalondrake," Dragon king of earth "Avalon" and evil castle "Avalon" from *Puzzle & Dragons (PuzzDra)*	2012 distributed	
Mobile game	Mobage and GREE (Japanese SNSs)	*The Knights of Avalon*	2012 (Mobage) and 2015 (GREE) distributed	Arthurian legend
Film	The Young Animator Training Project by the Japanese Agency for Cultural Affairs	*Little Witch Academia*	2013 released	Its setting is a Glastonbury-like place
Game application	Mixi (Japanese SNS)	Monster "Avalon" from *Monster Strike (Monst)*	2013 distributed	The names of monsters derive from myths and historical figures around the world.

Table 8.1 Avalon in Japanese pop culture

Amaterasu dance

The first thing that confused me when I started talking to the alternative people in Glastonbury was the image they have of "Japan." I had expected they would say anime, manga, geisha or judo, and was very surprised to learn that some thought Japanese food is pure vegetarian, all Japanese Buddhism is Zen, and that Shinto is the Japanese version of Paganism, since both worship many deities and nature. When I mentioned studying at Kyoto University,[8] several people said "I am a reiki master. Dr Usui trained and had a revelation in Kyoto!"[9] When I was invited to the local infants' school to teach *origami*, a Japanese paper craft, the teacher told the pupils that I wore *kimono*. I felt guilty because I was actually wearing a much more casual *yukata*.[10]

When talking with people involved in the Goddess movement, I learned new aspects of deities who were familiar to me in Japan. For example, I had never thought of Guan Yin's (Kannon) gender, but learned that she is known as the "goddess of mercy."[11] Furthermore, I had thought of Inari as a fox, and was surprised to learn that she is also worshipped as a goddess.[12] It also took time to accept Amaterasu as a popular sun goddess because she is known as an ancestor of the Japanese imperial family and is associated with nationalism.

As the theme of the 2009 Goddess Conference was "fire goddess," the organiser asked me to perform a dance of Amaterasu, a famous sun goddess from Japan. I created and performed an "Amaterasu Dance," although I had no experience of Japanese classical dance. I only remembered a local *Bon* dance[13] which I had learned in primary school. I contacted Ise Shrine, scholars of Shinto and mythology, the Japan Folk Performing Arts Association, and several tourist information offices seeking information about an Amaterasu dance, but they all said there was no such dance.

---

[8] One-third of them associated "Kyoto" with reiki, another third with the Kyoto Protocol (2005) because of their interest in environmental issues and the remaining third with many shrines and temples, knowing it was once the capital. That the word Kyoto was associated by a large number of people with reiki and Kyoto Protocol is perhaps because of the uniqueness of Glastonbury.

[9] I had never heard of reiki until then. Dr Mikao Usui is the founder of reiki, a form of energetic healing, and underwent strict training in Kurama mountain in Kyoto. Reiki was almost obsolete in Japan and became popular in the West. It has revived recently, but when I first went to Glastonbury in 2005, reiki was still not popular in Japan.

[10] *Yukata* is considered to be a casual version of *kimono*, but ordinary Japanese people distinguish between these two words. *Yukata* literally means bathing cloth and is made of cotton. It was traditionally worn after a bath at home and is still often worn at hotels and summer festivals. However, in 2020, I realized that a long Japanese garment which fastens in front was called *kimono* in the West.

[11] Guan Yin was originally a (male/masculine) god from India. After arriving in China, Guan Yin was revered as a goddess.

[12] In fact, the fox is a messenger of Inari, who is a goddess.

[13] The *Bon* dance was traditionally performed in the evenings during *Bon* season (13 to 15 August), when the spirits of ancestors are believed to return to their family, and people danced to calm them. The dancers form circles and dance with the *Bon* dance songs. Nowadays people enjoy *Bon* dances at local summer community festivals and school sports festivals. *Bon* dances can be new creations. The local *Bon* dance I learned was created in 1971 because local merchants decided to hold a summer festival and wanted an original *Bon* dance. We performed it at the sports festival every year at primary school, so I remembered the move.

According to Japanese mythology, Amaterasu, the supreme sun goddess, was upset with Susano'o, one of her younger brothers, because of his bad behaviour, so she hid in a cave. Darkness engulfed everything, and both deities and humans had difficulty getting by. Deities gathered in front of the cave, and Uzume, another goddess, performed a dance that revealed her sex organ, making all the other deities laugh. Amaterasu wondered what was happening outside the cave and opened the door slightly. She asked what they were doing, and the deities responded that they were welcoming an even more beautiful and splendid goddess than her and raised a mirror before her face. Not realising that the image was of her, Amaterasu leaned out to get a better view, when a strong god forced opened the door and asked Amaterasu to come out of the cave. This is a myth without clear evidence of this incident.

As describe above, the dancer in this story was Uzume, not Amaterasu. Although this myth became a staple of Japanese cinema – for example, (the Three Treasures, 1959), Kabuki[14] (Amaterasu, 2006–) and Takarazuka Revue[15] (Susano'o in 2004 and Mahoroba in 2007) – the dances were all recent creations. The closest performance seemed to be Kagura, believed to be based on the Uzume dance. Kagura is sacred music and dance which is performed at shrines and temples all over Japan. However, Kagura is not intended to worship deities, but rather to entertain them. Traditionally only males performed, but female performers are increasing because of feminism and a shortage of male performers. For example, all the performers of Nambu Kagura in Hiraizumi town, Iwate prefecture, were female in 2008 when I made contact.

I told the conference organiser who had invited me to perform that I had been unable to find an Amaterasu dance. I assumed she would create a dance or ask a professional dancer to create one (many followers of the Goddess believe that cultures and societies which celebrated femininity have been lost due to patriarchal domination and must be re-created). However, to my great surprise, she asked me to create one and perform it on stage, alone, though I hardly knew how to dance. She also said:

> I was thinking of some traditional Japanese music, with you in Japanese dress, as it's something that we in the West are unfamiliar with. We don't hear the echoes that you hear. For us it's just delightful and different. (personal email, 12 June 2009)

---

[14] A Japanese dance-drama started in the 17th century by a woman. Later women were prohibited from engaging in it, and now only men perform it.

[15] A Western-style all-female musical theater troupe from 1914.

Photo 8.1 Amaterasu Dance (30 July 2007)

I focused on the Goddess movement in Glastonbury for my PhD thesis. The organiser and others had helped my research. Therefore, I could not say no, regardless of how embarrassed I would be to dance in front of an audience. But, I did not have enough knowledge of Japanese dance, so I asked British people around me what images the term "Japanese dance" evoked for them. They mentioned using fans, wearing a *kimono* and smooth movements of arms and legs, images associated with "*geisha*" dancing. The organiser had allocated five minutes for my dance, so I chose a five-minute-long musical track from a CD of *gagaku*[16] which I borrowed from the local library. I created my dance based on the local Bon dance I had learned at primary school and a YouTube clip of Japanese classical dance by a women's university. Thinking of the moves of a *maiko*[17] I saw perform in Kyoto, I tried to smoothly move my body and the fan. Since it would not be easy to either travel with or wear a *kimono*, I chose to wear a *yukata*. The theme colour of the Goddess Conference that year was red, but I couldn't find a red *yukata*, so I bought a cheap pink one for 1000 yen (~10 US dollars). I also had a pink *heko obi*[18] and bought a dark red fan for 100 yen (~1 US dollar).

---

[16] Japanese classical music from the 7th century.

[17] Apprentice of *geiko*. The word, *geisha*, is hardly used in Kyoto.

[18] *Obi* is a type of belt that holds the *yukata* close to the body. The *heko obi* is usually for children, but is less bulky than an ordinary *obi*, and thus more suitable for my dance costume.

In July, I returned to Glastonbury and practised the dance every evening at home. On the morning of 30 July, the day of my performance, I walked to the town hall, wearing the pink *yukata*. People passing by told me that my "*kimono*" was beautiful. The speaker who preceded my dance introduced several goddesses, including Amaterasu, and explained her myth of the cave in detail.

The organiser asked whether I wanted to dance on the stage or on the lower stand in front of the stage. I chose the stage because my dance routine included kneeling and I thought the audience in the back rows could see me better. She nodded as if affirming my choice. I went on to the stage, and the spotlights came on. From the stage, there appeared to be more than one hundred people in the audience. It might be because I talked about my dance with many people who I met in Glastonbury and posted about it on Facebook. A lot of people had told me that they had been looking forward to my dance, and I found many familiar faces in the audience, therefore I felt relaxed and started dancing. I moved my hands and face, waved the fan and bent my knees to the floor.[19] While I danced, the hall was very quiet and solemn. Upon finishing, I received a storm of applause. Some stood up and applauded. I had thought they would be satisfied if I had yukata with fan and danced with Japanese classic music, but that roar of approval was quite unexpected. That was the best dance I have ever done.

My mother, at home in Japan, laughed at my "fake" dance, but many of my friends and informants said it was beautiful. One said it was reverent, and another said I held the energy of Amaterasu. One told me "It's uplifting, but smooth and elegant" and that my dance movements were completely different from any other dances she had seen. She compared it to belly dancing and hip-hop, which she said was faster and sharper, while the dance I created was very slow and smooth. The organiser later emailed to say: "Your dance for Amaterasu was delightful.

---

[19] 1) Placing the fan on the floor, I sat behind it and bowed to the floor. 2) At the first sound of Japanese drum (*taiko*), I lifted the fan and put it on my knees, stood slowly and slowly opened the fan. 3) When the Japanese free reed wind instrument (*sho*) began to play, I put my left hand on my right breast and reached my right hand forward. Then I turned to the right, put my right hand on my left breast and reached my left hand forward. After that, I turned to the back, put my left hand on my right breast and my right hand forward. Then I turned to the left, put my right hand on my left breast and my left hand forward. I borrowed this movement from the local *Bon* dance. 4) I faced the front again and waved the fan from side to side in a figure eight twice. 5) I raised the fan to the right and turned my face to the fan. I repeated the move on the left. 6) I stretched my right arm with the fan behind and to the right and turned the fan over twice. I repeated the move on the left. 7) I faced the front, held the fan with both hands and moved it back and forth (hiding my face) twice and up and down twice. 8) I held the fan with my right hand and turned a circle, moving the fan up and down. 9) I rotated the fan in front of my face. 10) Keeping the fan in front of my face, I sat down, keeping my spine upright and bending my legs beneath me. I moved my right hand with the fan on my left shoulder and showed the fan to the audience. I put my left hand on my right shoulder and moved my left hand back and forth. 11) I drew a circle with both hands, touched the fan with my left hand, folded the fan, left it in front of me and bowed, lowering my forehead to the floor.

Photo 8.2 & 8.3 Banners of Amaterasu (painted by Lydia Ruyle) (4 August 2019)

Thank you for taking the time to research Her story and forms of dance. It was what I hoped for." (personal email, 16 August 2009)

At the Goddess Conference the following year, some people told me "I liked your dance last year." I was surprised that anyone remembered it. I did not attend the Goddess Conference for several years after that. In 2019, ten years after my dance performance, the Goddess Conference focused on the Sun Lover Goddess. This reminded me of the Amaterasu Dance, and I posted a comment about my 2009 dance on Facebook. Some people commented that they still remembered it. The ceremonial group at the Goddess Conference that year re-created the myths of various goddesses and distributed a leaflet to the guests. One of the current organisers was writing about Amaterasu from the perspective of love. She said one reason that she chose Amaterasu was because she remembered my dance. To my big surprise, one of my friends, who held a workshop to revive the myth of Amaterasu as sacred drama, first encountered Amaterasu when she saw my dance. In fact, my performance had not ended in 2009, but lasted in the memories of those who witnessed it and influenced their re-creations of the myth.

Creating and performing this Amaterasu Dance also subtly changed me over these ten years. First, I came to accept Amaterasu as goddess, while disassociating her from nationalism. Second, I am more interested in the deities of each Shinto shrine that I visit. There is a board of names of deities at Shinto shrines, but many Japanese do not mind who they are worshipping. I had been disinterested before but am now curious about each deity.

Photo 8.4 Sufi charity shop which was run by the coordinator (29 Sept. 2011)

Chanting the Quran

173

During my stay in Glastonbury, I regularly attended a Sufi group and chanted the Quran. The Naqshbandiyya-Haqqaniyya order, which is based in Northern Cyprus, regards Glastonbury as a sacred place (cf. Draper 2004). South Asians, Southeast Asians, Westerners and people of other ethnic backgrounds hold meetings together. The female members meet every week, chanting the Quran then eating lunch and praying.

When I first attended a meeting in 2006, I asked the coordinator, a Scandinavian, to write the Quran on paper because I wanted to chant properly. She refused, saying it was not necessary because Muslim children learn the Quran by listening and chanting with adults. She also said it was not good to write the Quran in Roman alphabet since the Quran was written in Arabic, which made the Quran special. I thought it would be impossible to remember the Quran because I did not know any Arabic, but I concentrated on listening to the sounds at every meeting. To my surprise, I could chant two or three of the verses after several weeks. I wondered if the Quran might have special energy as she said.

I did not intend to research this group since there were many scholars who studied Islam, but I liked the sounds and the vibrations of the Quran. Therefore, whenever I had spare time in Glastonbury, I attended their meeting. Eventually the coordinator suggested I should visit Sheikh Nazim, their spiritual leader, in Northern Cyprus. He had frequently visited Europe, but as he got older, he stayed in Cyprus most of his time. She arranged transportation and accommodation, and I visited him, staying at his guesthouse for four days in 2009. Upon returning to Glastonbury, I noted that the members' attitude toward me changed slightly. They had always welcomed me, but I had felt a bit distant. They might have been suspicious of me for attending while not sincerely studying Islam. Perhaps I had been a mere curiosity for them. After returning from Northern Cyprus, there was still no pressure to convert, but they seemed to accept I came to the group with a serious interest in Sufism, not just for fun.

One day, I told the coordinator that I was going to Jerusalem. She suggested I visit the Temple Mount at a time when only Muslims are permitted, because the energy is very different. According to her definition of Muslim, I am a Muslim,[20] but I suspected the people in Jerusalem would not agree. In Jerusalem, I went to the Golden Dome. Three male soldiers stood with guns at the entrance. They told me to wait until the time for tourists. I told the soldiers her definition of a Muslim and started chanting the Quran. I chanted all that I remembered. They were surprised, but acknowledged my chanting, saying "good" and "right". However, they remained suspicious and asked me the names and times of the five prayers. Their guns scared me so much that I did not remember all of the names and was not admitted. I emailed her that evening to recount my experience at the entrance of the Temple Mount. She replied with regret, saying that they were too formal.

These days, when I meet a Muslim, I proudly tell them that I know the Quran and begin chanting, almost invariably to their surprise. One Muslim I met at an academic conference was very surprised and filmed my chanting to share with friends in his home country. I chanted the Quran for my students at university where I was teaching because most of them had never heard of it. I sometimes miss the chanting and am happy to find it as an audio program on planes from Islam countries. Although I still do not know the meanings of every phrase, I sometimes chant it when I am walking alone in the dark because I feel it might protect me.

---

[20] Although I had not converted to Islam, she said that anybody who believed in God, admitted Muhammad as one of the prophets and was a good person was a Muslim. Based on this definition, I am Muslim, as are most of the people in the world. She said that covering the hair and keeping rules about eating were just form, while what is important is the heart. It is worth noting that she had converted to Islam and sincerely kept the disciplines.

Discussion

Although these two cases do not directly relate to each other, my life in Glastonbury was a "patchwork" of different spiritual things. For example, it was not unusual to be back from the weekly Sufi chanting in the early afternoon and go straight to the Goddess Temple for volunteering. As I mentioned, there are various kinds of alternative spiritualities in Glastonbury. Glastonbury is a *ba* consisting of many special *bas*.

Like Prince, as a young woman in my 20s, some people regarded me as a spiritual seeker rather than a researcher. Yet unlike Prince and Ivakhiv, I suspect my presence was more notable in Glastonbury in general, and more particularly so in the settings for my fieldwork – the Goddess movement and Sufism – because of my "different" physical characteristics. And, like Sakai, English is the first language of most of my informants, but my second language. But I was not necessarily or automatically in a subordinate position. I was also an agent.

The act of performing the Amaterasu Dance co-emerged with the field of Glastonbury and the people who were involved in the Goddess movement, living in Glastonbury, and who supported my research. And I assume that the Amaterasu Dance performed on that day became a better dance because of the audience, especially those who knew me, and the *ba*. Although it is different from Schechner's "restored behavior" discussed in the Introduction (See pp.3–4), the vestige of my Amaterasu Dance was evident ten years later. Similarly, my chanting the Quran co-emerged from Sufi meetings and the people attending. Ten years later, I am still chanting the Quran in a university class that I teach in Japan and to the Muslims I meet.

These two cases reveal that *ba* (a field), the people in it, and I (a fieldworker) co-emerged. The performances, the Amaterasu Dance and Quran chanting, activated *ba*, from which emerged new *ba*. In other words, my agency co-emerges with *ba* and other people. We can detect the vestiges after many years; new *ba* emerges and changes my agency, which was already transformed by the original *ba*. Also, the vestige of *ba* can be found away from the original *ba*.

Fieldwork is the cooperation of a fieldworker, informants and *ba*. As a confluence of atmosphere, memory, language, sensuality and feeling, *ba* works on a person and changes their performance. My agency changed during the process of performing the dance and the chant, driven by *ba* – my field. In other words, ethnographic fieldwork is a process of changing the fieldworker's agency.

Conclusion

In the study of sacred places, energy or power is frequently mentioned. For example, a place of epiphany and hierophany (Eliade 1991), the difference of spot (Castaneda 1968), and leylines and the sacred places of Native American (Swan 1990).[21] In more recent studies, Ivakhiv analyses "ideas about Earth's 'power places' and about the people who have felt drawn to such places" (Ivakhiv 2001: x), and Marion Bowman, a religious studies scholar who has been studying Glastonbury for more than 25 years, says that the people of Glastonbury are united only by "their conviction of the special nature of the place itself" and "there is a growing consensus that *whatever* the stated reason or focus of pilgrimage, underlying it all is the greater timeless, universal pull of earth energies" (Bowman 2008: 279). The idea of places being sites of particular energy or power is typically treated as an alternative concept, but it bears similarities to the concept of fun'iki (atomosphere). Fun'iki is often used with *ba*, such as "atmosphere of *ba*" (*ba no fun'iki*).

Marcus and Fischer claimed that Anglo-American anthropologists were fantasising about "a reciprocal critical ethnography ... from the point of view of a radically cultural other" (1986: 156). My (non-Western anthropologist) attempt to analyse Westerners via a non-Western concept is intended as a contribution to realising that fantasy.

Acknowledgements

I appreciate the people and organizations who helped my research for the Amaterasu Dance, especially Professor Kazuo Matsumura, Ise Shrine, Kogakukan University, The Organization for the Preservation of Kabuki, Takarazuka Revue Information Centre, Hankyu Culture Foundation, the Japan Folk Performing Arts Association, Ise city tourist office, Imizu city office, Kyoto prefecture office, Nara visitors bureau and Hiraizumi town office. This paper is a significantly revised and expanded version of the third part of the book based on my PhD dissertation, titled *Goddesses in Glastonbury* (Kawanishi 2015) in Japanese. I appreciate all the friends and scholars who helped my research in and away from Glastonbury.

176

---

[21] The idea that certain places affect humans is also discussed by Tuan (1974) as topophilia.

Bibliography

Adams, Tony E., Stacy Holman Jones and Carolyn Ellis, 2015, *Autoethnography*. New York: Oxford University Press.

Akita Prefecture, 2015, *Akita ken jinkou bijon: 'koushitsu na inaka' wo omoiegaki nagara 'nihon ni koukensuru akita, jiritsusuru akita wo mezashite* (Vision of population in Akita Prefecture: Aiming at "Akita contributing Japan, Becoming self-reliant Akita" with imagining "high-quality countryside"). https://www.pref.akita.lg.jp/uploads/public/archive_0000010217_00/jinkou_vision.pdf (accessed 7 December 2019).

Akita Sakigake Shimpo, 13/4/2020, "Ken Jinkou genshouritsu, 7 nen renzoku de zenkoku Saikou, Soumu-shō no suikei 96 man 6 sen nin (Depopulation rate of Akita prefecture will be the largest in Japan for the past 7 years, According to the Estimate by Ministry of Internal Affairs and Communications" https://www.sakigake.jp/news/article/20200414AK0031/(accessed 20 May 2020).

Anderson, Benedict, 1983 / 1991, *Imagined Communities: Reflections on the Origin and Spread of Nationalism*. London: Verso.

Anderson, Benedict. R. O'G., 1990, *Language and Power: Exploring Political Cultures in Indonesia*. New York: Cornel University Press.

Anderson, Leon, 2006, Analytic Autoethnography. *Journal of Contemporary Ethnography*. 35(4): 373–395.

Auge, Marc, 1995, *Non-Places: An Introduction to Super Modernity*. London: Verso.

Aydın, Mehmet, 2017, *Göçebe Türk Kültürünün Son Temsilcisi Yörükler* (The last representative of nomadic Turk culture). Çıra Basın Yayın Ltd. Şti.

Bado-Fralick, Nikki, 2005, *Coming to the Edge of the Circle: A Wiccan Initiation Ritual*. New York: Oxford University Press.

Barrett, Leonard E., 1997, *The Rastafarians*. Boston: Beacon Press.

Barth, Fredrik, 1995, Other Knowledge and Other Ways of Knowing. *Journal of Anthropological Research*. 51(1): 65–68.

Bateson, Gregory, 1972, *Steps to an Ecology of Mind: Collected Essays in Anthropology, Psychiatry, Evolution, and Epistemology*. San Francisco, Scranton, London, Toronto: Chandler Publishing Company.

Bauman, Richard, 1975, Verbal Art as Performance. *American Anthropologist, New Series*. 77(2): 290–311.

Benedict, Ruth, 1946, *The Chrysanthemum and the Sword: Patterns of Japanese Culture*. Boston: Houghton Mifflin.

Bertram, Geoff and Raymond Watters, 1985, The MIRAB Economy in South Pacific Microstates. *Pacific Viewpoint*. 26(3): 497–519.

Bestor, Theodore C., 2004, *Tsukiji: The Fish Market at the Center of the World*. Berkley: University of California Press.

Bevacqua, Michael Lujan, 2017, Guam. *The Contemporary Pacific*. 29(1): 104–111.

Blacking, John, 1973, *How Musical Is Man?* Seattle and London: The University of Washington Press.

Blain, Jenny, Douglas Ezzy and Graham Harvey (eds.), 2004, *Researching Paganisms.* Lanham: AltaMira Press.

Blommaert, Jan, 2006, Applied Ethnopoetics. *Narrative Inquiry.* 16(1): 181–190.

Born, Georgina, 2013, Introduction – Music, Sound and Space: Transformations of Public and Private Experience. In Georgina Born (ed.), *Music, Sound and Space: Transformations of Public and Private Experience.* Cambridge: Cambridge University Press. pp. 1–70.

Bowman, Marion, 1993, Drawn to Glastonbury. In Ian Reader and Tony Walter (eds.), *Pilgrimage in Popular Culture.* Basingstoke and London: The Macmillan Press. pp. 29–62.

2000, More of the Same? Christianity, Vernacular Religion and Alternative Spirituality in Glastonbury. In Steven Sutcliffe and Marion Bowman (eds.), *Beyond New Age: Exploring Alternative Spirituality.* Edinburgh: Edinburgh University Press. pp. 83–104.

2005, Ancient Avalon, New Jerusalem, Heart Chakra of Planet Earth: The Local and the Global in Glastonbury. *Numen.* 52: 157–190.

2008, Going with the Flow: Contemporary Pilgrimage in Glastonbury. In Peter Jan Margry (ed.), *Shrines and Pilgrimage in the Modern World: New Itineraries into the Sacred.* Amsterdam: Amsterdam University Press. pp. 241–280.

Brisini, Travis and Jake Simmons, 2016, Posthuman Relations in Performance Studies. *Posthuman Relations in Performance Studies.* Special Issue. *Text and Performance Quarterly.* 36(4): 191–99.

Brisini, Travis, 2019, Phytomorphizing Performance: Plant Performance in an Expanded Field. *Text and Performance Quarterly.* 39(1): 3–21.

Butler, Judith, 1990, *Gender Trouble: Feminism and the Subversion of Identity.* New York: Routledge.

1993, *Bodies that Matter: On the Discursive Limits of "Sex".* New York: Routledge

Callam, Neville, 1980, Invitation to Docility: Defusing the Rastafarian Challenge. *Caribbean Journal of Religious Studies.* 3: 28–48.

Callon, Michel, 1998, An Essay on Framing and Overflowing: Economic Externality Revisited by Sociology. In Michel Callon (ed.), *The Laws of the Market.* Oxford: Blackwell. pp. 244–269

Casey, Edward S., 1996, How to Get from Space to Place in a Fairly Short Stretch of Time. In Steven Feld and Keith H. Basso (eds.), *Senses of Place.* Santa Fe: School of American Research Press. pp.14–51.

1997, *The Fate of Place: A Philosophical History.* Berkeley: University of California Press.

Castaneda, Carlos, 1968, *The Teachings of Don Juan: a Yaqui Way of Knowledge.* Berkeley: University of California Press.

Chatterjee, Partha, 2004, *The Politics of the Governed: Reflections on Popular Politics in Most of the World.* New York: Columbia University Press.

Chevannes, Barry, 1994, *Rastafari Roots and Ideology*. New York: Syracuse University Press.

Clifford, James and George E. Marcus, 1986, *Writing Culture: The Poetics and Politics of Ethnography*. Berkeley, Los Angeles and London: University of California Press.

Clifford, James, 1997, *Routes: Travel and Translation in the Late Twentieth Century*. Cambridge: Harvard University Press.

Coker, Caitlin, 2015a, Butō no nikutai: gendai nihon ni okeru butōkatachi no nichijōjissen to kyōdōseikatsu (Butoh and being a physical body: The daily practice and collective living of Butoh artists in Japan). *Jinbun Gakuhō* (The Zinbun Gakuho: Journal of Humanities). 107: 73–101.

2015b, Ayaui nikutai ni deau: butō to shō dansu to no kankei wo megutte (Encountering the precarious physical body: The relationship between Butoh and show dance). *Nihon Oral History Kenkyū* (Japan Oral History Review). 15: 217–244.

2018, The Daily Practice of Hijikata Tatsumi's Apprentices from 1969 to 1978. In Bruce Baird and Rosemary Candelario (eds.), *The Routledge Companion to Butoh*. London: Routledge. pp. 409–417.

2019, *Ankoku Butō no Shintaikeiken: affekuto to seisei no jinruigaku* (A physical experience of Ankoku Butoh: The anthropology of affect and creation). Kyoto: Kyoto University Press.

Connerton, Paul, 1989, *How Societies Remember*, Cambridge: Cambridge University Press.

Cresswell, Tim, 2004, *Place: A Short Introduction*. Malden, MA and Oxford: Blackwell.

Csordas, Thomas, 1993, Somatic Modes of Attention. *Cultural Anthropology*. 8(2): 135–156.

2011, Cultural Phenomenology of Embodiment: Agency, Sexual Difference, and Illness. In Frances E. Mascia-Lees (ed.), *A Companion to the Anthropology of the Body and Embodiment*. New Jersey: Blackwell Publishing.

Dahlquist, Paul, 1974, Political Development at the Municipal Level: Kiti, Ponape. In Daniel Hughes and Sherwood Lingenfelter (eds.), *Political Development in Micronesia*. Columbus: Ohio State University Press. pp. 178–191.

Division of Statistics, Department of Economic Affairs, 2002, *FSM National Detailed Tables: 2000 FSM Census of Population and Housing*. Palikir: The Federated States of Micronesia.

Dore, Ronald P., 1978, *Shinohata: A Portrait of a Japanese Village*. New York: Pantheon Books.

Draper, Ian K. B., 2004, From Celts to Kaaba: Sufism in Glastonbury. In David Westerlund (ed.), *Sufism in Europe and North America*. New York and London: Routledge. pp. 144–156.

Duranti, Alessandro, 1993, Intentions, Self, and Responsibility: An Essay in Samoan Ethnopragmatics. In Jane Hill and Judith Irvine (eds.), *Responsibility and Evidence in Oral Discourse*. Cambridge: Cambridge University Press. pp. 24–47.

1994, *From Grammar to Politics: Linguistic Anthropology in a Western Samoan Village*. Berkeley: University of California Press.

E.A.B.I.C., 1978, *Black Supremacy in Righteousness of Salvation*. E.A.B.I.C.

Edmonds, Ennis Barrington, 2003, *Rastafari: From Outcast to Culture Bearer*. New York: Oxford University Press.

Eliade, Mircea, 1991, *Images and Symbols: Studies in Religious Symbolism*. Princeton: Princeton University Press.

Embree, John F., 1939, *Suye Mura: A Japanese Village*. Chicago: University of Chicago Press.

Ezzy, Douglas et. al., 2015, Paths into Pagan Studies: Autobiographical Reflections. (Special Section) *The Pomegranate: The International Journal of Pagan Studies*. 17(1–2): 72–205.

Feld, Steven, 1996, Waterfalls of Song: an Acoutemology of Place Resounding in Bosavi, Papua New Guinea. In Steven Feld and Keith H. Basso (eds.), *Senses of Place*. Santa Fe: School of American Research Press. pp. 91–135.

Feld, Steven and Keith H. Basso, 1996, Introduction. In Steven Feld and Keith H. Basso (ed.), *Senses of Place*. Santa Fe: School of American Research Press. pp. 3–11.

Fischer, John, 1974, The Role of the Traditional Chiefs on Ponape in American Period. In Daniel Hughes and Sherwood Lingenfelter (eds.), *Political Development in Micronesia*. Columbus: Ohio State University Press. pp. 166–177.

Furuya, Yoshiaki, 2001, *Hybrid Modernities and Anthropology: From Latin-American Contact Zones*. Kyoto: Jinbun Shoin.

Garrard, Bruce, 1989, 'Glastonbury Hippies' – A potted history. In Ann Morgan and Bruce Garrard (eds.), *Travellers in Glastonbury: A series of articles written during the summer of 1989* [*The Glastonbury Gazette*]. Glastonbury: Unique Publications. pp. 4–5.

Gilroy, Paul, 1993, *The Black Atlantic: Modernity and Double-Consciousness*. Massachusetts: Harvard University Press.

Goffman, Erving, 1959, *The Presentation of Self in Everyday Life*. New York: Doubleday Anchor Books.

1986, *Frame Analysis: An Essay on the Organization of Experience*. Boston: Northeastern University Press.

Goldstein, Melvyn, 1997, *The Snow Lion and the Dragon: China, Tibet, and the Dalai Lama*. California: University of California Press.

Greenwood, Susan, 2000, *Magic, Witchcraft and the Otherworld: An Anthropology*. Oxford and New York: Berg.

Gupta, Akhil and James Ferguson, 1997, After "Peoples and Cultures." In Akhil Gupta and James Ferguson (eds.), *Culture, Power, Place: Explorations in Critical Anthropology*. London: Duke University Press. pp. 1–32.

Halbwachs, Maurice, 1992, *On Collective Memory*. Edited and translated from French by Lewis. A. Coser. Chicago: University of Chicago Press.

Hanks, William, Sachiko Ide, Yasuhiro Katagiri, Scott Saft, Yoko Fujii, Kishiko Ueno, 2019, Communicative Interaction in Terms of *Ba* Theory: Towards an Innovative Approach to Language Practice. *Journal of Pragmatics*. 145: 63–71.

Hanlon, David, 2017, Losing Oceania to the Pacific and the World. *The Contemporary Pacific*, 29: 286–318.

Harrison, Klisala, 2002, The Kwagiulth Dancers: Addressing Intellectual Property Issues at Victoria's First Peoples Festival. *World of Music*, 44(1): 137–151.

Hashimoto, Yoshio, 1995, *Nūdosan: Sutorippu ōgon jidai* (Burlesque dancers: The golden era of striptease). Tokyo: Chikuma Shobo.

Hastrup, Kirsten and Karen Fog Olwig, 1997, Introduction. In Karen Fog Olwig and Kirsten Hastrup (eds.), *Siting Culture: The Shifting Anthropological Object*. London: Routledge. pp. 1–14.

Hau'ofa, Epeli, 1994, *Tales of the Tikongs*. Honolulu: University of Hawai'i Press.

    1995, *Kisses in the Nederends*. Honolulu: University of Hawai'i Press.

    2005, The Development of Contemporary Oceanic Arts. *People and Culture in Oceania*, 20: 5–12.

    2008, *We Are the Ocean: Selected Works*. Honolulu: University of Hawai'i Press.

Hayashi, Kayoko, 2008, *Osuman teikoku 500nen no heiwa* (Five hundred years of peace in the Ottoman Empire), Tokyo: Kodansha.

Hendry, Joy, 1993, *Wrapping Culture: Politeness, Presentation and Power in Japan and Other Societies*. Oxford and Tokyo: Clarendon Press.

Henry, Rosita and Lawrence Foana'ota, 2015, Heritage Transactions at the Festival of Pacific Arts. *International Journal of Heritage Studies*. 21(2): 133–152.

Hereniko, Vilsoni, 1994, Representation of Cultural Identities. In Howe, K.R., Robert C. Kiste, and Brij V. Lal (eds.), *Tides of History: The Pacific Islands in the Twentieth Century*. Honolulu: University of Hawai'i Press.

    2010, Meditation on Epeli Hau'ofa. *The Journal of Pacific History*. 45(1): 141–144.

Hexham, Irving, 1981, New Age Thought in Glastonbury: Some Aspects of the Contemporary Search for an Alternative Society. [In Glastonbury, England, 1967–1971]. Unpublished M.A. thesis, University of Bristol.

Hirsch, Eric, 1995, Landscape: Between Place and Space. In Eric Hirsch and Michael E. O'Hanlon (eds.), *The Anthropology of Landscape: Perspectives on Place and Space*. Oxford: Clarendon Press. pp. 1–30.

Hughes, David W., 1992, "Esashi Oiwake" and the Beginnings of Modern Japanese Folk Song. *The World of Music*. 34(1): 35–56.

    2008a, *Traditional Folk Song in Modern Japan: Sources, Sentiment and Society*. Folkestone: Global Oriental.

    2008b, Folk Music: From Local to National to Global. In Alison M. Tokita and David W. Hughes (eds.), *Ashgate Research Companion to Japanese Music*. Aldershot: Ashgate. pp. 281–302.

Hymes, Dell, 1981, *"In Vain I Tried to Tell You"*: *Essays in Native American Ethnopoetics*. Lincoln: University of Nebraska Press.

Ihde, Don, 2007, *Listening and Voice: Phenomenologies of Sound (Second Edition)*. Albany, NY: State University of New York Press.

Ingold, Tim, 2011, *Being Alive: Essays on Movement, Knowledge and Description*. London: Routledge.

Islands Society, The Importance of the Festival of Pacific Arts for Guam. (http://islandssociety.org/community/regionalsocieties/pacific-islands-society/voices/pacific-education/the-importance-of-the-festival-of-pacific-arts-for-guam/) (accessed 20 July 2020).

Ivakhiv, Adrian J., 2001, *Claiming Sacred Ground: Pilgrims and Politics at Glastonbury and Sedona*. Bloomington: Indiana University Press.

Jakobson, Roman, 1960, Linguistics and Poetics. In Thomas A. Sebeok (ed.), *Style in Language*. MA: MIT Press. pp. 350–377.

Jamaica Gleaner 8/5/1997, 4/7/1998

Jolly, Margaret, 2001, On the Edge? Deserts, Oceans, Islands. *Contemporary Pacific*. 13(2): 417–466.

2007, Imagining Oceania: Indigenous and Foreign Representations of a Sea of Islands. *Contemporary Pacific*. 19(2): 508–545.

Kantorowicz, Ernest, 1957, *The King's Two Bodies: A Study in Medieval Political Theology*. Princeton: Princeton University Press.

Kataoka, Kuniyoshi, 2012, Toward Multimodal Ethnopoetics. *Applied Linguistics Review*. 3(1): 101–130.

Katsura, Hiroaki, 2003, Chi'iki ni okeru min'yō no ninawarekata: Akita-ken tazawako machi 'kyōdo geinou shinkoukai' no ba'ai. (The tradition of folk songs in local area: The case study of provincial performing arts association of Tazawako City in Akita Prefecture). *Memoirs of Faculty of Education and Human Studies Akita University, Humanities & Social Sciences*. 58: 41–48.

Kawanishi, Eriko, 2013, Alternative to taiji suru jimotomin (Locals face alternatives: A case study of new age business in Glastonbury, UK). *Shukyo to Shakai* (Religion and Society). 19: 1–15.

2015, *Glastonbury no megami tachi* (Goddesses in Glastonbury: An ethnography of alternative spirituality in England). Kyoto: Hozokan.

Kawano, Masaharu, 2019, *Ken'i to reisetsu: gendai mikuronesia ni okeru ikai shōgō to mibun kaisōchitsujo no minzokushi* (Chiefly authority, social hierarchy and the art of courtesy in Pohnpei, Micronesia). Tokyo: Fūkyō-sha.

Keating, Elizabeth, 1998, *Power Sharing: Language, Rank, Gender, and Social Space in Pohnpei, Micronesia*. Oxford: Oxford University Press.

2000, Moments of Hierarchy: Constructing Social Stratification by Means of Language, Food, Space and the Body in Pohnpei, Micronesia. *American Anthropologist*. 102(2): 303–320.

Kirshenblatt-Gimblett, Barbara, 2016, Performance Studies. In Henry Bial and Sara Brady (eds.), *The Performance Studies Reader (Third Edition)*. New York: Routledge. pp. 25–36.

Komine, Hideo, 1970, Akita no min'yō (Folk Songs in Akita). In Akita Sakigake Shinpō-sha Bunka-bu. *Akita no min'yō, geinō, bungei: Chihou bunka no genryū* (Folk Songs, performing arts, and literature in Akita: Origin of local culture). Akita: Akita Sakigake Shimpō-sha, pp. 1–101.

Kuwayama Takami, 2004, The "World-System" of Anthropology: Japan and Asia in the Global Community of Anthropologists. In Yamashita, Shinji, Joseph Bosco, and J. S. Eades (eds.), *The Making of Anthropology in East and Southeast Asia*. New York: Berghahn Books. pp. 35–56.

2017, Japanese Anthropology, Neoliberal Knowledge Structuring, and the Rise of Audit Culture: Lessons from the Academic World System. *Asian Anthropology*. 16(3): 159–171.

Lawless, Elaine J., 1993, *Holy Women, Wholly Women: Sharing Ministries of Wholeness Through Life Stories and Reciprocal Ethnography*. Philadelphia: University of Pennsylvania Press.

Leahy, Joycelin, Joyce Yeap-Holliday and Bill Pennington, 2010, *Evaluation of the Festival of Pacific Arts*. Noumea: Secretariat of the Pacific Community.

Lindstrom, Lamont and Geoffrey White, 1997, Introduction: Chiefs Today. In Geoffrey White and Lamont Lindstrom (eds.), *Chiefs Today: Traditional Pacific Leadership and the Postcolonial State*. California: Stanford University Press. pp. 1–18.

Lord, Albart, 2000, *The Singer of Tales: Second Edition*. Cambridge: Harvard University Press.

Low, Setha M., 2017, *Spatializing Culture: The Ethnography of Space and Place*. New York: Routledge.

Low, Setha M. and Denise Lawrence-Zúñiga, 2003, Locating Culture. In Setha M. Low and Denise Lawrence-Zúñiga (eds.), *The Anthropology of Space and Place: Locating Culture*. Malden, MA and Oxford: Blackwell. pp. 1–47.

MacAloon, John. J., 1984, Introduction: Cultural Performances, Cultural Theory. In: John. J. MacAloon (ed.), *Rite, Drama, Festival, Spectacle: Rehearsals Toward a Theory of Cultural Performance*. Philadelphia: Institute for the Study of Human Issues.

MacCanell, Dean, 1973, Staged Authenticity: Arrangement of Social Space in Tourist Settings. *American Journal of Sociology*. 79(3): 589–603.

Mackley-Crump, Jared, 2015, *The Pacific Festivals of Aotearoa New Zealand: Negotiating Place and Identity in a New Homeland*. Honolulu: University of Hawai'i Press.

Magliocco, Sabina, 2004, *Witching Culture: Folklore and Neo-Paganism in America*. Philadelphia: University of Pennsylvania Press.

Malkki, Liisa, 1995, *Purity and Exile: Violence, Memory, and National Cosmology among Hutu Refugees in Tanzania*. Chicago: University of Chicago Press.

Mara, Kamisese Ratu Sir, 1997, *The Pacific Way: A Memoir*. Honolulu: University of Hawai'i Press.

Maraldo, John C., 2019, Nishida Kitarō. In Edward N. Zalta (ed.), *The Stanford Encyclopedia of Philosophy (Spring 2019 Edition)*. https://plato.stanford.edu/archives/spr2019/entries/nishida-kitaro/

Marcus, George E., 1989, Chieftainship. In Alan Howard and Robert Borofsky (eds.), *Development in Polynesian Ethnology.* Honolulu: University of Hawaii Press. pp. 175–209.

Marcus, George E. and Michael M. J. Fischer, 1986, *Anthropology as Cultural Critique: An Experimental Moment in the Human Sciences.* Chicago: University of Chicago Press.

Massey, Doreen, 2005, *For Space.* Los Angeles: Sage.

Matsubara, Masatake, 1988, *Toruko no hitobito: kataritsugu rekishi no naka de* (People in Turkey: An oral history), Tokyo: Nihon Hōsō Shuppan Kyōkai.

1990, *Yubokumin no shouzou* (The portrait of nomads), Tokyo: Kadokawa Shoten.

2004, *Yuboku no sekai: Toruko-kei yubokumin Yörük no minzokushi kara* (World of nomads: From ethnography of Yörük, Turkish nomads), Tokyo: Heibonsha.

Minzoku Geijutsu Kenkyūsho (ed.), 2013, *Akita min'yō sodate no oya kodama gyōson* (The foster father of Akita Min'yō, Kodama Gyōson). Akita: Mumyō-sha.

Mori, Akiko, 1999, *Tochi o yomikaeru kazoku* (Family and its interpreted land: A historical ethnography of a Carinthian parish). Tokyo: Shin'yosha.

2004, Jo-Europe jinruigaku no kanosei (Introduction: The possibility of an anthropology of Europe). In Akiko Mori (ed.), *Europe jinruigaku* (Anthropology of Europe: From the field of reorganising the modern period). Tokyo: Shin'yosha. pp. 1–24.

Morris-Suzuki, Tessa, 1998, Gurobaru-na kioku, Nashonaru-na kijutsu (Global memory, national description), *Shiso.* 890: 35–56.

Motofuji, Akiko, 1990, *Hijikata Tatsumi to tomoni* (With Hijikata Tatsumi). Tokyo: Chikuma Shobo.

Na'puti, Tiara R. and Sylvia C. Frain, 2017, Decolonize Oceania! Free Guåhan!: Communicating Resistance at the 2016 Festival of Pacific Arts. *Amerasia Journal,* 43(3): 2–34.

Nettleford, Rex, 1970, *Mirror Mirror: Identity, Race and Protest in Jamaica.* Kingston: LMH Publishing.

Newland, Arthur, 1994, *The Life and Works of King Emmanuel Charles Edwards.* Unpublished.

Nihon Hōsō Kyōkai (ed.), 1992, *Nihon min'yō taikan tōhoku hen* (Conspectus of Japanese folk song Tōhoku Volume). (Reprint). Tokyo: Nihon Hōsō Syuppan Kyōkai.

Nishida, Kitaro, 2012, *Place and Dialectic: Two Essays by Nishida Kitaro,* Translated by John Krummel and Shigemori Nagatomo. Oxford: Oxford University Press.

Ogashiwa, Yoko, 2000, Taiheiyou toushoshokoku kankei to chiiki kyouryoku (Relations of Pacific Island nations and regional cooperation). In Yamamoto, Matori (ed.), *Oceania Shi* (History of Oceania). Tokyo: Yamakawa Shuppansha.

Osawa, Masachi, 2007, *Nasyonarizumu no yurai* (The origin of nationalism). Tokyo: Kodansha.

Oxford University Press, 2005, *Oxford Dictionary of English* (Second Edition revised). Oxford: Oxford University Press.

Ozawa, Shoichi, 1969, *Watashi ha kawarakojiki/ kō* (I am an entertainer, a riverside beggar: A report). Tokyo: Iwanami Shoten.

1977, *Geinin no Shōzō* (Portrait of an entertainer). Tokyo: Chikuma Shobo.

Ozawa, Shoichi and Tetsu Hijikata, 1981, *Geinō Nyūmon / kō: Gei ni ikiru* (An introduction to entertainment: A report: living one's craft). Tokyo: Akashi Shoten.

Paerregaard, Karsten, 2002, The Resonance of Fieldwork. Ethnographers, Informants and the Creation of Anthropological Knowledge. *Social Anthropology*. 10(3): 319–334.

Parman, Susan, 1998, Introduction: Europe in the Anthropological Imagination. In Susan Parman (ed.), *Europe in the Anthropological Imagination*. Upper Saddle River: Prentice Hall. pp. 1–16.

Petersen, Glenn, 1982, *One Man Cannot Rule a Thousand; Fission in Ponapean Chiefdom*. Ann Arbor: University of Michigan Press.

Pike, Sarah, 2001, *Earthly Bodies, Magical Selves: Contemporary Pagans and the Search for Community*. Berkeley: University of California Press.

Prasad, Mohit (ed.), 2006, *Dreadlocks Vaka Vuku. Special Issue: Proceedings of the Pacific Epistemology Conference 2006*. Suva: University of the South Pacific.

Prince, Ruth and David Riches, 2000, *The New Age in Glastonbury: The Construction of Religious Movements*. New York and London: Berghahn Books.

Ribeiro, Gustavo L., 2006, World Anthropologies: Cosmopolitics for a New Global Scenario in Anthropology. *Critique of Anthropology*. 26(4): 363–386.

2014, World Anthropologies: Anthropological Cosmopolitanisms and Cosmopolitics. *Annual Review of Anthropology*. 43: 483–498.

Rice, Timothy, 2014, *Ethnomusicology: A Very Short Introduction*. Oxford: Oxford University Press.

Riesenberg, Paul, 1968, *The Native Polity of Ponape*. Washington: Smithsonian Institution Press.

Roach, Joseph, 1995, Culture and Performance in the Circum-Atlantic World. In A. Parker and E. Sedgwick (eds.), *Performativity and Performance*, New York: Routledge.

Roemer, Stephanie, 2008, *The Tibetan Government-in-Exile: Politics at Large*. London: Routledge.

Rountree, Kathryn, 2004, *Embracing the Witch and the Goddess: Feminist Ritual-Makers in New Zealand*. London and New York: Routledge.

Sakai, Tomoko, 2011, Contact zone to shiteno life story (Life story research as contact zone: Methodological considerations on interviewing in second language). In Masakazu Tanaka and Toru Funayama (eds.), *Contact zone no jinbungaku I (Contact zone I: Problematique)*. Kyoto: Koyo Shobo. pp. 79–102.

2015, *Funsou toiu nichijo* (Conflict as daily life: An ethnography of memory and storytelling in Northern Ireland). Kyoto: Zinbun Shoin.

Salomonsen, Jone, 2002, *Enchanted Feminism: Ritual, Gender and Divinity among the Reclaiming Witches of San Francisco*. London and New York: Routledge.

Samuels, David W., Louise Meintjes, Ana Maria Ochoa, and Thomas Porcello, 2010, Soundscapes: Toward a Sounded Anthropology. *Annual Review of Anthropology*. 39: 329–345.

Sarı, Cemali, 2013, Batı Toroslar'da Yaylaların Fonksiyonel Değişim Süreci Ve Yayla Şenlikleri (The functional changing process of Yayla in Western Toros). *Marmara Coğrafya Dergisi* (Marmara Journal of Geography). 27: 242–261.

Sarı, Cemali and Mustafa Ertürk, 2017, Batı Toroslarda Yörük Göç Yollarının Turizm Amaçlı Kullanımına Yönelik Planlama (Planning of tourism utilization of Yörük migration paths in Western Toros). *Journal of Turkish Studies*. 12(24): 159–178.

Sasaki, Shōgen, 2008, *Kikiaruki akita no uta* (Listening around Akita Folk Song) Vol.1/2. Daisen: Shoshi Mugura.

Schechner, Richard, 1985, *Between Theater and Anthropology*. Philadelphia: University of Pennsylvania Press.

2003, *Performance Theory*. London: Routledge.

2013, *Performance Studies: An Introduction* (3rd edition). New York: Routledge.

Secretariat of Pacific Community, http://www.spc.int/ (accessed 20 January 2014).

Sen, Arijit and Lisa Silverman (eds.), 2014, *Making Place: Space and Embodiment in the City*. Bloomington and Indianapolis: Indiana University Press.

Shiga, Nobuo, 2008, Hijikata Tatsumi: butō/kyabarē shikō (Hijikata Tatsumi: Thoughts on Butoh and the cabaret). *Corpus: Shintai Hyōgen Hihyō* (Corpus: A review of physical expression). 4: 41–45.

Shimizu, Akitoshi, 1982, Chiefdom and the Spatial Classification of the Life-World: Everyday Life, Subsistence and the Political System on Ponape. In Machiko Aoyagi (ed.), *Islanders and their Outside World: A Report of the Cultural Anthropological Research in the Caroline Islands of Micronesia in 1980–1981*. Tokyo: St. Paul's (Rikkyo) University. pp. 153–215.

1987, Feasting as Socio-Political Process of Chieftainship on Ponape, Eastern Carolines. In Iwao Ushijima and Ken'ichi Sudō (eds.), *Cultural Uniformity and Diversity in Micronesia*. Osaka: National Museum of Ethnology. pp. 129–176.

Shimizu, Hiroshi, 1993, Biological Autonomy: The Self-Creation of Constraints. *Applied Mathematics and Computation*. 56(2–3): 177–201.

1995, "Ba-Principle": New Logic for the Real-Time Emergence of Information. *Holonics*. 5(1): 67–79.

2003, *Ba no shisou* (The thoughts of "ba": Creative stages of life). Tokyo: University of Tokyo Press.

Shioji, Yuko, 2003, *Eikoku countryside no minzokushi* (The creation of Englishness: Sensing boundaries and the preservation of cultural heritage in the Cotswolds of England). Tokyo: Akashi Shoten.

Simone, Abdoumaliq, 2005, Urban Circulation and the Everyday Politics of African Urban Youth: The Case of Douala, Cameroon. *International Journal of Urban and Regional Research*. 20(3): 516–532.

Simpson, George E., 1955, The Ras Tafari Movement in Jamaica: A Study of Race and Class Conflict. *Social Forces.* 34: 167–171.

Small, Christopher, 1998, *Musicking: The Meanings of Performing and Listening.* Hanover and London: Weslyan University Press.

Smith, M., R. Auguer and R. Nettleford, 1960, *Report on the Rastafari Movement in Kingston, Jamaica.* Mona, Jamaica: University College of the West Indies.

Smith, Robert J., 1974, *Ancestor Worship in Contemporary Japan.* Stanford: Stanford University Press.

Snook, Jennifer, 2015, *American Heathens: The Politics of Identity in a Pagan Religious Movement.* Philadelphia: Temple University Press.

Somerset Intelligence, 2012–2013, Census 2011. http://www.somersetintelligence.org. uk/census2011. (accessed 10 August 2016).

SPACLALS, 1999, *Imagining Oceania.* Suva: University of the South Pacific.

Statistical Institute of Jamaica, 2014, *Population and Housing Census 2011 General Report Volume 1.* Regional Census Coordinating Committee.

Stevenson, Karen, 1999, Festivals, Identity and Performance: Tahiti and 6th Pacific Arts Festival. In Barry Craig, Bernie Kernot and Christopher Anderson (eds.), *Art and Performance in Oceania.* Honolulu: University of Hawai'i Press. pp. 29–36.

Sullivan, Kirk Ernest, 2014, *Representations of Pacific Identity at the 2012 Festival of Pacific Arts.* Master thesis at the University of Maryland, College Park.

Suzuki, Nanami, 1999, *Shussan no rekishi jinruigaku* (Historical anthropology of childbirth: From the dissolution of midwifery to the movement of natural birth). Tokyo: Shin'yosha.

Swan, James A., 1990, *Sacred Places: How the Living Earth Seeks Our Friendship.* Santa Fe: Bear.

Taguchi, Hidekichi, 1983, Akita no sousaku min'yō to shūhen: obone'a dashi to denbetodo (Folk songs created in Akita and its surroundings: Obone'a Dashi and Denbetodo). *Akita Minzoku.* 9: 26–30.

Takahashi, Erika, 2013, *Oi o ayumu hitobito* (People who walk toward aging: An ethnography of Finland's welfare state from the everyday life perspective of elders). Tokyo: Keiso Shobo.

Takahashi, Yuuichiro, 2005, *Shintaika sareru chi* (Embodied knowledge: The study of performance), Tokyo: Serika-shobo.

Takeda, Shunsuke, 2001, Min'yō no rekishi shakaigaku: rōkaru na aidentiti/nashonaru na souzouryoku (Historical sociology of Min'yō: Local identity/National imagination). *Sociologos.* 25: 1–20.

Takeuchi, Tsutomu, 2018, *Nihon min'yō jiten* (Encyclopedia of Japanese folk song), Vol.1. *Hokkaidō & Tōhoku.* Tokyo: Asakura Shoten.

Tamura, Ulara, 2018, Toruko nanbu no yubokumin Yörük no genzai: seigyou wo meguru henka wo chushin ni (The current status of Yörüks, nomadic people in Southern Turkey: The changes in their occupation). *Nihon Seitai Gakkai Newsletter* (The Society for Ecological Anthropology newsletter). 23: 82–88.

187

Tanaka, Eisuke, 2018, Iboku no kako no bunka isanka: Toruko chichukai chihou no teijuka shita Yörük no jirei kara (Heritage-making of the Transhumance past in the case of Yörüks who adopted sedentary life in Mediterranean Turkey). *Fukuoka Jogakuin Kiyou Jinbun-gakubu hen* (Fukuoka Jogakuin University Bulletin). 28: 203–229.

Tanaka, Masakazu, 2006, Mikuro-Jinruigaku no kadai (The task of micro-anthropology). In Tanaka Masakazu and Matsuda Motoji (eds.), *Mikuro- Jinruigaku no Jissen: Eijensh i/Nettowāk/Shintai* (The practice of micro-anthropology: Agency/ network/body). Kyoto: Sekaishisōsha. pp. 1–37.

Tedlock, Dennis, 1983, *The Spoken Word and the Work of Interpretation*. University of Pennsylvania Press.

Terado, Junko, 2006, *Lourdes shobyosha junrei no sekai* (Universe of the sick pilgrimage of Lourdes). Tokyo, Chisen Shokan.

Thomas, Deborah, 2004, *Modern Blackness: Nationalism, Globalization, and the Politics of Culture in Jamaica*. Durham: Duke University Press.

Tuan, Yi-Fu, 1974, *Topophilia: A Study of Environmental Perception, Attitudes, and Values*, Englewood Cliffs: Prentice-Hall.

Turino, Thomas, 1999, Signs of Imagination, Identity, and Experience: A Peircian Semiotic Theory for Music. *Ethnomusicology*. 43(2): 221–255.

2008. *Music as Social Life: The Politics of Participation*. Chicago and London: The University of Chicago

Turner, Victor, 1987, *Anthropology of Performance*. New York: PAJ Publications.

Tuztaş-Horzumlu and Ayşe Hilal, 2017, Yörük Kültürünü Tanitmak: Dernekleşme Faaliyetleri Ve Yörük Şenlikleri (Introducing Yörük culture: Organizational activities and Yörük festivals). *Türkiyat Mecmuasi* (Turkish Journal). 27(2): 239–255.

Van Dijk, F.V., 1993, *JAHMAICA - Rastafari and Jamaican Society*. One drop books.

Vatan, Ahmet and Burhanettin Zengin, 2018, Söğüt İlçesi'nde Kültürel Miras Ve Yerel Halkın Turizme Bakiş Açisi (Cultural heritage in Söğüt County and the locals' viewpoint towards tourism). *Akademik Sosyal Araştırmalar Dergisi* (Journal of Academic Social Research). 3(10): 634–650.

Watanabe, Fumi, 2014, *Oceania Geijutsu: Red Wave no Ko to Shugou* (Art of Oceania: Individuality and collectivity of Red Wave). Kyoto: Kyoto University Press.

Webster, Anthony K., 2015, Cultural Poetics (Ethnopoetics). *Oxford Handbooks Online*. https://www.oxfordhandbooks.com/view/10.1093/oxfordhb/ 9780199935345.001.0001/oxfordhb-9780199935345-e-34. (accessed 22 May 2019).

Wesley-Smith, Terence (ed.), 2010, Epeli's Quest: Essays in Honor of Epeli Hau'ofa. *The Contemporary Pacific*, 22(1): 101–123.

Wetherell, Margaret, 2012, *Affect and Emotion: A New Social Science Understanding*. London: Sage Publications.

White, Geoffrey, 2008, Foreword. In Hau'ofa, Epeli, *We Are the Ocean: Selected Works*. Honolulu: University of Hawai'i Press.

Yamamoto, Matori, 2006, The Eighth Festival of Pacific Arts: Representation and Identity. In Yamamoto, Matori (ed.), *Art and Identity in the Pacific: Festival of Pacific Arts (JCAS Area Studies Research Reports, No.9)*. Osaka: The Japan Center for Area Studies.

Yasui, Manami, 2009, Taiheiyou geijutsusai ni miru identity no souzou (Creation of Identity at the Festival of Pacific Arts). In Endo, Hisashi et al. (eds.), *Oceania Gaku* (Oceanic Studies). Kyoto: Kyoto University Press.

Yomiuri Shinbun Akita Shikyoku (ed.), 1979, *Min'yō no sato: ora ga akita no uta ga kikoeru* (Villages of Min'yō: Hearing my Akita folk songs). Akita: Mumyō-sha.

Zips, Werner, 2006, 'Repatriation is a Must!' The Rastafari Struggle to Utterly Downstroy Slavery. In *Rastafari a Universal Philosophy in the Third Millennium*. Kingston: Ian Randle Publishers. pp. 129–168.

189

Index

Subject

Personal Name